SINEMA

"An adult needs pornography as a child needs fairy tales."
—Henri Poincaré, quoted by
Alain Robbe-Grillet, "For
a Voluptuous Tomorrow"

SINEMA

AMERICAN PORNOGRAPHIC FILMS AND THE PEOPLE WHO MAKE THEM

KENNETH TURAN AND
STEPHEN F. ZITO

PRAEGER PUBLISHERS   New York · Washington

To the memory of our fathers

Published in the United States of America in 1974
by Praeger Publishers, Inc.
111 Fourth Avenue, New York, N.Y. 10003

Library of Congress Cataloging in Publication Data

Turan, Kenneth.
  Sinema: American pornographic films and the people
who make them.

  1. Erotic films—History and criticism. 2. Moving-
pictures—United States. I. Zito, Stephen F., joint
author. II. Title.

PN1995.9.S45T8   791.43′0909′3538   73-18750
ISBN 0-275-50770-X

Printed in the United States of America

CONTENTS

ACKNOWLEDGMENTS

First, our deep gratitude to those producers, directors, and participants who not only agreed to extensive interviews but trusted us with their psyches by being totally frank in their answers. Without their full cooperation, there wouldn't have been any book at all.

After them, thanks in equal measure to:

- Sam Kula, former archivist of the American Film Institute, who originally put us in touch with Praeger Publishers; our agent, David Obst; John Hochmann, for his initial interest, and the staff at Praeger, especially Lois O'Neill and Joan Tapper—all of whom always believed this book would eventually make its way to print

- Harold Fairbanks of *The Advocate*, J. J. Proferes of Washington's Metropole Theater, *Variety*'s Addison Verrill, and, most especially, Bruce Williamson of *Playboy*, for putting us in touch with people who generally prefer as much anonymity as possible

- The management of the *Washington Post* and especially the editor of the *Post's Potomac* magazine, Shelby Coffey, III

- Paul Lindenschmit of Universal Pictures, who was invaluable in clearing up the persistent rumors linking John C. Holmes with the "Leave It to Beaver" show

- Ellen Darabaner of the American Film Institute and, from Georgetown University, Professor Joel E. Siegel and Dr. Irving Schneider, who allowed us access to his comprehensive files and knowledge

Two areas call for special and extensive thanks.

• The first includes individuals who have previously written on sex films: Bruce Williamson, Addison Verrill, and Harold Fairbanks; Hollis Alpert of *Saturday Review/World;* Arthur Knight of *Playboy*; Anthony Gambino, Jim Buckley, and Al Goldstein of *Screw*; and William Rotsler of *Adam Film World*

• Second, for stills used in the book, the filmmakers and participants themselves. Also essential were Richard Henshaw, Ernest Burns of Cinemabilia, Dan Faris of San Francisco's Cinema Shop, Don Velde of Donald L. Velde, Inc., Lorraine Borden of Great Scott Advertising, plus the staffs of Movie Star News, the Memory Shop, and Consolidated Poster

Saved for last and most special thanks are:

• Nila Sanders, who typed half the final manuscript, and Diane Shapiro, who typed the other half and was simply indispensable in carefully transcribing close to thirty hours of hectic tape recordings

• The U.S. Government, which printed the *Technical Reports* of the President's Commission on Pornography and Obscenity, source of the most varied and unlikely information, and instigator of the obscenity hearing that brought the two of us together

And finally, to Connie Holland and Joanna Zito, a gratitude for which words are inadequate.

God bless you, every one.

KENNETH TURAN
STEPHEN F. ZITO

Washington, D.C.
June, 1974

INTRODUCTION: THE LIFE AND MAYBE DEATH OF DIRTY MOVIES

The pornographic film is not a topic your mother would want you to write about. In fact, if she were any kind of mother at all she wouldn't even want you to see the nasty things and risk having your nice clean mind perverted by God knows what kinds of filth.

Apparently, however, the moral authority of mothers is not what it used to be, for pornographic films have become something of a national obsession, a highly visible aspect of increased public attention to all things sexual. Two startlingly explicit films, *Deep Throat* and *The Devil in Miss Jones*, were among the top ten money-makers of 1973, outperforming almost all of Hollywood's overblown attractions, and the venerable *New York Times* found itself the coiner of a phrase, "porno chic," to describe the growing fascination with cinematic sex. As Paul Bender, general counsel to the Presidential Commission on Obscenity and Pornography, said of Potter Stewart's famous "I know it when I see it" definition of pornography, "If Justice Stewart knows it when he sees it today, he either sees it everywhere or he doesn't see it at all." Where would it end?

In one sense, at least, it ended one day in June 1973 when the Supreme Court, in a series of 5 to 4 decisions, noticeably broadened its definition of pornography and the means suitable for quashing it by making *local* rather than *national* community standards the touchstone for obscenity convictions. The ultimate impact of that day will not be clear for some time, perhaps years, as old laws, new laws, and various appeals wend their way through the courts, but one effect was immediate: The production of high-budget, explicit sex films of superior technical quality came to a halt. For who, faced with a crazy quilt of conflicting and contradictory state and local standards, would invest in a film whose chances for profits were problematical. The cheap stuff, made in someone's garage for a total cash outlay of $27.50, would still be around, as always, but the era of class theatrical pornography was, to all appearances, over.

It was an era that saw vast changes in the popular definition of *pornographic*, a word the dictionary says comes from the Greek *pornographos* or writing about prostitutes. It officially means forms of communication intended to excite lascivious or lustful feelings—whatever turns you on, man—but what that has meant in practice has varied greatly. When the first major theatrical sex film, Russ Meyer's *The Immoral Mr. Teas*, went into general circulation in 1960, simple nonfrontal nudity of a type that can occasionally be seen today on educational television was enough to throw the New York State Board of Censors, to cite one example out of many, into a howling fit.

Films gradually got more and more explicit, and it became necessary to differentiate between hard- and soft-core pornography. Soft core features nothing more than extensive nudity and a huffing-and-puffing, obviously simulated variety of sex. Hard core shows people really doing it, make no mistake about it, meaning that erection, penetration, and sometimes ejaculation are featured in all-too-living color. No value judgment, pejorative or otherwise, is implied. One person's morally uplifting pastoral romp is quite likely to be another's dirty movie.

Films of this type are often exhibited under the most depressing circumstances, in seedy, malodorous theaters with names like the "Sho-Mor" and "Tom Cat." They show perhaps every sexual act and combination known to humankind with the possible exception of necrophilia (though some of the actresses in question are so unresponsive that there is perhaps room for doubt). Although the films often have strange, delightful titles like *The Adventures of James Bondage*, *The Gayru*, or *Runaway Hormones*, nobody is laughing, or at least not very often. Going to pornographic films tends to be a solitary and sometimes odd activity, seldom inviting the intellectual involvement or imaginative participation of the viewer. With few exceptions, these films are quite difficult to watch, and reactions to them generally include disgust, indifference, embarrassment, and, most of all, boredom. So why do people go to see them? And why write a book about them?

For one thing, there *are* those moments, bright electric moments, when it all works, when the film on the screen by some accident of luck and talent transcends itself, becoming simultaneously drama, eroticism, and cinema, and producing a sexual sequence of riveting emotional intensity. Every follower of celluloid sex can name his favorites, and though isolated sequences do not make a work of art, they definitely do indicate that the potential for one exists. Moreover, it is highly unlikely that the lavishly praised erotic sequences in *Don't Look Now* or *Last Tango in Paris* could have existed without there already having been some five thousand sex-exploitation films made within the last fifteen years.

An additional incentive for writing a book is that the pornographic film industry, on the outside a seamy monolith populated exclusively by greasy men with big cigars and pimply, heroin-addicted actors and actresses, is, in fact, the home for as diverse and totally open a group of people as can be found anywhere, fascinating for their backgrounds, their life-styles, and most of all their overwhelming, leerless honesty concerning what is traditionally the murkiest of areas, one's own sex life. They form a very legitimate slice of Americana, as deftly revealing in its way about the type of country the United States has become as any group you can name.

Ultimately, though, the very fact that there is a theatrical sex-film industry to chronicle is the main reason we have chosen, from the dual vantage points of journalism and film history, to chronicle it. Less than two decades ago, sex films meant totally anonymous productions, black-and-white shorts shown only clandestinely in the dead of night. Within that length of time not only did the product improve technically to the point where some sequences are on a par with Hollywood, but the films themselves came to be shown theatrically in reputable movie houses all across the country.

Although many of the films are admittedly dreary, detailing little more than the random copulations of two bored people, the species as a whole improved so much and so rapidly before the Supreme Court decision, it seemed only a matter of time until there would appear truly fine pornographic films for which no one would have to apologize. People, including actors, directors, and producers, were putting their real names on them and becoming wealthy and famous in the process, and audiences had increased in sophistication to the point where, just as with non-pornographic films, the names of certain directors and stars in the ads were enough to draw a crowd. By the '70s, "dirty movies" had become a staggering and bona fide phenomenon, and that is fascinating for what it says about changes in American mores and morals, and for what it tells us about the nature and quality of our erotic fantasies, motives, and experiences.

PART 1

UNCERTAIN

INNOCENCE

1

THEY WEAR NOTHING BUT THE WIND

NUDIES AND NUDIE-CUTIES

Photographic processes have long been used to record erotic activity in order to educate, arouse, or entertain humankind. The earliest still photographs of a sexual nature are dated circa 1850, and there were erotic films within two years after the first public showing of motion pictures in 1894. One of the best-known early American films showed Fatima recreating the dance that had made her famous at the World's Fair of 1893. It was considered daring, and some prints were released with bars across the offending portions of the dancer's anatomy. The censorship of this film was exceptional, however. There was almost no societal control over motion pictures during the first decade of their existence, and early films, particularly those designed for peep-show viewing, were often relatively risqué. Although there was no overt sexual content to peep-show films like *As Seen on the Screen, Behind the Screen, Her Morning Exercise, One Way of Taking a Girl's Picture, The Pajama Girl,* and *Waiting for Santa Claus,* for his penny the viewer could see a woman, clad in undergarments, negligee, or tights, walk about, undress, or exercise. For the turn of the century, that was exciting.

The first municipal censorship boards came into being in 1908. Within ten years most cities and states in this country had some form of prior censorship, and motion pictures became increasingly discreet in terms of overt sexual action or display. As the art of cinematic narrative developed, however, films on such subjects as white slavery, drug addiction, venereal disease, sex education,

3

birth control, and abortion began to be made. Universal Pictures, for example, in 1913 released *Traffic in Souls,* based on the report of the Rockefeller White Slavery Commission. The film grossed $250,000 and was one of the great financial successes in early motion-picture history. The example of Universal was quickly followed by other companies, and the next several years saw the release of *Port of Missing Women, The Lure of New York, The Shame of the Empire State, The Thorns of the Gay White Way,* and *The Serpent of the Slums.* Most of these films on sexual or sex-related subjects were produced and distributed by small, independent companies and were sold on the sensational value of the subject matter rather than star power or artistic excellence. Thus was set the pattern by which marginal operators in the motion-picture industry supplied a product to exhibitors that was franker and more explicit than films produced by major companies.

A third form of erotic cinema that began to be manufactured at an early date was stag films. In *A History of Eroticism,* Lo Duca identifies a French pornographic film as early as 1908, and the Kinsey Institute houses in its collection *A Free Ride* (also known as *The Grass Sandwich*), an American film that has been dated circa 1915. Stag films were to remain a separate industry. They were not exhibited theatrically and, since home projectors were largely unknown, they were generally shown to fraternal groups by itinerant showmen whose presence was informally sanctioned by local authorities. Stag films had no influence on the form or content of films for general release until the mid-'60s.

After the Hays Office, chartered to police the motion-picture industry, was established by the principal Hollywood studios in 1922, the major companies were forced to observe guidelines that restricted or circumscribed what could be shown on the screen. The small independent companies were not bound by these covenants, however, and continued to produce exploitation features and shorts that featured sex themes, daring plot situations, and—occasionally—nudity. The coming of sound in the last years of the '20s did not alter the content of the sex-exploitation films, but the additional cost of sound recording did force the producers to upgrade the quality of product. Exploitation films from the '30s, therefore, became equal in quality to the action melodramas being produced by the legitimate companies that worked on Hollywood's "poverty row." One of the most interesting films from this period is *Child Bride,* a well-photographed exposé of the evils of child marriage in Kentucky, in which a lovely adolescent girl frequently bares her pubescent breasts. The film was competently directed by Harry Revier, a craftsman whose one other notable film was *The Slaver* (1927), in which, according to a *Variety* review, "A Negro tribal chieftain on the coast of Africa makes a deal with a dissolute sea captain to buy a white girl."

The exploitation market remained relatively stable during the '30s and '40s. Production and distribution of sex films remained in the hands of a small number of men, known among themselves as "the Forty Thieves," who annually released and rereleased a few pictures each to the so-called grind houses that would play them. Some of the films produced by these men were serious and well-intentioned. *Damaged Lives*, for example, was a study of the dangers of syphilis and gonorrhea based on the Pulitzer Prize-winning reports of New York *Daily News* reporter Carl Warren. The plot was designed to reveal the dangers of ignorance and false modesty in relation to social diseases; a doctor (played by Jason Robards, Sr.) gave a lecture about the dangers and treatment of venereal disease. Another sober picture was Kroger Babb's sex-education film, *Mom and Dad*, directed by William Beaudine, who at various times in the course of a long motion-picture career, also directed Mary Pickford, the Dead End Kids, and Lassie. The film featured the birth of a baby and was one of the most successful motion pictures ever released. (David F. Friedman, who owned the rights for several years in the late '50s, estimates that the total grosses for the film were about $40 million.) *Mom and Dad* was followed by *Street Corner, Because of Eve*, and *The Story of Bob and Sally*. All four films propounded the thesis that ignorance about the facts of life could lead to unwanted pregnancy and ruined lives.

Few films released to the exploitation market were serious, however; many treated sex in a highly melodramatic and unrealistic manner. Representative titles include *Wages of Sin, Forbidden Oats, Souls at Pawn, Honky Tonk Girl, Devil's Harvest, The Woman Is a Fool, Forbidden Desires, Hopped Up*, and *Test Tube Babies* (a film that asked, "How would you solve the problem of not being able to fulfill your marital obligations?"). Kroger Babb, producer of *Mom and Dad*, made an anti-drug picture starring Lila Leeds, an actress who was arrested on a marijuana charge with Robert Mitchum in 1948. The picture, first called *Wild Weed* and later *She Should Have Said No*, was not very good, but Babb made his money back by exhibiting it at midnight shows at which Leeds would appear on stage and speak against the evils of marijuana. Babb also made a picture with Ruth Warwick on alcoholism called *One Too Many*. Both films were peopled with young innocents (boys and girls together) who were led from the straight and narrow path by the vile influence of drugs, bad company, liquor, and lecherous adults. The exploitation films were basically didactic and Victorian in outlook, upholding the virtues of cleanliness, chastity, marriage, and family life.

The '50s saw two major changes in the exploitation industry. One was the brief vogue for burlesque films, the other the growing popularity of nudist-camp films. Burlesque reels had been made since World War II, but it was not until the '50s that full-length features, filmed off the boards of burlesque houses, were put into release. Burlesque houses had closed in many cities, so movies were the only means by which patrons could see favorite performers. The burlesque films were among the least cinematic of exploitation genres, using camera techniques that went out of date in 1903. What the patron saw was a photographed record of a stage performance, and what may have worked well before a live audience did not necessarily work well frozen on the silver screen. The burlesque film declined in popularity in the late '50s, partly because of repetition and partly because several of the big burlesque names began to appear in Nudie and Nudie-Cutie films.

Never have so many paid so much to see so little. That is basically the story of the nudist film. It had several variations, played for a while to good grosses, and died of its inherent limitations: Nothing ever happened. Or almost nothing. Naked men and women (and sometimes young children) played spirited games of volleyball and ping-pong; there was sunbathing, and water sports, and a lot of strenuous moving around. And that was all. No touching; no kissing; no looking "down there." There was, in fact, a strictly observed ban on sexual activity or even the suggestion of sexual activity. Looking at these films today, it is amazing that anyone, anywhere, ever objected to their manufacture or screening. But people did object.

As is so often the case with sex-exploitation films, the coming of age of the nudist-camp film was the direct result of a court decision. The decision was handed down by the Court of Appeals of the State of New York on July 3, 1957, in the matter of *Excelsior Pictures Corp.* v. *Regents of the University of the State of New York,* the latter being ultimately responsible for the prior censorship of all films shown in the state of New York. The film involved in the case was *Garden of Eden,* a nudist-camp film made in 1955, which reconstructed the activities of a nudist colony in a remote region of Florida. The film had been denied a license for exhibition by the Motion Picture Division of the New York State Education Department (a decision upheld by the Board of Regents, the plaintiffs). The opinion in the case, written by Judge Charles Desmond, asserted that *Garden of Eden,* despite having been found obscene and indecent by the Department of Education, could

6

nevertheless be shown because, under law, nudity *per se* was not indecent. One of the key portions of Desmond's opinion set the standard that was observed by motion-picture producers anxious to have their wares displayed in New York State, a market that was estimated to generate up to 30 per cent of the sex-film gross. Desmond wrote:

> There is nothing sexy or suggestive about it. . . . In it the nudists are shown as wholesome, happy people in family groups practicing their sincere but misguided theory that clothing, when climate does not require it, is deleterious to mental health by promoting an attitude of shame with regard to natural attributes and functions of the body.

Among the precedents that Desmond cited was *Joseph Burstyn, Inc., v. Wilson*, the case in which the Supreme Court declared that "expression by means of motion pictures is included within the free speech and free press guarantee of the First and Fourteenth Amendments." Desmond also appealed to contemporary community standards in his decision by citing the fact that very respectable magazines such as the *National Geographic* regularly featured nudity as part of their stories on primitive tribes. What Desmond did not say was that American motion-picture censors, both state and local, had previously adhered to a double standard with regard to nudity, for it was quite all right for the breasts and buttocks of nonwhite women to be exposed to the patrons of the grind houses. (For example, a film directed by Charles T. Trego, originally called *Bali* and later rereleased under several other titles, in wide circulation since 1932, featured the customs of that island paradise, whose female population walked about naked to the waist.) Judge Desmond struck a blow for racial equality in his decision by making it possible for theaters in the state of New York to show films in which all shades and hues of men and women—black, white, and yellow—could appear in the nude.

The nudist-camp films were doubly exempt from prosecution: Normal people (unclothed) went about their daily tasks and recreations, and certain ideas, primarily dealing with the benefits of nudism, were openly advocated. Whatever the baser motivations of the men who made the nudist films, the movies paid more than lip service to the basic tenets of what has become known as social nudism—the rules designed to keep people from becoming sexually aroused. Social nudism may not be one of the ten great ideas of Western civilization, but it is an accepted practice, and the producers of nudist films accurately reflected that back-to-nature philosophy. And faced with the awesome task of finding material to use for the soundtracks of their films, they endlessly and faithfully repeated the platitudes of the sunbathing magazines that spiced up the counters of bookstands and barbershops of the time.

The decision in the *Garden of Eden* case had a remarkable effect on the production of nudist films in the United States and greatly stepped up the importation of nudist films from abroad, primarily from France and Great Britain. *Garden of Eden* had played in thirty-six states before it was finally licensed to play in New York State, but besides being the biggest single market for sex films, New York often set standards by which other states licensed films. (In particular, Maryland, Virginia, Pennsylvania, and Ohio often followed the lead of the New York censors.) So when New York permitted the nudist film, independent American producers began making low-budget movies with such titles as *My Bare Lady*; *For Members Only*; *Nature Camp Diary*; *Fanny Hill*; *Hollywood Nudes Report*; *International Smorgasbord*; *She Should Have Stayed in Bed*; *Nudes Around the World*; *1,000 Shapes of a Female*; *Career Girls on a Naked Holiday*; *The Nude and the Prude*; *Mr. Peek-a-boo's Playmates*; *Wild Gals of the Naked West*; *The Barest Heiress*; *Naughty Shutter*; *The Calico Queen*; *The Bare Hunt, or My Gun Is Jammed*.

David F. Friedman, the director of a nudist musical called *Goldilocks and the Three Bares,* says of the industry at this time:

> When I got into the exploitation distribution business in the late '50s, there were four of us in the country—Bill Mishkin and Joe Brenner in New York, myself in Chicago, and Dan Sonney in L.A. —and the total output in the whole United States was about eight to ten pictures a year in this market, so that the fifty or sixty theaters that had to play this stuff every year played each one of these pictures ten to twelve weeks, gave you a fair percentage, and you made a fortune with it. I bought a drive-in in Joliet and I had one of the first Nudie houses in Chicago back when Chicago had a very tough police censorship board and everything had to be submitted to that board. And I dare say it was more profitable then than it is today when you don't have to submit anything and they're playing hard core in Chicago.

The nudist-camp films following the *Garden of Eden* decision in 1957 established certain customs and formulas. There was no frontal nudity—the male and female sex organs were never shown —and what the viewer saw was rather a great deal of bare breast and buttock. Although many of the nudist films were sold as documentary studies of nudist camps, most of the actors were, in fact, professional models working for the standard fee of $100 a day and the chance to get a uniform suntan. (Sad to relate,

8

the nudist producers discovered that the authentic nudist often was not photogenic enough for films.) And while the only reason-for-being of the nudist film was nudity (and there was a great deal of it for the standard admission price of three dollars), many of the films developed a slim story line to keep the audience awake between the volleyball matches that showed body contact without erotic overtones.

One of the formula nudist plots tells of the proverbial sweet young thing (of which there was a seemingly inexhaustible supply) who is initiated into nudism by a kindly, more experienced woman. It is a natural theme, and one that allowed for the gradual, cruelly tentative undressing of the heroine (a kind of inept striptease) as well as an opportunity for the narrator to mouth platitudes about the virtues of nudism. Next in popularity is the story of the outsider who visits the nudist camp looking for something—the journalist in search of a story or the detective in search of a missing heiress.

Only a few nudist-camp films attempted to go one step further and give the audience something new. That "something new" was presented rather belatedly to a doubtfully breathless American public in 1966 by John Lamb, who produced and directed *The Raw Ones*. It featured frontal nudity, albeit in a nonerotic context, and when it opened at the Paris Theater in Los Angeles, it grossed $3,400 in one screening on one night. It also did well in other cities. The Guild Theater in Albuquerque, New Mexico, reported to Art Films International that it doubled the ordinary house take; at the Crescent Theater in Dallas, Texas, the film had the longest run in that city's exploitation film history; and the Astor Art Theater in Charlotte, North Carolina, reported that the $3,487.50 gross was more than twice the house average of $1,500. Lamb's daring, astute advertising campaign, stressing that the film was uncut, unretouched, and showed what had only been whispered about (and covered up) in past years, packed them in. Lamb was, in fact, referring to his supposed topic—nudism—and even though the copy was obviously designed to be read and understood as dealing with total nudity and the exhibition of the male penis and female pubic hair, his purpose was more serious than the film or the advertising suggests. There is no story and no sex in the film, but there is a very competent narration that speaks up for nudism and argues against censorship, quoting such eminent civil libertarians as Albert Ellis, Hugh Hefner, Bertrand Russell, Thomas Jefferson, and Supreme Court Justice Hugo Black. Despite the discreet, sincere manner in which the nudity in the film was handled, *The Raw Ones* ran into a certain amount of trouble with the law. It won these court cases, however, because nudity was presented in a nonerotic context, and nudity *per se* (even total nudity) was not

9

obscene under Supreme Court guidelines. On October 2, 1967, the film was even cleared for showing in Maryland by the State Board of Censors.

John Lamb followed *The Raw Ones* with *She Did It His Way*, a film that featured Kellie Everts, Miss Nude Universe herself, and a number of other contestants at the Miss Nude Universe pageant. The film offered both frontal nudity and a story about "the life and loves of Miss Nude Universe." There was drama (two outlaw bikers rough up Kellie, viciously tearing off her dress to reveal her breasts), cleanliness (Kellie washes off with a hose), and love (Kellie, quite naked, kisses a bearded man in a swimming pool). As the press book said, it was a "penetrating and uninhibited exhibition of pageantry and pulchritude."

The Nudie-Cutie was born in 1959, the year Russ Meyer, a one-time army combat cameraman and cheesecake photographer, raised $24,000 and made *The Immoral Mr. Teas*, the most important and notorious erotic film released in the United States until *I Am Curious (Yellow)* was put on the market by Grove Press in 1968. It is almost impossible to overestimate the importance of *Mr. Teas*. It set the formal and thematic standards for a new genre of narrative films that featured female nudity and poked gentle fun at the inept and sweaty participants in the game of love. *Mr. Teas*, which prompted a good deal of legal controversy and critical comment and returned about $1 million profit on its initial investment, was bankrolled on an even-dollar basis by Russ Meyer and Pete DeCenzie, the owner of the El Rey Theater, an Oakland burlesque house. It was not the first time the two men had worked together, however, for Meyer had previously photographed *The French Peep Show*, a burlesque film featuring Tempest Storm, shot on the stage of the El Rey.

The Immoral Mr. Teas was largely improvised over a period of four days, and Meyer used what was at hand. He gave the starring role to an old comrade-in-arms and sometime comedian, Bill Teas, borrowed the office of a dentist acquaintance as the main set, and hired a number of beautiful models, including Marilyn Westly, Ann Peters, Dawn Dennelle, and Michele Roberts. It was directed and photographed in Eastmancolor by Russ Meyer, and the accordion music and sly, ironic narration for the 63-minute film were credited to Edward Lasko.

The plot of *The Immoral Mr. Teas* centers on a delivery man for a dental supply house who bicycles around town to deliver false teeth. This fellow, clad in pink coveralls and a straw boater, is an inveterate girl-watcher, ogling each and every girl who goes by, and a compulsive daydreamer, who mentally undresses some of the women. He goes to a dentist to have a tooth pulled and is given an anesthetic. After he leaves the dentist, each woman he meets—receptionist, dental assistant, waitress—appears to him in the nude. On a weekend fishing trip he sees three nudes sporting in a field and stream. He also goes to a burlesque house and then to a beach where he watches a beautiful model being put through her erotic poses and paces by a professional photographer. Teas becomes resigned to his fate when he goes to see a female psychiatrist and sees her nude also.

The Immoral Mr. Teas created a scandal when it was released, partly because of the nudity and partly because it was a great financial success. The initial trade-paper notices on the film praised its quality, but one cautioned exhibitors, "It packs more female nudity than ever before in any motion picture, including those devoted entirely to nudist camps and burlesque." The same article also ran this estimate of the film: "GOOD NUDITY NOVELTY FOR SPOTS THAT CAN SHOW IT." But it was precisely by playing theaters that had never played sex-exploitation films before that *Mr. Teas* was to create a whole new market for sex films. "There was an interesting vacuum there," Meyer has said.

> The public was waiting for something new. I think they were becoming disenchanted with the so-called European sex films, like some of the early Lollobrigida pictures, in which there's a lot of promise but never any kind of real fulfillment . . . they would always cut to the curtain blowing and things of this nature. So there were a number of secondary art houses that were floundering and they were looking for product. It was this field that we were able to jump into. Once this goddamn picture caught on, it was booked all over the country in these art houses and the picture would just hang in there for a year and play incredibly.

And the fact that *The Immoral Mr. Teas* played in theaters that had never before played erotic films made it the subject of a considerable amount of journalistic comment. When it played at the Monica Theater in Los Angeles in January 1960, Charles Stinson wrote a short notice in the *Los Angeles Times* that stated, "Last Friday evening the Peep Show finally moved across the tracks from Main Street, and to judge by the concourse of solid-looking citizens, presumably all aged 18 or over, the film is going to be a GREAT success." Stinson goes on to discuss the plot and dismisses the film as "a montage of calendar art." *Mr. Teas* later opened on Market Street in San Francisco, and after it had played an extended run there Paine Knickerbocker, the well-known critic for the *San Francisco Chronicle*, reviewed the film by noting, "It is an innocent film, presenting its unclad beauties with unabashed delight. The commentary . . . is occasionally amusing and sly, the photography is excellent, and Teas, with his bug-eyes, his preoccupations and his beard, is a whimsical performer." *The Immoral Mr. Teas* also caught the fancy of literary critic Leslie Fiedler, who wrote a long review for *Show* magazine, which said in part:

> In "Mr. Teas" there was not only no passion, but no contact, no flesh touching flesh, no consummation shown or suggested. For pornography the woman's angle of vision is necessary, but here were no women outside of Bill Teas's head; and Bill Teas was nobody's dreamed lover, only a dreamer, with his half-modest, half-comical beard, his sagging pectoral muscles, his little lump of a belly creased by baggy shorts or hidden by overalls. And Mr. Teas could touch no one—not in lust or love or in the press of movement along a street. Once in the film he lays his hand on flesh, the shoulder of an eight-year-old girl working out with a hula hoop, and she beans him with a rock. Any really nubile, desirable female is doomed to disappear into the ladies room or the arms of some lover whose face we never see—as unreal, finally, as the girl he embraces. Mr. Teas conducts his odd business and carries his frustrated dreams through a world of noncontact and noncommunication. As old restrictions crumble in our society, the naked flesh assumes its proper place among the possible subjects for movies, the place it has always held in the other, less public arts; but meanwhile, in the United States, we have been long corrupted by the pseudo arts of tease and titillation, conditioned to a version of the flesh more appropriate for peeking than love or lust or admiration or even real disgust. Its makers have not attempted to surmount the difficulties which confront the American movie-maker who desires to make nakedness his theme; but they have, with absolute good humor, managed at once to bypass and to illuminate those difficulties. The end result is a kind of imperturbable comedy, with overtones of real pathos.

The only real similarity between *The Immoral Mr. Teas* and the nudist-camp films was that both genres featured nudity. The nudity in *Mr. Teas*, however, occurs in an everyday context (at work, at home, and on the streets), and there is no attempt to rationalize nudity as a unique and beneficial life-style (as was done in the nudist films). The naked women in *Mr. Teas* are simply there to entertain the grind-house audiences, a fact that was played up in the advertising. The posters for the film included copy like: "A RIBALD FILM CLASSIC . . . MADE IN HOLLY-WOOD, THE PICTURE ITALIAN OR FRENCH MOVIE MAKERS WOULDN'T DARE TO MAKE." They invited the audience to "a peeping Tom's dream of ravishing beauty" and advised that the film was for "unashamed adults only." The

nudity and notoriety of the film naturally made *Mr. Teas* subject
to prior censorship and court cases across the nation. Meyer and
DeCenzie won the court cases, but several censor boards, including the key one in New York state, cut the film before it could be released. (New York cut eleven minutes; Maryland banned it outright for several years.) A lot of people ultimately saw the film, however, and Meyer went on to become a millionaire and a filmmaker of repute whose collected works have been shown in a retrospective at Yale University.

The great success of *The Immoral Mr. Teas* altered the course of the sex-exploitation industry. In the following years what had been a cottage industry, supporting only the Forty Thieves, became a thriving business. Anyone with a movie camera and a few naked women could make a Nudie-Cutie and then make a few dollars selling it. It has been estimated, for example, that more than 150 imitations of *Mr. Teas* were made in the three years following its first release. Meyer himself made several of these—including *Eve and the Handyman, Erotica, Europe in the Raw, Wild Gals of the Naked West*, and *Heavenly Bodies*—and a number of other producers came into the business as well. Dave Friedman made *The Adventures of Lucky Pierre*, Ted Paramore released *Not Tonight, Henry*, Bob Cresse produced *Once Upon a Knight*, Robert Gurney, Jr., made *The Prude and the Parisienne*, and Jack Harris filmed *Paradisio* (in 3-D). Other titles in the Nudie-Cutie sweepstakes were *The Saucy Aussie* (called a "bargain basement *Cleopatra*" by the *San Francisco Examiner*), *The Naked World of Harrison Marks* (with Marks, a renowned nude photographer, impersonating, among others, Toulouse-Lautrec and Al Capone); *The Wonderful World of Girls* (the ad line read: "Stop the World, I Wanna Get On"); *The Nude and the Prude* ("Through his telescope, Harry Truehart learns the bare facts of life"); *Babes in the Woods* (filmed in Ogle-Scope); *Everybody Loves It*, a spoof of television that included nude commercials; *Sinderella and the Golden Bra* (a retelling of the old legend, produced by Paul Mart, one of Hollywood's better second-unit and stunt directors); and *Uncle Tomcat's House of Kittens*, the story of a policeman who tangles with five women who wreck his life. The general level of achievement in the Nudie-Cutie field was not particularly high, but films of this genre generally were notable, at the very least, for the two qualities that made *The Immoral Mr. Teas* a success: a lot of very pretty women in various stages of undress and a humorous approach to the generally strained relationship between men and women. There was no erotic touching, but there were innumerable incidents that brought together men and women in situations in which the women were not clothed. Several of the Nudie-Cuties deserve to be remembered for a special mixture of vaudeville comedy and lovely women.

One of the best, *Kipling's Women*, was also one of the first after *Mr. Teas*. Its good photographic and dramatic qualities can be attributed to its producer, Harry Smith, a veteran Hollywood sound man who had worked with Gary Cooper on *Return to Paradise* and with Glenn Ford on *Jubal*. The story of *Kipling's Women* was based on the Rudyard Kipling poem in which a retired British Army officer reminisces about the women he has known: the "sisters-under-the-skin" Colonel's Wife, Doll-in-the-Teacup, Girl of Sixteen, and Shiny She-Devil. The film has the charm of faded postcards. The women are very beautiful (especially Malia Olandag as the little Chinese girl), and the narration lends a certain class.

The film was released in two versions, one sixty-two and the other seventy-two minutes long, the shorter version omitting some of the full nudity shown in the complete film. The advertising campaign for the film, handled by Kroger Babb and designed to broaden the appeal of the film and make it acceptable outside of the big-city grind houses, is a model of its kind. Babb thought of everything, including the provision of complete sets of slides for the projectionists so they would not clip frames out of the film, a common practice that has persisted to this day. The catchlines for the film were straightforward and not overly suggestive: "THEY WEAR ONLY THE WIND" and "THE KIND OF GIRLS MEN LIKE—BUT SELDOM MARRY." Babb also carefully prepared trailers and radio ads—twelve 1-minute spots and twenty-five "time break" 12-second spots—as well as a variety of ad mats and newspaper stories that could be run before the film opened. Claiming that *Kipling's Women* was the first American art film and therefore inoffensive to public taste, Babb suggested that regular theaters play the film first on a midnight-show basis and later move it in as a regular feature. This would make it possible to judge local reaction (in the courts and at the box office) and, if all went well, to lay the groundwork for a successful legitimate run. Babb's campaign was a smashing success, and *Kipling's Women* not only did well financially but also broke down resistance to sex films in many localities.

Another of the important early Nudie-Cuties was *Not Tonight, Henry,* a wacky comedy, produced by Ted Paramore and Bob Heidrich, starring veteran comic Hank Henry, a corpulent MC at the Silver Slipper in Las Vegas, who was a close friend of Frank Sinatra and had previously appeared with him in *The Joker Is Wild, Pal Joey, Ocean's 11,* and *Pepe.* Henry, besides doing legitimate films, had appeared on the TV shows of Ed

Sullivan and George Gobel. He has a crazy, slapstick style, and his broad burlesque was a significant factor in the success of *Not Tonight, Henry.* The plot centered on a fat, lovelorn husband who, frustrated sexually by his disenchanted wife, dreams of amorous escapades with several glamorous figures of history including Cleopatra, Napoleon's Josephine, Delilah, Pocahontas, Lucrezia Borgia, and an anonymous cavewoman. The film was quite discreet, but it did feature a certain amount of breast nudity and ran afoul of the California courts and the New York State Board of Censors. It was eventually cleared of obscenity charges by a jury in Beverly Hills but was not so lucky in New York State, where, according to an article in *Variety,* the Board of Censors reportedly ordered cuts that would eliminate all but eleven minutes of the film including the titles. Despite this entanglement with censorship boards and the high cost of legal fees, *Not Tonight, Henry* on an initial investment of $40,000 (a production figure that was higher than average because Paramore used union crews and known talent like Henry, Little Jack Little, Follies star Valkyra, and Daurine Dare, who had previously appeared in United Artists' *Terror in a Texas Town*) grossed, by the estimate of the Los Angeles Police Department, more than $500,000 on the West Coast alone.

So it was that the Russ Meyer formula for presenting nudity without explicit sexual content but with sexual overtones was developed by the men who followed him. The first significant wave of Nudie-Cuties was successful in finding and amusing an audience. As Arthur Knight and Hollis Alpert pointed out in *Playboy* (June 1967),

> . . . the Nudie-Cuties of the early Sixties offered a broad burlesque of sex—purveying asexual nudity and depicting the male as a bumbling buffoon rather than a lover. . . . The voyeuristic nature of these early nudies is perhaps the most striking thing about them. The hero does not crave sex; he just wants to look—and the devices of the filmmakers . . . remove all suggestion of sexuality from the leading male character.

The formula was set early, and those who followed kept well within its limits. The best of the subsequent Nudie-Cuties were marked by the skill with which the conventions of the genre were manipulated. Director-writer John McCarthy, for example, made two films that were among the best examples of their types: *The Ruined Bruin* and *Pardon My Brush. The Ruined Bruin* (produced at a cost of $35,000 by actor Bob Felderman) told the somewhat bizarre tale of Buddy, a bear who escapes from a zoo because he wants to be human. He makes an unsuccessful pass at a pretty nurse in a park, takes male hormone pills in an attempt to transform himself into a man, and attends the annual Artists and Models Ball in Hollywood where, mistaken for a real man in costume, he almost makes love to a couple of girls. *The Ruined Bruin* was full of nudity but no sex. There were twenty-one models hired to take parts, and the big scene in the film was shot around a borrowed swimming pool.

Pardon My Brush starred Maureen Gaffney, a 42-24-34 red-head who had been featured both on the Red Skelton Show and on the Tonight Show with Johnny Carson. The plot concerns two housepainters (loosely based on Abbott and Costello) who work for the Peekaboo Paint Company and are hired to paint an apartment hotel inhabited solely by beautiful career women. Vanishing cream is inadvertently mixed with the paint, and walls become transparent when it is applied. The painters watch the girls go through their daily chores, exercises, and ablutions, until they are finally chased off by the irate owner of the apartment house. It was all done with style, and the knockabout comedy was amusing.

One of the most extraordinary figures to come out of the Nudie-Cutie era was Barry Mahon, a New York producer who had been associated with Errol Flynn in the final tragic years of his career. Mahon got into the Nudie business early, and by 1962 he was producing between fifteen and twenty cheaply made pictures a year (the average budget was $15,000, low even for Nudies). The films were all in color, and they were among the first Nudies to have "dramatic" rather than comic plots. Mahon would be the first to admit that the films were not very good, even by the standards of other exploitation films being produced at the same time. "We have not aimed for the single picture that is going to make us rich," Mahon said in a *Film Comment* interview. "We are looking for the business that's like turning out Ford cars or anything else. If there is a certain profit per picture and we make so many pictures, then we have established a business that is on a basis that's economical." Mahon's gross return on most pictures was between $40,000 and $60,000, and he did much of the creative work himself: He was producer, director, cameraman, editor, casting director, and whatever else was necessary to make pictures quickly, cheaply, and of a certain standard. One of the things contributing to Mahon's success was the technical and dramatic quality of his films. Mahon estimated that they could be booked into the five or six hundred theaters (besides the four hundred or so grind houses) that would play pictures that were not too salacious. Nevertheless, the Mahon oeuvre is large and generally unexceptional. Typical Mahon products of the early '60s were *1,000 Shapes of a Female,* featuring "the artist at

16

work" and "live models as they pose!"; *Nude Scrapbook,* the story of a New York photographer of nudes and a cinematographic equivalent of the pin-up picture; *Nude Las Vegas,* a film that featured the well-known and talented nude photographer Bunny Yeager at work setting up the tasteful photographs for which she was known; and *Naughty, Naughty Nudes,* the story of a college art class. A one-man industry, Mahon made well over sixty films and, for the most part, played it safe—some nudity, no sex, some laughs, all sweetness and light. The only Mahon Nudie-Cutie that went a little beyond the standards of the New York State Board of Censors was *She Should Have Stayed in Bed,* a comedy that lacked the usual "safe" framing story to place its nudity in a nonerotic context. Mahon spent $15,000 defending it in court before he temporarily shelved it because the limits of prurient appeal, set by the New York State Board of Education, were too unclear to provide him with an accurate guide as to what was within the law.

Bachelor Tom Peeping ran into the same kind of trouble in California. It opened with a gala premiere at the Paris Theater in Los Angeles and was promptly withdrawn by the exhibitor when the representatives of the L.A. County Sheriff's office threatened seizure unless the picture was taken off the screen. The producers of the film, Corsican Productions, took the case to federal court, charging that the sheriff's action was illegal harassment compounded by wrongful determination of obscenity. Judge Pierson M. Hall found the film to be not obscene and restrained the sheriff's office from further interference with the booking of the film. Despite the legal problems, *Bachelor Tom Peeping* was nothing special, and its main offense would seem to have been the publicity with which the film opened up in Los Angeles.

By 1964 the Nudie-Cutie had about run its course. The market was flooded, and exhibitors were beginning to show double bills in order to attract an audience. The public's declining interest in the Nudie-Cuties led some producers to increase investment greatly in order to provide star names and glossy production values to silly, unreal stories that remained mere showcases for nudity spiced with vaudeville jokes and burlesque routines. Perhaps the most famous of the expensive Nudie-Cuties was *Promises, Promises* (1963), a film produced by funnyman Tommy Noonan, for an alleged $80,000. It starred Jayne Mansfield in a tale about a writer (Noonan) married to a woman (Mansfield) who desperately wants to have a baby. The only problem is that he is impotent. This basic situation is worked out—the film ends happily, with Mansfield pregnant by the revitalized Noonan—by means of a variety of vaudeville gags and *double entendres.* But

Promises, Promises did well at the box office primarily because a Hollywood star of Jayne Mansfield's stature was willing to take off her clothes in an exploitation film.

Only five years after *Mr. Teas* had changed the erotic-film market, the most innocent and gentle of all sex-exploitation genres was losing popular interest. Nudity was no longer enough, not even in Eastmancolor.

2

BLOOD LUST

GHOULIES, ROUGHIES, AND KINKIES

About the same time Russ Meyer's early films were losing their shock value, other exploitation moviemakers were turning to hard, crude, sex-and-violence pictures—lowbrow items known in the trade as Ghoulies, Roughies, and Kinkies. They feature rape and murder, dismemberment and disfigurement, torture and kidnapping, domination and flagellation, bondage and leather orgies. Limbs are hacked off, virgins violated, whole families slain, rural innocents humiliated and degraded. The icons of this genre are boots, chains, ropes, knives, hatchets, and all lethal instruments, both sharp and blunt, and the characters are motivated by lust and avarice. These products of the dark underside of the erotic imagination have been deplored, cut by the censors, and sometimes completely forbidden. But they have made money, and they continue to be made, recent examples including *The Last House on the Left, Don't Look in the Cellar, Corpse Grinders, I Eat Your Flesh,* and *I Drink Your Blood.* The all-American theater of blood and cruelty, perhaps the most stable of the exploitation genres, illustrates Gershon Legman's thesis in *Love and Death* that violence is the ultimate sublimation of sexual impulse: that "sadism . . . is complete in itself. It can dispense with all earthly relation to sex—can even dispense with orgasm—thus allowing its adherents publicly to preen themselves on the 'purity' of their ruthless delights."

One of the first and most important producers to introduce violence into sex-exploitation films was David F. Friedman, an independent who realized early that the market for nudist-camp films and Nudie-Cuties was about to dry up from overexposure and saturation of product. Friedman developed an idea for a new kind of film that would concentrate on blood and gore. Inspired by a performance of the Grand Guignol in Paris, Friedman produced a film worthy of that source. *Blood Feast,* the first of the Roughies, was released in the autumn of 1963, with a script by Friedman and direction and photography (accomplished in four days) by Herschell G. Lewis. Connie Mason was the star of *Blood Feast,* and her subsequent appearance in a *Playboy* centerfold (with mention of the film) helped at the box office, where returns, according to Friedman, totaled more than $1.2 million, making a significant profit over the movie's $20,000 cost.

Dave Friedman quickly followed *Blood Feast* with *Color Me Blood Red* and *Two Thousand Maniacs.* These films used the same formula (seldom has Eastmancolor been exploited to better effect) and were also very successful at the box office, having a particular appeal for drive-in audiences, which traditionally have been receptive to blood and guts.

The second film in the Friedman "blood" trilogy, *Two Thousand Maniacs,* was a spectacular production Friedman and Herschell Lewis shot on location in the town of St. Cloud, Florida, with design and sound recording by Friedman, and writing, direction, photography, and music by Lewis. The star once again was Connie Mason, and the plot, an outstanding example of the genre, is a crude but effective variation on the Brigadoon theme.

Six people from the North are detoured into a small Southern city that is celebrating a Civil War centennial. They are invited to be the guests of the townspeople and, one by one, four of the Yankees are brutally murdered. The two who are left, discovering that they also are to be the victims of this blood-vengeance rite, kidnap a small boy and eventually escape, going to the state police for help. The police return to the place and, finding no trace of the town, inform the men that there has been no town there since the entire population was slaughtered by Northern troops during the Civil War. As the film ends, it becames clear that the town materializes only once every hundred years for the "celebration" of the ritual murders.

This action is handled, as in the other Friedman-produced films, directly and brutally. One of the women has her thumb cut off with a knife, and, dragged in hysteria to the sheriff's office, is then hacked to pieces with an axe. Other deaths include those of a man who is drawn and quartered and a woman crushed by a boulder. *Two Thousand Maniacs* was considered too rough by the Kansas State Board of Censors, and several cuts were ordered, including all scenes depicting amputations and a shot of a running horse with a man's leg attached to a rope. These cuts softened the film, but in essence it remained intact—exploiting the gross violations of the wills and bodies of innocent victims who scream in protracted agony at what is being done to them. Nudity was kept to a minimum, but the film shows a lot of hard-breathing rape, romance, and sadism—all faintly trashy and violent, featuring hot-blooded women (who are killed) and cruel, virile men.

Color Me Blood Red, the third Friedman-Lewis "blood" film, tells the story of a demented artist who murders his models and uses their bright blood for the red in his canvases. There is a certain amount of gallows humor, as when the painter remarks just before killing a girl, "This painting will be you."

The "blood" triology is the most violent and grotesque of Friedman's work, but his other films often contained elements of bizarre, cruel sex. *The Defilers,* for example, has a plot inspired by John Fowles's novel *The Collector.* The film was written and produced by Dave Friedman, with direction and photography by R. Lee Frost, a highly skilled exploitation director who has made many of the most interesting sex-exploitation films of the last decade. Frost began his career in Nudies and Nudie-Cuties and before directing *The Defilers* was the creative talent behind *Surfside 77* and Bob Cresse's *The House on Bare Mountain.*

The Defilers is shot in a dark, claustrophobic style, and Frost's handling of the material brings out some of the same tensions that can be found in Fowles's novel. This parodistic use of high and popular culture in the films he produces sets Friedman apart from other producers of exploitation films. Several of his films are based on previously existing material: *Starlet* is the archetypal Hollywood story; *She Freak* is based on Tod Browning's *Freaks*; and the legendary characters of Fanny Hill, Trader Horn, and Zorro the Avenger have inspired other Friedman films.

The same pressures and ambitions that drove Dave Friedman into making Roughies were also instrumental in Russ Meyer's eventual move into the business of exploiting violence and sadism. After his great success with *The Immoral Mr. Teas,* his subsequent films, such as *Eve and the Handyman* and *Erotica,* were only moderately successful. Finally, his *Wild Gals of the Naked West* fell on its face, probably because it had more belly laughs than buttocks.

What Meyer did then was produce *Lorna,* a strong melodrama in which sex, nudity, and violence were carefully integrated. It was his conscious intention to convince theater bookers that *Lorna* was not just another sex-exploitation film, but an action picture with a lot more action than usual—sexual and otherwise. Meyer was once again successful and helped to create a vogue for

21

Gothic dramas in which sex took second place to violence. As Meyer tells it, "I said, now I must do something like the foreign films, only it will be Erskine Caldwell and it will be a morality play and we'll borrow heavily from the Bible and I'll find a girl with giant breasts."

Meyer wrote the original story and acted as producer, director, photographer, and editor. Lorna Maitland, a sometime dancer with a sweet face and watermelon breasts, one of 134 women who answered Meyer's casting ad in *Variety,* won the starring role of Lorna, a voluptuous young woman who has been faithfully, unhappily married for a year to a naïve young man unable to satisfy her. Only when she is raped by an escaped convict does she first experience sexual satisfaction, and she brings her assailant back to the couple's run-down shack. The husband returns unexpectedly, and both the convict and Lorna are killed during the ensuing fight. The moral of this story is pointed out by a "man of God," who appears now and then to give warnings and make dire predictions. There is relatively little nudity in the film beyond a brief, startling exposure of Miss Maitland's remarkable anatomy, but this elemental revenge fable is crudely effective. As the press book for *Lorna* astutely states, it is "a primitive work of art in which black is black and white is white and there is no shading or distortion. The characters in *Lorna* are simple; their lives reflect the basic emotions of man: love, lust, jealousy, fear and desire."

The film did well at the box office, playing an extended run at the Rialto Theater on Times Square, and was booked into theaters that had not previously been willing to play Meyer's Nudie-Cutie product. The trade press reviews were complimentary, and there has been a considerable amount of subsequent critical comment about *Lorna* as well, most of it favorable. *Lorna* was included in a retrospective of Russ Meyer's films held at Yale University in 1970, and it is still in spasmodic distribution in certain parts of the United States. Film historian Richard Schickel, who saw the film at Yale, has described *Lorna* as "a film of preachment against hypocrisy, exhibiting no more skin than the plot absolutely requires . . . crudely vigorous in development."

The great success of *Lorna* prompted Russ Meyer to make several more films in the same genre, including *Mud Honey* (also known as *Rope of Flesh*); *Motor Psycho*; *Faster, Pussycat! Kill! Kill!* (also known as *The Leather Girls* and *The Mankillers*); and *Common Law Cabin* (also known as *How Much Loving Does a Normal Couple Need?*). These films were shot primarily on location in black and white and in a severe cinematographic style; they have rough, coherent stories that feature murder, rape, beatings, whippings, hangings, arson, and fights; characters are motivated primarily by lust and hate; nudity is functional; and sexual motivation is realistically integrated into the plots. Meyer has spoken of the manner in which his films were shot: "There's an excitement. It's a style, it moves very fast, they're not overly long. I like violence in films. I think it's highly entertaining." The films are still rather crude and uncertain in intention, but Meyer's growing control over his narrative material, his consistency of vision, and his considerable technical skills make the hard-surfaced fables sometimes arousing and sometimes moving experiences. Professor and writer Fred Chappell, for example, has compared *Faster, Pussycat! Kill! Kill!* to the work of Thomas Kyd, the most bloody of Elizabethan dramatists. Writing of Meyer's work, Chappell cites its "very odd, serious attempts, full of big, gloomy archetypes and Gothic puzzlements."

Besides Friedman and Meyer, so many people at so many levels of competence were making Ghoulies and Roughies that there have been approximately 750 films of this kind released in the United States alone. Most of the films are crudely made, and they contain many of the standard themes and situations of classic pornography and erotic folklore, including gross sadism toward members of the opposite sex.

Many films from the mid-'60s deal directly with male dominance and brutality. Typical is *Invitation to Ruin,* a film directed by Kurt Richter, which relates the story of Ernie Polaski, who lures young innocents to Mama Lupo's establishment where Mama Lupo—played by Bertha Bigg, who weighs in at three hundred pounds—trains them to be high-class whores, after which they are sold to the highest bidder. Apart from bondage and whipping, the featured attractions of the film are the castration of the hero and the insertion of a hot poker into the vagina of one of the tortured girls. Also following this bloody pattern is *The Sadistic Lover,* in which a peeping Tom goes to a psychic adviser and tells of beating an exotic dancer to death and of locking a pair of lovers in the trunk of their automobile and setting it on fire. The adviser attempts to turn him over to the police but is killed by the voyeur, who then finds time to rape a secretary before the climactic shoot-out with the cops.

A few years later, the team of Anna Riva and Julian Marsh produced, wrote, and directed the Kinkies called *The Touch of Her Flesh* and *The Curse of the Flesh*—the latter one of the kinkiest of its kind, a revenge drama in which a demented man arranges to kill off some people he does not care for. What is remarkable about the film is how the people are killed. The protagonist smears a cat's paws with poison and quickly drags the animal across the naked stomach of the woman with whom he has just had intercourse. The cat scratches the woman and she

23

dies. Two women make love, and one is killed by a spring knife in the dildo her partner has inserted into her vagina. The protagonist marries a girl and, the morning after the wedding, kills his wife with a harpoon gun after watching a pornographic movie in which she masturbates with a squash. The film ends with the castration of the hero by a machete-wielding fellow bent on revenge.

The American Film Distributing Corporation in Manhattan made three of the most violent and vulgar Kinkies of the '60s—*Olga's Girls, Olga's Massage Parlor,* and *White Slaves of Chinatown*—all of which were produced by George Weiss and directed by Joseph A. Mawra. The sadistic story of *White Slaves of Chinatown* is typical: There is Chinese water torture, bondage, and whipping; women are put in stocks, beaten with rubber hoses, hung by their wrists, forced to endure the pain of a metal bit in the mouth, strapped down, and thumbscrewed by Olga Petroff, a brothel-keeper, and her sinister Chinese assistants. These films were very popular, as were other films made to exploit similar fantasies. In *The Daughters of Lesbos,* a secret society devotes itself solely to female dominance. At one of the dinners this society holds each week, two women tell how men have taken advantage of them: One woman was drugged and raped, the other assaulted by the maintenance man in her building. The Daughters vote to castrate the maintenance man (who is sitting in the corner of the room, completely naked and tied firmly to a chair with a black hood over his face) and then carry out the sentence. The rest of *The Daughters of Lesbos* is devoted to solitary masturbation and lesbian lovemaking, all within the limits then prevalent in the industry (much implied, little actually seen). Another film featuring castration was Barry Mahon's *Prostitute's Protective Society.*

The image of the woman in these films, and numerous others like them, is that of the classic, castrating bitch-heroine described by critic Gershon Legman as the woman who enacts "her dominance in more clearly physical ways, taking upon herself all the virility the man has forfeited, whipping him, torturing him, and finally doing him to death. . . . Enviously phallic, she can achieve her forlorn maleness only by castrating men." Women in the Roughies are victims of male lust and dominance; they are to be used and abused, trained in their duties and hard pleasures in much the same way a dog is trained by a cruel master, with a lot of pain and a few slim rewards. The parameters of this sadistic fantasy also include another, seemingly paradoxical element very much in keeping with bondage and whipping fantasies: the image of the castrated male. Women in Roughies are something to be feared and therefore to be subdued, so that castration becomes simultaneously the realization of one's worst suspicions and a kind of rationalization for the harsh manner in which women are treated.

Unlike the Friedman and Meyer films, which dealt in violence but had some artistic merit, the Roughies and Kinkies of the middle '60s generally represent the nadir of the sex-exploitation film, ugly in spirit and appealing to the worst instincts of humankind. The death rattle of the woman with the severed leg replaces the unfettered cry of ecstasy, and blood rather than semen becomes the symbolic fluid of erotic expression. Paradoxically, these grotesque films, featuring neither complete nudity nor loving sexual contact, were largely exempt from the wrath of the censors, possibly because the United States has traditionally been a country that censors sex but tolerates violence.

3

KING LEER

AN INTERVIEW WITH RUSS MEYER

"Well, I'll tell you," Russ Meyer says, thoughtful, a long thin cigar in one hand, a Rob Roy straight up on the table in front of him. "One thing this life has given me which almost everybody wants, if I never have another piece of ass, I've had more than my share and they all were great looking broads. And I tell you, if nothing else has happened in my life, I've known some great women, exciting beautiful women, and I wouldn't have had it if I hadn't been in this business. So it can't be all bad."

This is the Russ Meyer of legend, the man the *Wall Street Journal* called "King Leer," the doyen of skin-flick makers, whose first film, *The Immoral Mr. Teas,* started the whole wave of cinematic sexual permissiveness back in 1959, and whose most famous *Vixen,* produced for $72,000 in 1968, has grossed over $7.5 million, making it, "on the basis of what it cost, the most successful film that's ever been made; there is not a picture that has ever been made that would approach that." To the President's Commission on Obscenity and Pornography, he is "the leading exponent and pioneer in the exploitation market," but to the American public Russ Meyer means celluloid sex. It is that simple.

Recently turned fifty, hair graying a bit at the temples, he gives off an air of hearty, take-charge masculinity. He looks, critic John Simon has said, like "a former prizefighter now operating a successful chain of South American brothels," but the judgment there is too harsh. For Russ Meyer, despite his Hey-I-don't-mess-around sturdiness, is a pleasant, relaxed fellow, forthright, a straightshooter, above all, a pal.

He may make amoral movies, but there is a strong sense of morality, of doing what's right, about him. He was incensed when an actress who worked for him dumped on the film she was in; it infuriated him because he had considered her a friend. "Here's a person I liked; I couldn't believe what I was hearing." He feels extremely responsible to the people who invest in his films, to the point where "I would never let anyone lose money; if I made another film they'd get it some way. It's easier to walk away from them and say, 'Oh, fuck it,' but it's a thing, a code I have, if someone entrusts me with their money, it's very important." And while he's making a film, there comes a time, "I'm not trying to make it sound like the second coming of Christ or anything, but there's a moment of truth every day you make a film—it comes at 4:45 in the afternoon, it comes at that time where you have to say, 'Okay, let's go, now let's try harder and let's do it again.'" It's the thing that must be done, and Russ Meyer does it because "in the final analysis you have to be a man, you have to, you know. Otherwise you ain't worth a shit if you don't really finally stand up to something, to something you believe in."

While he was married to Edy Williams—*la dernière bombe sexy* in *Cine-Revue*'s estimation, "the last of the lust queens" in his own—he delighted in making entrances. "We were kind of an anachronism—you know, voluptuous flashy girl and here she is with a dirty old man, it's marvelous, marvelous. All these men are sitting around with a lot of haggard, dumpy-looking women, you know, and I walk in, here I am, I'm living the part. So what's wrong? I think it's funnier than hell."

Yet despite his reputation, despite girls coming to his office and asking, "May I show you my body?" despite one actress taking her breast out of a low-cut gown asking, "You know any new tricks?" Russ Meyer insists, "When I was with a woman that was the only one I was with." And on his film sets, he's "always had a big thing about being the scoutmaster, making sure the women are not molested. You couldn't make as slickly made a film as I do if you fucked around." He even went so far as to tell his wife Edy when they were planning a movie that "we're just not gonna sleep together when we make the picture. I think we're gonna make a better picture if we don't."

For at bottom he is the hard worker, the man who calls himself "determined, stubborn, dedicated, resourceful, ambitious. I have an incredible amount of energy; I can outlast those twenty-year-olds. I mean it's like the neutron, you know, just a burning seed I have in my bosom. I'm a doer, I make things move and all that."

The result of all this toil has been a source of real pride to Russ

Meyer. "Listen," he says, "what else have I got to sell except Russ Meyer and some good camera work and a style—some people loftily call it a genre. But I compete, I can compete, there are damn few filmmakers that can slug it out toe to toe with the majors. I'm very proud of that. There's the orgasm, that you did it, you did it under any kind of adversity and critical condemnation." Then, after a pause, "But I tell you, there's nothing more electric than to sit in a theater, walk up and down and see people laugh. You made a bunch of people laugh. It's a great thing."

Also nice is the fact that critical recognition has come, albeit late, into Russ Meyer's life. The Yale University Law School Film Society ran a two-day festival of his best; highbrow critic Raymond Durgnat wrote an analysis of his work Meyer was amused to admit he couldn't make head or tail of; and most gratifying of all, "An Evening with Russ Meyer" was held at the Museum of Modern Art. "It was one of the most exciting nights I can ever remember. It was fantastic, it was like at a bullfight," the guest of honor remembers. "The people that were inside had all seen the film *(Beyond the Valley of the Dolls)* many times, they're real buffs of the picture. And they would stand up and scream the lines out before the actors would. And God, they were just trying to rip Edy's clothes off. It was just a fantastic thing."

This is where the real payoff comes for Russ Meyer. Always feeling he was serious about what he was doing—"meaning, if you work hard you're serious"—he would be offended when "people would hack at me"; when critics would say, "Like, who's this guy kidding?"; when women would "take great offense to what I've done"; when Charles Keating of Citizens for Decent Literature would attack *Vixen* so strongly that it would cost Meyer a quarter of a million dollars in legal fees to defend it. But his great reward, his justification and triumph, the thing that motivates him above all else is that people like his films like there was no tomorrow. "Russ Meyer, he may have made a critical piece of shit in *Beyond the Valley of the Dolls,* but wow, a lot of people went to see it, you know. Why? How come?" he says, momentarily taking the third person. "The most important critical acclaim is the box-office reaction, that people will want to go and lay down some money to see a picture. I feel pretty good about that."

Not only do people go to see them, they don't stop. "Films that have played, ten, twelve times in given theaters—they go back and they do great business, they play just as aggressively and just as strongly as they did before. People in Griffin, Georgia, and Terre Haute and Muskegon, they accept them, they go on a rainy night in Georgia and the theater does $1,400 with *Vixen* after it's played half a dozen times. Out there is an enormous following for my kind of films."

And most satisfying, his films have surmounted what he sometimes calls "any kind of critical bludgeoning," or, alternately, "a critical kick in the ass." Russ Meyer people are drive-in people, and drive-in people "do not read reviews. They're influenced by a shrieking, shouting radio spot, bombastic TV spot, and bigger-than-life ads. They go and they eat the tacos and hamburgers and maybe make out a little bit, and it's just a nice place to go. So those people don't give a shit about Judith Crist or Rex Reed. Who are they, you know?" The point is not so much that the films make money, but that they survive, they survive "even though you may get kicked in the balls." The films, like the man who made them, are tough enough.

Russ Meyer got his first movie camera at age fourteen in Oakland, California. To buy it, "my mother actually hocked her engagement ring," he remembers. "We were not particularly well off, but when I took an interest in a motion-picture camera, she being the type of gal she was, made sure I got one." And, according to a Twentieth Century-Fox studio biography, he promptly used it to take pictures of "neighborhood children, pets, and town drunks."

When World War II overtook his generation, Meyer had dropped out of college and was working as a messenger to support his mother and sister. Still interested in the movies, he read that the Signal Corps was looking for applicants to be combat cameramen. "It all sounded very romantic and exciting, and I realized that the infantry wasn't too far away," so he applied. But in the end, he nearly didn't go, nearly didn't get into motion pictures at all, because of a fishing trip, of all things.

"I've always been very fond of fishing in the mountains, and I was torn between going away fishing for a week and then returning and being drafted, or forgo the trip and go to Los Angeles" for Signal Corps interviews. Someone talked some sense into his head, and the fishing trip was postponed.

Training at first was "a complete hoax. We had an inane course in which we only exposed a hundred feet of film, and we were instructed in a camera that we never even saw again, none of us knew shit from shinola. But I placed second highest in my class, and I got what was called a T-3, which was a staff sergeant. I was nineteen, didn't know a fucking thing, except little 8mm movies, the Ice Capades, and Yosemite National Park, that sort of thing."

Finally, after reporting to the 166th Signal Photographic Company in Missouri he got some actual training, from Art Lloyd, who had shot most of the "Our Gang" comedies, and Joe Ruttenberg, who had filmed *Mrs. Miniver*. He was sent to Europe, and after landing at Normandy shortly after D-Day with the First Army, he went through most of the war with General Patton's Third Army. Some of his newsreel footage, of a Free French division headed by Jacques Le Clair entering liberated Paris, was used in the movie *Patton*. "Those scenes, as a cameraman they're indelible in your memory," he says. "You see them, and you know them."

Other footage Meyer shot also found its spot in movie lore, for it was of a group that ended up being immortalized in the immensely popular and often revived *The Dirty Dozen*. "They were twelve GIs who were convicted of capital crimes, rape, and murder, and apparently it was the brainstorm of some colonel somewhere that it would be a hell of an interesting thing to get these men together and train them and drop them on D-Day with specific missions and complete exoneration if they survived," Meyer says, a bit wryly. "I remember they were very surly, uncommunicative. I went in there and exposed a couple hundred feet of guys just laying on the ground glowering at me. And the guy says, 'We call them the Dirty Dozen because they vowed not to bathe or shave for the period of time they were there.'"

The actual end result, however, was not nearly as glamorous as Hollywood's. "There is no record of any mission having been accomplished by the Dirty Dozen, there were no heroes involved or anything, they dumped them out of an airplane and nothing ever was heard again, nobody ever turned up," Meyer reports. "I suspect one of them is, you know, down in Marseilles somewhere running a bar."

Russ Meyer talks at length about his war experiences, talks about them with care and feeling. They were, he says, the formative experiences of his life and have made him the ultimate Old Army Buddy. He is still very close with a number of his Signal Corps pals, seeking them out in odd corners of the country to have dinner and talk over old times. "Those two, three years I spent in the service were magnificent, exciting, marvelous; it was just Tom Swift and everything rolled into one," he says with great and careful emphasis. "There's nothing that I will ever do that will begin to approach that experience."

There were specific events, like meeting Ernest Hemingway in a small French town a few days before the liberation of Paris, or "being the only GI in town and the whorehouse says, 'Come on over,' and it's all that kind of Guy de Maupassant kind of whorehouse, you know, with the big fat madam and fifteen girls in sorts of negligees or nothing, that kind of beautiful whorehouse." But more than that, it was an era-of-good-times feeling that overwhelmed everything else. "See, it wasn't that unpleasant kind of war where you have jungle rot and crud and no matter where you were someone was going to ambush you," Meyer explains. "There were fixed conditions, and you could be relatively sure you could spend a pretty good night somewhere with some safety. And the next day was a new day and a new town, and you got in your jeep, and went down the road. There's a little danger and that's wonderful, you know, never thought for a minute that anything would happen to you. There was some gunfire, and you would get out in the trenches and try and somehow get pictures of explosions or artillery and hopefully get some guy shot or something, that kind of thing. It was a very romantic, very exciting moment."

With this kind of experience behind him, it was inevitable that Meyer would find fault with the immediate postwar world, and when the Hollywood film unions "just said 'fuck off' " he went back home to the San Francisco area and began making industrial movies, films for oil companies, railroads, and the like. One day an old Signal Corps buddy, Don Ornitz, asked him, " 'Why don't you start shooting girls?' And so I did, and I dug it, I really dug it. I had kind of a bombastic style, very mild by what's considered strong today, but I got into it hammer and tongs," becoming one of the top cheesecake photographers of the day, shooting stills for burlesque star Tempest Storm as well as some of the early *Playboy* centerfolds. It was also during this period that he made the acquaintance of burlesque entrepreneur Pete DeCenzie, "who was always after me to do a nudist film, and I was always rejecting it. He wanted me to do some kind of schlock picture—volleyball and croquet." Then Russ Meyer got an idea, the idea for *The Immoral Mr. Teas.*

"At the time," he remembers, "there was a lot of interest in voyeurism ard the common man and the big broads and put yourself in this position, you don't have to be twelve feet tall with a physique like Adonis, you too can enjoy the fruits of life." Acting on that premise, he and DeCenzie got together $24,000— the amount has become as legendary as the $24 spent for Manhattan Island—and in four or five days made a film starring an old Army buddy named Bill Teas. Innocent but leering, it was made, Meyer relates, "for fun. We made it like we were a couple of UCLA cinema graduates, just having a good time making a film."

The Immoral Mr. Teas was to make movie history of a sort, but not quite at once.

"When we finished it, we couldn't get a release anywhere; everyone was afraid because in those days this film was extremely bold," Meyer says. Six months went by, and Pete DeCenzie found himself in Seattle, Washington, with a print of the film. "Seattle had a censor board, and Pete met a fellow *paisan* who was one of the board members. And he said, 'Well, why don't we come up to my room and bring the board up there and I'll get a lot of wine and we'll eat some raviolis and I'll show you the film,' which was a most unusual way for a censor board to review a picture. So the fellow *paisan* says, 'Atsa nice,' and they all went up there and they passed the picture in the hotel room."

From there on in, all hell broke loose. *Teas* played for two years in Seattle, for almost three in Los Angeles and San Francisco. It was censored, banned, confiscated, and snipped to pieces, but the more than $1 million it made in its initial run was phenomenal for its day. It inspired endless imitators, not the least of whom was Meyer himself. "I immediately made another film with a lot of nudity and big tits and all that stuff. I copied myself maybe ten, eleven more times," he says now.

Overall, Russ Meyer is sentimental about his films. In his office, along with cutting equipment, odd pieces of film, and a tuxedo—"I'm ready to go anytime"—are mementos mounted on wooden plaques: Teas's hat, a straight razor from *Finders Keepers, Lovers Weepers,* a can of Treesweet grapefruit juice from *Vixen,* because one of the actors insisted on drinking it instead of water on location "and nearly broke me." But Russ Meyer also has a clear idea of which of his pictures really meant something. "'There were four important films in my life," he says, carefully, and after *Mr. Teas* the next one was *Lorna,* circa 1964. When that movie showed at Amherst, Massachusetts, witnesses swear that the crush was so thick in the lobby that the side wall mirrors actually cracked under the strain.

Big picture number three came four years later and started with a conversation Meyer had in a laundromat, where "I said we must really make the most erotic film that anybody's made." The result was *Vixen,* which succeeded royally because "it was the first film that I made that appealed to women. Unwittingly I made a film on behalf of women's lib. Because this woman calls all the shots. And she made everything better, people got back together, and it was all wonderful and marvelous."

It also paved the way for the final big picture. Twentieth Century-Fox mogul Darryl F. Zanuck saw *Vixen* in New York, liked it, and had son Richard invite Meyer in for a talk. Not one to take things too seriously he drove up for the interview in an unprepossessing Jeep and promptly fell asleep in Zanuck's outer office. "I was," he says, "real loose." When he awoke he made the beginnings of a deal that ended with him signing to make *Beyond the Valley of the Dolls* for $2 million, a giant jump in both budget and prestige for the erstwhile King of the Nudies.

Greeted by and large with a torrent of critical disgust, *Beyond* is nevertheless beloved by its creator. "I think I'm more proud of that picture than any film I've made. I think it is the best," he says. "It's made $11 million gross so far, it's played two years in London, there's a cult that follows this picture. You might say, 'How can you be so crass as to say it made $11 million,' but that still is the name of the game."

The technique that gets all these people to put down their money is based on one simple standard: "things or positions or attitudes that personally excited me physically." Take, for example, his use of women with breasts that "just boggle the mind. I dug it, I really dug it. I thought that it was really great. That was to me the ultimate, superwoman. I've been accused of degrading womanhood, but I don't look upon it that way. I just think that everyone that's built like that should be enormously fun-loving and just, you know, deliver all the pleasure one possibly can." And so these women inevitably end up "making love like a football scrimmage, always under difficult circumstances."

His stories, he admits are "morality plays. I feel pretty strongly about people getting their just desserts, if you do something bad you gotta pay for it." But the style—the style is something else. Originally used, Meyer admits, to help camouflage acting deficiencies, it has evolved into a fast, rambunctious, aggressively brazen manner where "I never let the story get in the way of the action.

"The people are all far out, the girls are outrageous, and they get right down to business in a hurry. And I think people can relate to that and say, 'Wow, Jesus, if I could just find something like that,' or the girl'll say, 'Mmm, look at that guy, he looks like something else.' It's a blending of violence, melodrama, hoke, parody, satire, really unbridled sex, the kind of sex that people fantasize about. You'd like to walk into a bar and there's a gal sitting there and she goes like that and there's that chemistry and pow, they're in the hotel in the next ten seconds. I have just this sixth sense with regard to rambunctious sex. And anytime that I've steered from it, it has not been altogether successful for me."

There is a large twinge of sadness in that last remark, for his next film, *The Seven Minutes*, based on the Irving Wallace novel about censorship, was the least titillating of all the Meyer epics and "my biggest disappointment, just an enormous disappointment. No matter how hard I try it would appear that the only thing I can make is some kind of half-assed comedy or satire or parody. It's like my reputation preceded me, my fans were let down, I did not give them what they wanted.

"I decided to take a great slap at Charles Keating, of the Citizens for Decent Literature, and that was stupid. I said, 'I'll do it, I'll do it, and I'll really make the common man understand the problems he's faced with as far as free speech.' But it went over like —well, it didn't go. Who gives a shit, who gives a shit about being lectured to? The common man is not concerned about censorship, not until they finally say, 'Sorry, you can't see any more R-rated movies.' So that was a mistake, it was a mistake, and I gotta watch that."

Meyer and Fox parted company after *Seven Minutes,* not so much because of the one failure, or because, as incorrectly rumored, he disliked working with a major studio crew—"It's wonderful, wonderful to have fifty-five people under foot, oh it's great"—but simply because his protector, Zanuck, was booted out in a studio coup and because some people were still offended that he had been offered work at a major studio at all, a kind of collective "How dare this man think he could come into these hallowed halls?"

Back as an independent, Meyer came face to face with a wave of pornography that, ironically, could be traced back to his original *Teas.* Remembering when he had been condemned as "that smut merchant," Meyer feels it would be presumptuous of him to condemn hard core, but just the same, it obviously doesn't appeal to his tastes. He archly calls *Deep Throat* a "highly publicized movie on cocksucking, with a girl that has no finesse at all, she's like a piston motor" and says he himself is "not interested in making hard core under any circumstances. It has no appeal to me whatsoever, God, love, nor money," the reason being, "it leaves nothing to the imagination. Once you show the zone you don't see anything else but that. I mean you see the cock and the mouth, you see the terrible looking pussy and the joint going in and . . . to me sex has to be taken with a grain of salt and not terribly seriously, that's all. And I just don't see the humor in some guy being sucked off. I think there are other ways."

When the Supreme Court moved heavily against sex in the movies, giving censorship authority back to the states, an action Meyer had predicted would be "just fucking poison," he was forced to cancel his next film, a $400,000 epic called *Foxy* that was to star Edy Williams and be distinctly on the racy side. After the court decision, he reasoned, it "might end up as the most expensive home movie ever made." And Edy herself filed for divorce, accusing Russ of "disappearing acts," adding "I am a sex symbol and I don't want to be alone." He took it all philosophically, commenting waspishly, "I don't think that I would care to continue within her guidelines, shall we say. It probably wasn't in the cards, a couple of egomaniacs impacted and rebounded."

With his latest movie, *Blacksnake* (later renamed *Sweet Suzie*) not breaking any box-office records, Meyer is unsure about the future. He's planning nothing more for now than getting in some of that fishing he's owed himself since the pre–Signal Corps days. As far as films go, he is trying to "come up with something now that people will buy tickets to see. I have to be practical, I have to work within the framework, but my whole thing is films, you know. I gotta make films and the Supreme Court be damned." With plain old X-rated movies, "you can't play as many theaters. It's like a prior indictment, like the skull and crossbones. The days of making a picture for $72,000 are gone. You can't do it now, because there is no longer the curious oddity of being a first."

He wants to make them "like I used to make it, where I shoot it, where there's an umbilical cord between me and the actors and the camera. I want to bust my ass, I want to make a simple film, and I want to make a very sensual, a very erotic film, that's my intention. And one who makes films must ask himself, 'Why does someone want to come to see my picture?' And the answer may lie in 'Where does Russ Meyer find those big girls?' I've always had one girl, and now maybe I should get about seven big girls, you know, whether it's an ingenue or a grandmother, they all have 46-inch busts." Whatever it turns out to be, Russ Meyer feels "I'm at a critical time in my career, I gotta come up with a big winner. I can coast very well, but I gotta come up with one that once more makes them say, 'Wow.' That's necessary."

So it is that Russ Meyer, the man who started it all, feels himself inexorably squeezed out of the picture. "The idea of Brando, the Academy Award winner, in there putting butter up some broad's ass and jumping her and you see his ass twittering as he's on top of her, it's hard to compete with that." Caught between the more explicit films made by major studios and the all-out pornographers, Meyer sighs and admits, "I don't know frankly if there are any more frontiers left. That's where I question, I really question, What is there left?"

35

4

"DICK NIXON DOESN'T HAVE AS MUCH FUN"

AN INTERVIEW WITH DAVID F. FRIEDMAN

"Hollywood is a showman's paradise. Showmen make nothing; they exploit what someone else has made. But the showmen in Hollywood control the making—and thereby degrade it."
— Raymond Chandler, "Writers in Hollywood"

"I put the film in one end of the projector and out of the other end comes money."
— David F. Friedman

At the very top of one of the storied Hollywood hills, David F. Friedman stands on the terrace of his splendid personal Xanadu and looks down on a view that could choke a horse. Arrayed below him in the madly twinkling evening lights are the houses of such as the Jackson Five, Johnny Mathis, Dorothy Provine, even Liberace. Dave Friedman views it all with equanimity. "I piss on 'em," he says, and then he laughs.

"Do I look like I have any lack?" he asks back inside, playing with a plate that allows him to gamble in the million-franc private circle at Monte Carlo. Besides the house and the three acres of near-priceless land it occupies, there are a dark Mercedes and a green-and-white Cadillac Coupe de Ville, both the latest model with personalized license plates "so you can tell it's the boss's car." Plus the $2,200 gold mesh watch, the gold engraved name bracelet, the gold wedding band, the gold and diamond pinkie ring. His clothes are tastefully obstreperous: "Everything I wear, though it may not look it, is the most expensive that money can buy." He travels extensively overseas, is an opera buff, occasionally flying to San Francisco just to see a good production. "I suppose I could liquidate my personal holdings for a million dollars," he says. "There's nothing that I want that I can't buy or that I don't buy for myself. I am probably one of the lucky few."

In the exploitation film industry, Dave Friedman is very much one of the powers that be. He is the president of Entertainment Ventures, Inc., the oldest and largest sex-film producing and distributing company in America, referred to, depending on Friedman's mood, as either "the Mighty Monarch of the Exploitation Film World" or "the oldest established permanent floating crap game in Los Angeles." He not only produces but writes, directs, and runs the publicity campaigns for his films, which, though not widely reviewed and "about as hard-core as *Mary Poppins*," formed the meat and potatoes of the soft-core market. Movies like *Starlet, Thar She Blows, Trader Hornee,* and *The Erotic Adventures of Zorro,* each made for less than $100,000 and returning about half a million dollars each, led to yearly EVI grosses that climbed to $2.5 million in fiscal 1972. To the French he is the pre-eminent *specialiste de films nudistes;* in America he has been called "the Great Clown Prince of Dermapixville" and his exploitation compatriots have elected him president of the Adult Film Association of America for four years running, but, characteristically, he says it's only because "I can't get anybody else to take the job." For Dave Friedman, being earnest and sincere is the only sin for which there is no forgiveness. "If I ever make a picture and take myself seriously," he says, "I'm gonna be in trouble."

He delights, for instance, in telling of his adventures in France, "where everybody is a journalist. I've never seen so many journalists. My God, they start calling for interviews and suddenly there're a dozen of them sitting around your hotel room, asking you these questions. 'What did you feel when you . . .?' 'Was the motivation . . .?' Are you kidding? Then you've got to invent these stupid answers. What the hell did somebody ask me on this last trip, 'Was the motivation de Maupassant?' or something. And do I feel 'a kinship to Buñuel'? I said, 'Who's Buñuel?' Oh, God, they can make so much of it. Most people make a picture to make money. I never wanted to be and I hope I never become either pompous or pretentious, because there is nothing to warrant any pretentiousness on my part. I've made a few bucks, I live a nice life, I'm having a ball."

Friedman maintains, by his own proud admission, "the highest profile in this industry," including cameo appearances in his own films, making him "the Hitchcock of the crotch operas." But all his public statements have the same brunt—things like, "P. T.

Barnum was wrong, there is more than one sucker born every minute," or "Did you know that no one has ever asked for his money back after seeing one of my movies?" or "I am probably guilty of promulgating more of the most disgusting garbage on the American public than anyone has ever done." His words strongly reinforce the image Friedman has of himself and would like the world to share. "I'm a showman, I am not an introvert by any means. Say something good or say something bad but for God's sake say something," he says. For to Dave Friedman the big bonus of the exploitation business is not the money or the acclaim, both of which he treats as incidental, but what he calls "the eternal con. I get a big kick out of being in a quasi-legal business. Mencken said, 'Nobody ever went broke underestimating the taste of the American public,' which Friedman has proved, and Lincoln said, 'You can fool some of the people all of the time and all of the people some of the time, but you can't fool all the people all of the time,' and Friedman adds to that, 'but you can try.' With the garbage I make and the money it brings back, I've got to be a con man."

Even as a kid hanging around carnivals, Friedman was admittedly fascinated by "concessionaires beating some farmer out of a whole winter's earnings and they sit there and rationalize it that 'if I didn't take it from him, he'd take it from me.' And this is the last syndrome extant where you can still do that. Don't get me wrong, I probably couldn't do something like Glenn Turner or some of these people that really hurt a lot of people and hurt them big. I rationalize it that what the hell, all I'm taking away from them is two and a half bucks and a couple of hours.

"In another time and another place I probably would have been running a shell game through the backwoods of Mississippi and Louisiana, one step ahead of the sheriff. The only difference is that I don't have to hook on the back of some passing freight anymore, just ahead of the posse. I now fly transcontinental jet, first class."

And Friedman plays the role of the successful flimflam man, the mogul, the enterprising entrepreneur with great enthusiasm, down to nonchalantly saying to a temporarily needy friend, "Let me lend you a grand" and immediately writing out the check. He is a big tipper who lists gambling and drinking—"When you come to interview Friedman, come prepared to drink"—as his main habits, the type who is personally known to everyone from the doorman to the headwaiter in the clubs he frequents. Sitting in his office in front of a collage of posters from some of his more colorful films—*The Lustful Turk, Brand of Shame, The Notorious Daughter of Fanny Hill*—he can answer any one of the three phones that compete for space on his massive desk with an executive pencil box, a canister of genuine Havana cigars, and signs that say "Big Boss" and "It's hard to be humble when you're as great as I am."

That desk sits in the cluster of faceless one-story buildings that serve as EVI headquarters, utilitarian blocks of brick and concrete located in downtown Los Angeles in what was the hub of Hollywood film activity half a century ago. Though there are no big fancy signs to indicate it, the buildings form a 34,000-square-foot exploitation film complex, an endless series of rooms and more rooms, where every aspect of the industry, from the storing of negatives to the production of stills, press kits, and posters to the screening of feature films, is handled with tender loving care. And to Dave Friedman, bow-tied, cigar-smoking, and just turned fifty, his body getting fuller at the middle, his hair graying but longish in the back, it is one great big toy. Gleefully padding from room to room, showing it all off, he becomes a cross between W. C. Fields and a teddybear, the Great High Pooh-bah of the exploitation industry. "This job may not pay as well, but I bet Dick Nixon doesn't have as much fun."

Though indifferent toward the paraphernalia of his own work —"I don't get sentimental about those pieces of crap; if I kept everything I'd need forty warehouses"—there is a segment of the exploitation industry whose every scrap Dave Friedman relishes. In a back room of his empire there are film clips and posters, old, yellow, and curling, that trace the entire history of the business. Stuff from vaguely contemporary films like *Nudes of All Nations* and *Christine Keeler Goes Nudist* to the World War II vintage *Atrocities of Manila,* which Friedman renamed *Beast of the East,* to really classic '30s vehicles like *Wages of Sin*—"The picture that hits you between the eyes"—and *Sinful Souls*—"She got in trouble, who was to blame?"—Friedman comes close to revering this aged stuff, for to him it signifies a time when men were men and exploiters really exploited. "I don't want to concentrate on myself or the rest of us nickel-and-dime guys that are running around now making like something important," he says. "I want to talk about the real characters that were in this business."

The original character, the man who in 1921 founded the company that later became EVI and whose photograph sits in the corporate lobby, the man who right on the very spot all those buildings now occupy made some of the first exploitation films, was an Italian immigrant named Louis Sonney. According to Friedman he arrived in the United States around the turn of the century, worked in the coal mines of Pennsylvania, and ended up in Centralia, Washington, where he was "the biggest, toughest miner in all of the state. They made him the town sheriff because he was the only guy who could handle the lumberjacks." One fine day in 1919 Sonney was walking down the streets of his town "and a guy goes by with bandages all over his face. Sonney looks back, and as he looks back the guy looks back. Sonney says, 'Hey you, just a moment, you acta very suspicious.' The guy says, 'Leave me alone.' Sonney says, 'I thinka you Roy Gardner.' Sonney takes him to the police station, pulls the goddamn bandages off the poor guy, and it's Roy Gardner."

Gardner, for those whose memories do not extend back to 1919, was "the most wanted man in America at the time, used to rob mail trains single-handed. There was a big reward on him, the Northwestern Railroad had a $5,000 reward, and the United States Government had a $5,000 reward. It was headlines all over the world, 'Officer Sonney Captures Roy Gardner.'" In 1921 a film was made of his exploits, entitled *The Smiling Mail Train Bandit,* the first of more than four hundred films that Sonney Amusement Enterprises was to produce. But that was all in the future. First Sonney went on the Pantages vaudeville circuit, traveling around, showing the film, and lecturing on how he captured old Roy Gardner. "He always had these 'Crime doesn't pay' shows, 'I'm a shoota him, he's a shoota me,' he always wore his cowboy hat," says Friedman, smiling to himself. And though Elmer, the mummified body of "some Oklahoma outlaw that some posse shot" and one of the features of Sonney's show, is now gone from its former place of honor in the EVI offices, there remains an aging, hand-painted sign from the old days that reads as follows: "Officer Sonney, Whose aim in life is to benefit all Mankind. To prove that crime is a disease and to abolish Capital punishment are his great Hobbies." So much for law and order.

All this continued rather uneventfully until one day in the '30s, when, in a small town in Montana, it began to dawn on Sonney that "people aren't interested in crime. But there's a guy down the street with sex, and he's doing all kinds of business. So the old man goes down and buys the sex show—the guy had models of VD, you know, diseased cunts and diseased pricks put in the lobby—and from then on the old man was in the sex business." He went back to Los Angeles and began making the *Wages of Sin*–type exploitation classics, items like *Gambling with Souls,* and *Forbidden Oats,* where titillation was given under the guise of moral instruction. "All of these pictures just hoped that through this showing of this great picture through the length and breadth of our beloved land that the evils of prostitution will be stamped out, or the evils of child marriage or the evils of dope," says Friedman delighted at the chicanery. "Whatever the subject was it was always an evil."

Distributing these films around the country were that group of characters who referred to themselves as "the Forty Thieves."

The time was the '30s, and they were road-show men, "traveling from town to town in their territory or they'd jump their territory —there was not one of them could read a map. They'd book the picture, play the date and bring all the publicity stuff, sit with the exhibitor, and at the end of the engagement share up with him in cash, one for you and one for me." Though the plots verged on the inane—*Wages of Sin,* for instance, has a fighting morals reformer sneaking out to the whorehouse and finding his daughter —these films were relatively well-made, starred a group of stock players, and played for a night or two in as many as two thousand theaters across the country. To keep the audience happy, a "square-up" reel, featuring plenty of nudity, would be slipped in once the police left. "It was very, very remunerative," says Friedman wistfully. "They absolutely got a percentage of every date they played because they were sitting right there. These guys made more money than the major studios ever dreamed of."

Following the Forty Thieves came the character who enthralls Friedman more than any other, the man he feels he is the direct descendent of, "the most fabulous showman America ever saw, a gentleman by the name of Kroger Babb." Babb's strong point was salesmanship, with a great big S, and the things he decided to sell were called "birth-of-a-baby" pictures, or "clap operas," little vehicles extolling the need for sex education and usually showing an actual birth on the side. After touring with lesser vehicles for some years, Babb in 1944 "conceived the idea of making *Mom and Dad,* the supreme birth-of-a-baby picture of all time." Along with the film, supersalesman Babb always had a guest lecturer, plus "a broad dressed up in a nurse's costume," whose joint task it was to sell the book—"how to do it, how not to do it, when to do it, why to do it, how not to get the clap, how to get the clap"—that Babb had printed to accompany the movie. Was it successful? Don't ask.

"This fucking *Mom and Dad* is everywhere," says Friedman, the excitement rising in his voice. "There ain't a theater in America that didn't play this picture. They had a show for women at two o'clock in the afternoon, another show for women at seven o'clock, and then a show for men at nine, and everybody had to listen to the lecture, and everybody bought a book—no, two books. We bought out Babb in 1956, and as near as I could figure out then, the picture had grossed in film rentals somewhere in the neighborhood of $40 million—God knows what the book sales were."

Not content with this success, Babb tried the same tack on other subjects, like drugs and alcohol. He went down to Lawton, Oklahoma, and filmed a local passion play, but when he found the country dialect too thick he redid the sound—"the first time English has ever been dubbed into English"—and when he

41

finished, came out "with a fucking campaign that is unbelievable, a title *The Prince of Peace,* the artwork is Christ on the cross, the nails through the palms, blood dripping. And no matter what, Babb always had something to sell. What were we selling? The New Testament the size of a postage stamp and a four-color picture of Jesus Christ, our Savior, suitable for framing." Following that bonanza, Babb got hold of some film shot in the Congo of a tribe called the Karimoja, "a pretty disgusting bunch who'd cut the throats of their cattle and drink the warm blood as it came out and rub themselves with the dung of the animals to ward off evil spirits. Ugh! The first thousand feet everybody throws up," but Babb recut it and released it as *Karimoja.* "Made a fucking fortune on it."

And so it goes, on and on, endless tales of the days when great things still remained to be done. "It was a much more fascinating business back in the '30s and the '40s and the '50s," Friedman says. "Men like Babb who made really big money, nobody ever chronicled anything they did, they were relatively unknown, and today they're ancient history. And we are all pimples upon the asses of the Kroger Babbs of this world."

Despite this tough-guy talk, and despite a varied career that has included writing speeches for former Alabama governor Big Jim Folsom and making a film with stripper Virginia "Ding-Dong" Bell—"Miss 48-24-36, her act was she walked across the stage and fell down, face first"—Dave Friedman was born into relatively affluent circumstances on the day before Christmas, 1923: "My mother was expecting a second Jesus; she got fooled." His grandfather had been a captain in the Civil War, his father was the editor of the conservative Birmingham, Alabama, *News* and a friend of Supreme Court Justice Hugo Black. His parents were divorced when he was eight, and "by the time I was eleven years old I was hanging around the theaters," conveniently owned by his uncle. He spent the weekends with his father, who lived in a hotel, and "got to like the life of living in a hotel, sleeping until noon every day, staying up all night, and seeing all the shows. A couple of times I ran away from home in the summer. I traveled with a carnival, traveled with circuses through friends of my father's." He graduated from Cornell with a degree in electrical engineering—"I couldn't change a light bulb today"— and joined the army during World War II. "Brilliant career, I think I shot myself in the foot." After the war he worked in notorious Phenix City, Alabama, as a craps dealer, bummed around a bit, and ended up as a press agent for Paramount in Chicago when he decided to go into the business of being an independent film distributor. "I walked away from a pretty good job," he says, but he has hardly been sorry.

The things that Dave Friedman began to produce, direct, and distribute covered an incredible amount of exploitation territory. He made perhaps the first post–*Mr. Teas* Nudie, *The Adventures of Lucky Pierre,* and distributed the first Ingmar Bergman film shown in America, *Monika,* as a sex picture. He spent three years traveling with his own versions of the birth-of-a-baby films and made about half a dozen nudist-camp films.

"I spent more time in nudist colonies than any nonnudist in the world," Friedman says with wry pride, proceeding to detail his experiences with "Zelda, the queen of the nudists," the proprietress of a camp he was interested in using. "Here's this old hag in her fifties, had a pair of tits that hung down below her belly button, and we're talking to her about this picture and how it's gonna extol the virtues of nudism. Yes, they were very interested, but they wanted $5,000 for the use of the camp, and everybody would have to take off their clothes and sign the nudist pledge. Oh my God, it was like a masonic order. We have lunch, and they're having spaghetti, and here's Zelda's tits in the spaghetti, nosing their way in, and I said, 'Fuck this.' So we found another camp."

Friedman's subsequent creation of the genre known as the Ghoulies was greatly helped by a new type of artificial blood that "really photographed like blood for the first time. It was viscous; it looked like you'd really sliced a vein."

Friedman, "not ashamed of anything I've ever done," finds it ironic that his Ghoulies had infinitely less trouble passing censor boards than anything with sex or nudity in it and, in fact, have gone on to become "classic pictures that every backwoods drive-in plays year in and year out." He is not one of those people who "come out and formally say, 'Which would you rather see, someone getting killed or slaughtered or someone making love?' That's a device. I say if somebody wants to see somebody getting killed, let him see that, same as you see him getting fucked. If you're gonna defend a person's right to see sex, you're gonna have to defend his right to see anything."

Be that as it may, Friedman left the Ghoulies behind and began turning out regulation soft core with titles like *My Tale Is Hot, The Master Piece, The Big Snatch,* and *Come One, Come All.* The formulas for all of them, he likes to say, "are as rigid as a medieval morality play. A heterosexual scene, an S-M scene, a lesbian scene; oldest thing in show business, something for everybody." But the people who came to Dave Friedman's films, they got something more.

For though he calls his stuff "back-alley pictures" and worse, though he claims that "everything that I have ever spewed forth is garbage," and that the whole exploitation business is "a big fucking joke anyway," he will admit under slight pressure that his efforts are "the best the market has to offer, twenty times better than most of the shit that was coming out. I do not shoot these fucking things in a hotel room. Every one of these at least looks like a movie and sounds like a movie. The sound is crisp and clear, the photography is good, there is a semblance of a story. There is more than just fucking and sucking, and I can prove that, because I can cut out the fucking and sucking and still have a motion picture that can play to an audience somewhere."

In addition to all this, there is the unmistakable Dave Friedman trademark: a very zany sense of humor. It appears in the way he writes about himself in EVI promotional literature: "America's Fearless Young Showman . . . The sounds of audience laughter and ticket-machine clicking all over the world ring in Friedman's circumspect ears, stimulating a continuing creative output." It appears in his poster campaigns, where he calls *Zorro* "the only picture rated Z" and *Trader Hornee* "The film that breaks the law of the jungle . . . Convivially consummated in color . . . The film that proves you don't need talent, just nerve." It appears in the names he makes up for his cast and his crew, names like Mona Lott and Joy Boxe for his co-scriptwriters, Lance Boyle and Heidy Ho (as Brunhilde) for his stars in *The Long Swift Sword of Siegfried*, and in calling "the most feared tribe in all the Dark Continent" the Meshpokas (the Yiddish word for "clan") and having the character Phil Latio (Sgt. Felipe Latio in *Zorro*) appear in all his films as a running joke. And most of all, the humor surfaces in the quarter-hour trailers Friedman makes for his films with his very own hands, efforts so zippy that he has been asked to show them to the students who attend the American Film Institute's summer seminars. In the *Trader Hornee* clip, for instance, a stentorian voice booms niceties like "No animals on the ark to rival these," and "This ship isn't the Mayflower but several beautiful girls have come across on it," and "A story that will drain your emotional fountain." Friedman himself enjoys the trailers as much as anybody, guffawing along with guests whenever they're shown. "Most people are making pretentious garbage or crummy garbage," he says between chuckles. "I make funny garbage."

While others went on tours with their female stars, puckish Friedman went one better, going around with John Alderman, his major male lead. "And Christ almighty, the reception was unbelievable. It was amazing, these poor suckers would come up to him in the lobby of theaters and say, 'Gee, Mr. Alderman, I've seen all your movies, and I love the way you handle girls, and I've never had a date with a girl and I need a . . . .' But the guy handled himself beautifully, and he talked to these poor suckers and gave them

44

autographs and told them how to meet girls and what to say to them. Oh, it was tragic, but that actually happened."

All of which confirmed Friedman's suspicions as to whom he was making his films for. "You are pandering to the most horrible of all human emotions, loneliness," he is wont to say. "The average guy, why does a guy buy a dirty book, why does a guy buy a girlie magazine? A guy buys a dirty book primarily to take home or wherever he is and masturbate while he reads it, because it creates a fantasy. If you were a lonely guy, let's say you were on the road, you're in a strange town, not one guy out of a thousand knows how to get a date unless he's paying for it, and even when it comes to paying for it, he's too embarrassed to ask. So he goes to a Nudie theater and he fantasizes."

For a while Dave Friedman and a handful of other entrepreneurs had this market all sewn up, and a very loyal market it was. "The same guys came every week to the same theaters," he says fondly. "I had theaters that I could go down on opening day and call the roll. They came back week after week, because that was the whole secret of the exploitation business. 'Well we didn't see it this week, but boy, we're sure gonna see it next week.' " More of the old con, you understand, and it worked fine until catastrophe struck: "A few assholes decided to go hard-core and gave away the last act."

Dave Friedman's opposition to hard core is hardly on moral grounds, for though politically conservative—"I voted for Nixon six times; the poor guy needs all the help he can get"—he is a bleeding heart liberal on the censorship issue. "I was fighting these battles when most of these people were pumping gas or still in grammar school," he says, referring to the ancient days when the biggest enemy a film had was the Roman Catholic Church. "In those days the priest would call the theater owner, 'Don't you dare play this picture!' and the guy would sit and shake in his boots," Friedman says, recalling an incident in Mandan, South Dakota, where the Knights of Columbus came out to picket one of his films and "burned the goddamn screen down and nobody said a word. The cops didn't come out, nothing happened." His problem is rather a fiscal one, a feeling that explicitness killed the goose that laid the golden exploitation egg.

"I hope they roll things back ten years, I dare say it was more profitable then than it is today," Friedman says, claiming it was possible to make more money "when you got flesh and tit than when you can show a guy eating a girl's cunt." Because showing everything put minimum values on the type of technical polish Friedman pushes and meant that "everybody in the world who can fire a camera and find a broad that will fuck will make one, and every guy who can find a 30-foot storefront will open a theater.

Business isn't worth a tinker's damn." He also has little patience with what he considers the hard-core people's arrogance, "all these guys who will tell you how many millions they've made." And as to the possibility of legalization, he feels that it would finish his end of the industry by bringing in the major studios. "If they make a picture with Ali McGraw and Steve McQueen— I'm just using a couple of names—who in the hell will see our broads with the pimples on their back and their dirty feet. Because the majors can spend two hours making her up every time she's gonna suck a cock and there isn't gonna be a pimple, there isn't gonna be a drop of sweat or an asshair showing. It's gonna really be sucking and fucking with kid gloves on and ain't nobody gonna go see Linda Lovelace if they can see Ali McGraw."

The Supreme Court decision leaving everything up to the states is fine with Friedman, who has the facilities to tailor his film fifty different ways if necessary. And, anyway, Entertainment Ventures, Inc., has been primarily involved with R-rated ventures like *Bummer: A Far Out Trip Through a Hard Rock Tunnel* for the last two years, even recutting some of its X-rated features for rerelease with an R rating. The reason, again, is strictly economics, for R films can get, Friedman says, two thousand more bookings than X films, adding half a million dollars to the grosses, and that is nothing to sneeze at.

But as Dave Friedman sits around talking about his financial solvency, something seems to be missing. A man who gets his biggest kick being "in the forbidden fruit business, the same business the bootleggers were in during Prohibition," he knows that, traditionally, "the only reason for your existence, your total *raison d'être* is that you do something that the majors never touched." And now, with the majors into just about everything, what will give David F. Friedman that extra little jolt that merely making money just doesn't provide?

"There was a time that I had a patent on this exploitation market in that I would do something that nobody else would do, and now there ain't nothing that nobody else won't do, including the majors," he says, brooding a bit. His thoughts turn to strange films he's seen around in the past, a circumcision epic called *Slash of the Knife* and a murder mystery called *Chained for Life* starring genuine Siamese twins. "I ought to go back and really do something vile and disgusting, I mean, to really shake up the American public," he says, thinking it out. "Maybe I'll go back and start doing something that nobody would dare touch." He pauses now, and thinks some more. "Then the question is, what subject matter is there in human life today that nobody would dare touch?"

5

SOFT-CORE SENSUALITY

MADE-IN-AMERICA AND FOREIGN FILMS

During the '60s, the producers and directors of American sex-exploitation films grew increasingly skillful in dealing with erotic themes, and as a result "dirty movies" turned to more daring themes and images, revealing the contours of the human form in their frank treatments of human sexuality. It was the golden age of soft-core erotic fantasy, an innocent time during which movies showed all but the Real Thing. As the courts and the press began to take a very close interest in the erotic motion picture, foreign films became a significant factor in the sex-exploitation market, running up large grosses and hastening the maturation of the American sex film.

There is no absolutely accurate count of the total number of foreign films that played on American screens over the years, but it is literally in the thousands. Many of these films, neither titled nor dubbed, were intended for showing in ethnic enclaves—to Polish audiences in Paterson, New Jersey, and to Spanish-speaking audiences in towns along the Mexican border. Of the many foreign films, however, that were dubbed and released to the American public, almost all were merchandised on the real or imagined nature of their erotic qualities—Fellini's *La Dolce Vita,* for example, played on a double bill with *Platinum High School* at a drive-in in rural Virginia, and David F. Friedman distributed Ingmar Bergman's *Monika* with the subtitle *The Story of a Bad Girl,* playing up the sexual nature of Bergman's tender, moving study of a troubled, indiscreet Swedish adolescent. The art and exploitation market in the late '50s really expanded with the release of films like *Hiroshima, Mon Amour*; *Breathless*; *Les Liaisons Dangereuses*; *Love Is My Profession*; *Les Cousins*; *Lady Chatterley's Lover*; and, perhaps most significant of all, *And God Created Woman*, starring Brigitte Bardot. Director Roger Vadim, then Bardot's husband, carefully constructed a highly profitable personality for Bardot: She was the new woman—sensual, sometimes childlike, sometimes dangerously adult, permissive, and open. Despite the "cool" versions of certain nude scenes in *And God Created Woman*, the film grossed $4 million on the American market.

The careful preparation by Vadim of two separate versions of the same scene (in one she is raped, but her body is not exposed, in the other she is raped and her breasts and underwear shown) points up the difficulty of actually getting a foreign film into the United States. A U.S. Customs Service film reviewer inspects all motion-picture film entering the country and notes any he finds obscene or pornographic in intention. This decision is reviewed by a higher official, and, if the senior officer concurs, the film is seized. To show the film, the importer must then go to court and prove that the film is not obscene, an expensive delay that leads most importers to bring in only those films that will, in all likelihood, pass the customs inspectors. State and local censorship boards form another block to the exhibition of foreign films in the United States, and in the '60s certain theater circuits, fearing a company-wide boycott, would refuse to book a movie that might be condemned by the Catholic Legion of Decency.

Compared to American films of the era, the foreign product was shocking indeed, dealing realistically and in a mature fashion with prostitution, extramarital sex, homosexuality, rape, incest, pedophilia, sexual dysfunction, abortion, and birth control. It was left to certain distributors to fight the court battles that would make them available, if not in every local theater, at least in those art houses that catered to a smaller, adult, urban audience that would not be deterred by the Catholic Church. The rewards to be gained, in the form of large box-office grosses, attracted some of those companies that had been involved with sex films since the '50s—Entertainment Ventures, Inc., Audubon, Boxoffice International, Hollywood Cinema Associates, Eve Productions, Sherpix, Times Film Corporation, William Mishkin, Distripix, the Cresse conglomerate—whose owners are now banded together into a loose, professional association, the Adult Film Producers Association.

One of the first important foreign films to get into censorship trouble was a British-French coproduction of *Lady Chatterley's Lover*, imported to the United States in 1959 by Kingsley International Pictures Corporation. When the film was submitted to the Motion Picture Division of the New York Education Department for licensing, several nude and partially nude scenes were found objectionable. Rather than submit to cuts, Kingsley International appealed the case to the Regents of the University of the State of New York, who concurred with the ruling. The decision was later annulled by an appellate court, upheld by the Court of Appeals of New York, and eventually considered by the Supreme Court, where Justice Potter Stewart delivered the final opinion. Remarkably, the Court agreed almost to a man on the issues involved:

> What New York has done is to prevent the exhibition of a motion picture because that picture advocates an idea—that adultery under certain circumstances may be proper behavior. Yet the First Amendment's basic guarantee is of freedom to advocate ideas. The State, quite simply, has thus struck at the very heart of constitutionally protected liberty.

The language of the opinion is remarkably straightforward, but the Court did not address itself to several questions raised by the defense, namely, the vagueness of the language in the New York Penal Code definition of obscenity and the validity of censorship of a film prior to its public showing. These questions were to surface again in the five years following the Kingsley decision, as a number of controversies arose over what, specifically, could be shown on the screen.

Among the films that got into trouble was *Les Amants*, a critically praised film by Louis Malle that, in advocating adultery, depicted nudity in a manner that went beyond the customary limits of candor. Nico Jacobellis, a theater manager in Columbus, Ohio, was charged with possessing and exhibiting an "indecent and immoral" motion picture that offended "against the peace and dignity of the state of Ohio," and his conviction was appealed all the way to the Supreme Court. This time Justice William Brennan raised the question of community standards, defining them on a national scale, and found the movie not obscene within the standards enunciated in *Roth* v. *United States* and *Alberts* v. *California*.

This decision, handed down in June 1964, coupled with the earlier ruling that nudity *per se* was not obscene, opened the way for films that were more explicit than any seen on American screens since the enforcement of the Production Code in 1934. The impact of the Court's decision was not lost on the American distributors of foreign films, who from the early '60s had begun to buy and develop a relatively large number of theaters—around

500 for routine films and 1,500 to 2,000 for blockbusters like *La Dolce Vita*—in which to show imported movies.

Physical distribution was worked out in several ways. Large distribution companies often handled, and continue to handle, the booking and print shipping of films on a national basis, backing the movie with countrywide advertising in the motion-picture trade press. Smaller distributors, because of the difficulty of supervising nationally the disposition of film prints and the division of the house take, generally have preferred to handle a film only in their own region of the United States.

Most theaters that show sex-exploitation features do not rent films outright from distributors. Instead, they take a percentage of the house take (minus the distributor's share of advertising costs) on a predetermined basis. The better the film, the more money will proportionately go to the distributor of the film, but in most instances the lion's share goes to the exhibitor. Understandably, this form of profit sharing occasionally creates a troubled relationship, with distributors often accusing exhibitors of giving inaccurate counts of the house take by reusing tickets and adding box-office receipts onto the figures for popcorn sales. Eve Meyer, president of Emco Films, one of the oldest and most prominent sex-exploitation distributors, claimed in a *Hollywood Reporter* interview:

> I have been stolen from by everybody over the years. . . . There are so many ways for them to steal, so many ways. I've tried checking, and they buy the checkers. They pay them off, so they get paid off at both ends. . . . They just don't pay you. When you get the box-office figures, which are probably false to begin with, and you talk about getting paid, they say, "Well, I'd like to give you 5 per cent less." Well, the hell with 5 per cent less. It's an honest debt.

Conversely, theater managers agree that the product sometimes sent into theaters is so bad that they must revise the sliding scale or the theater will operate at a loss for the week. The arbitrary method of cost accounting may be unethical but perhaps is necessary in a business where some unscrupulous, fly-by-night distributor will buy a very old film, juice it up with some Nudie or hardcore inserts totally unrelated to the story, add a new title, and rent it to a theater owner who has already played it ten times.

The prospect of poor prints, archaic distribution methods, potential police harassment, and censorship did not deter Radley Metzger, who, with his partner, Ava Leighton, founded Audubon Films in 1960 and immediately began to import foreign films to sell on the exploitation market. From the first film Metzger bought

—Mademoiselle Striptease, a French film starring Agnes Laurent
—his choice of product paid off. To avoid confusion with an
identically titled Brigitte Bardot film on the American market,
Metzger toyed with changing the name of the film to *The Nude
Set,* but because newspapers in California wouldn't carry the
word "nude" in advertising, he finally settled on *The Fast Set.*
Metzger vividly recalls his difficulties with the film:

> There was nothing raunchy, no kissing, no shaking hands . . .
> but it did have some striptease and bare breasts, of course. Some-
> one asked a professional sex distributor, and he said the content of
> the film would limit it to about ten theaters in the United States.
> That's what a bare breast was considered.

But *The Fast Set* played many more theaters than the predicted
ten. It made enough money to convince Metzger to buy another
Agnes Laurent film, *Les Collégiennes,* that was released in the
United States as *The Twilight Girls.*

The original version of the film had no overt sex in it, so
Metzger shot some inserts of nude women and matched them to
the original footage, an addition that escaped notice in thirty-five
states before it caught the attention of the New York State Motion
Picture Commission when the film was submitted for licensing in
that state. Despite Commission objections to "various scenes in
which the lesbians embrace and show their interest in this type
of sex perversion," Metzger eventually won his case in the New
York State Court of Appeals.

Another Audubon film released at this time, *I Spit on Your
Grave,* ran afoul of local Memphis police for depicting a steamy
love affair between a black man and a white woman set in that
city. In an interview at the time Metzger said:

> It does show some citizens of Memphis behaving in perhaps an
> uncomplimentary manner; but, under the guise of restraining some-
> thing that is sexy, you have a regulation of a social comment on the
> citizens of Memphis and those citizens of the South who support
> lynching.

This film was followed by *Warm Nights and Hot Pleasures,
Sweet Ecstasy, Days of Sin, Nights of Nymphomania, Soft Skin
on Black Lace, The Weird Lovemakers,* and, one of the strangest
and most successful films in the Audubon catalog, a French import called *Sexus,* directed by Jose Benazeraf. Radley Metzger's
taste for the esoteric, the erotic, and the elegant is nowhere more
evident than in *Sexus,* a bizarre, surreal gangster melodrama full
of rape and murder, lesbianism and grand larceny. The film is a

parody of American thrillers, but the slow, arty direction, full of pauses and shots of clocks, kills the logic and dramatic momentum of the plot. The only sex in *Sexus*, other than rape, sadism, and shots of Dany Carrel changing clothes, consists of two startling numbers in a lesbian nightclub in Paris. The first is a dance of love between a black woman and a white woman that ends with lips and bodies entwined and almost lives up to the movie's advance billing as "a study of sexual excess." In the second dance, one woman, with dark, close-cropped hair and stripped naked to the waist, caresses her partner, a full-figured blonde, with a cat-o'-nine-tails. This sadomasochistic number was a sensation at the time and is still remembered as one of the high points of the erotic cinema—suggestive, disturbing, and exciting. The scene's effectiveness emerges from a lucid, carnal representation that is graphic but not gross.

The great success of these foreign films in the early '60s soon had an impact on the nature of the American sex-exploitation film, and before long audiences were being treated to U.S.–made movies featuring nudity and direct intimacy in the sex act: *The Sins of Mona Kent*; *Too Young, Too Immoral*; *Unwed Mothers*; and *Wild for Kicks*. Like their forerunner, *Mom and Dad*, these offspring preached against such abuses as forced prostitution, ignorance about sex and birth control, teenage promiscuity, and drug abuse.

One of them, *White Slavery*, produced and directed by Barry Mahon, got its raw sex and nudity past the censors only because of the seriousness with which a narrator deplored the workings of the ruthless syndicate that used force, intimidation, brutality, and humiliation to turn respectable women into whores. Mahon later attributed the success of the picture to the large number of women viewers who seem to have been attracted by a fearful curiosity about sexual abduction.

Another film from this period, *Strange Compulsion*, remains one of the great oddities of the genre. It dealt with the voyeurism of a troubled, young medical student (Preston Sturges, Jr.) who is afflicted by the overwhelming desire to observe women both clothed and naked ("I don't want to touch them . . . I just want to watch them"). Aware that this fixation will ruin his career, he seeks help from a psychiatrist, who has the young man discuss his erotic past (seen in flashback). Gradually, the doctor uncovers the compelling reasons for the young man's behavior. Typically, the producers of *Strange Compulsion* were at pains to justify the nudity and sex in the film, and, disclaiming the movie's audience, advertised, "This is *not* a picture for the cheap thrillseeker, snickering, slavering ogler of female flesh. . . . The producers have set their sights higher and have aimed at a more ambitious target, namely to present the story in a realistic manner."

The Orgy at Lil's Place, made in 1964 by longtime New York movie distributor William Mishkin, continued to break new ground for sex-exploitation movies. Mishkin's formula for success—he parlayed an investment of $35,000 into gross profits of more than $300,000—was simple and direct hard sell of soft sex in the framework of a highly puritanical morality play. Like numerous other films of this genre, the innocent heroine, an actress, falls on hard times, works at a trade with sexual overtones (here, as an art model), is almost raped at a party that turns into an orgy, and has her virtue finally rewarded by marriage to a writer. Unlike many similar films, however, *The Orgy at Lil's Place* did have its erotic moments: nudity in the art classes, an attempted rape, a whipping scene, a vice raid, beautiful girls wrestling, and the final orgy at Lil's place (shot in color) that really did look a little like an orgy. The direction by J. Nehemiah was competent, and Carrie Knudson, fresh from the *Playboy* centerfold, acted the part of the heroine in what was perhaps the most daring American film, and certainly one of the most successful, made up to that time.

The same year, 1964, Radley Metzger directed his second film, *The Dirty Girls* (his first, *Dark Odyssey,* had been a total flop), a two-part study of European prostitution shot with a certain erotic elegance on location in Paris and Munich. (The cinematography was by Hans Jura, one of Europe's finest cameramen.) The first story involves a young French streetwalker who, in the course of her business, runs into a variety of men: a shy boy, a sadist, and a masochist. The second focuses on the love life of a high-priced call girl.

The success of *The Dirty Girls* inspired Metzger to make *The Alley Cats* with Peter Fernandez, who had also written *The Dirty Girls,* and with photography once more done in Europe by Hans Jura. Again the collaboration was successful, and profits were substantial. As Metzger explained to Richard Brown in an interview in *Today's Film Maker:*

Ordinarily, a producer sees possibly 10 per cent of what his pictures bring in, because the income has to be cut into so many small pieces. In my case, I didn't have to realize so much on my pictures because I saw 100 per cent of what was coming in, and I didn't have an enormous bureaucratic structure to support.

Metzger made good use of the corporate income of Audubon, and in 1966 he produced an Eastmancolor film called *Carmen,*

Baby, based on the original story by Prosper Merimée. Shot on location in Yugoslavia, and starring Uta Levka and Barbara Valentine, the picture was perhaps the first of Metzger's films to fully display the thematic and stylistic preoccupations that distinguish his best work. The story of a faithless woman who is killed by her jealous lover apparently interested Metzger because of the multiple deceptions and betrayals and the chance to explore erotic themes and images. In one extraordinary love scene, photographed through rows of colored bottles in a series of slow, dream-like tracking shots, the erotic charge is contained not in the explicitness of the image—it is, in fact, difficult to know exactly what is going on between the lovers—but in the constantly shifting colors and textures of glass and flesh. Characteristically, Metzger avoids the cheap, fleshy two-person shot in preference to the imaginative use of plastic materials, and the suggestiveness and tactility of the image override the importance of physical lovemaking.

While Radley Metzger was directing the first of his erotic movie fantasies, David F. Friedman put into distribution a film that was to be one of his most successful, *The Notorious Daughter of Fanny Hill*. The picture, made under a bewildering variety of pseudonyms by men whose collective credits include *Kiss Me Quick, Knockers Up, Woman of Pleasure, The Wonderful World of Girls,* and *My Tale Is Hot,* showed nudity and direct physical contact between the sexes, with erotic scenes played for both thrills and laughter. It relates the fabricated adventures of Kissy Hill (Stacey Walker), daughter of the famous English courtesan, and herself a skilled, cynical professional who provides "special" services catering to the fantasies and fetishes of the rich and titled men who purchase her favors. Obviously influenced by Tony Richardson's *Tom Jones* (there was a gross, suggestive eating scene as well as a heroic love bout that knocked pictures off the wall), *The Notorious Daughter of Fanny Hill* was a costume picture shot in color with quality equipment and with more than usual care to details of sets and costumes. The attention paid off; the picture has remained one of the most financially successful ever released by Entertainment Ventures, Inc., along with *The Defilers, A Smell of Honey, A Swallow of Brine,* and *She Freak*.

In the wake of these comparatively memorable films there followed an extraordinary number of cheaply made sex-exploitation movies that were not very good. Many were probably seen only by a handful of patrons, but certain titles are noteworthy for the people who worked in them. *The Sweet Smell of Sex*, for example, was directed by Robert Downey (who later made *Putney Swope* and *Greaser's Palace*) at a time when he was broke and his wife was pregnant. Downey recalls, in an interview with Professor Joel E. Siegel of Georgetown University:

> I did *Sweet Smell* in three days for the bread—$750. But it wasn't worth it! I rounded up every freak I knew and we all freaked out together. I've written all of my movies, but this one was winged. We screened the final cut at the Bleecker Street Cinema with no soundtrack, just Beatles records, and it was really funny. Then the guy who produced the film put a narration on it and terrible music. [Tom] O'Horgan showed up with some jazz-men, took one look at it, and winged a score that doesn't fit—all in one session. The music is just terrible. I couldn't salvage the film. It's not mine—I don't own it. The producer [Bernard L. Sackett] was furious with what I'd done. The sex theaters didn't want to show it because it didn't have the kind of sex they wanted in it. I was doing all these strange, wild things with chickens and dogs, and it was funny. But the producer, who had done other sex films, kept referring to his past movies as one-, two-, and three-hatters. Which refers to how many hats the old creeps who go to these movies bring into the theatre to, like, make it in. The producer saw my film, said it was a no-hatter, and that was that.

The plot of *The Sweet Smell of Sex* bears little resemblance to the story lines of more ordinary sex-exploitation films. Bebe Katsafannis, the bumptious heroine "with normal tastes," encounters various men who use her: a bold man in a limousine, a fat man who keeps pigeons in his apartment, a cabdriver who rapes her. After a wild party featuring a sadistic version of the Frug, Bebe prepares to leave town, but she meets Joe, a regular guy whom she has shunned for the wild life. They return to his apartment, where Joe strangles her. As advertising for the film put it: "For all the weirdos Bebe toyed with, the ordinary Joe—who looked so straight—left the most lasting impression on Bebe."

Whatever the soft-core films lacked in quality was made up in staggering quantity, for there were about 1,000 exploitation movies released during the '60s. Most of the titles have long been forgotten, but a few of the more memorable are *Body of a Female*; *The Seducers*; *The Sexploiters*; *Lip Service*; *Moving Violation*; *Overdose of Degradation*; *Lonely Sex*; *All of Me*; *Skin Deep in Love*; *Sex Family Robinson on the Farm*; *I Feel It Coming*; *Girls That Do*; *Invitation to Lust*; *Bad Girls Go to Hell*; *She Came on the Bus*; *Love Now, Pay Later*; and *After the Ball Was Over*. These films, intended exclusively for the sex market, were remarkably consistent in the development and deployment of erotic themes and situations. The obligatory "hot parts"—the sole selling point and reason for being of erotic films—were usually handled by directors in the same way; such sex scenes also appeared generally in the same order, moving from solo sex to conventional sex to unconventional sex.

By the mid-'60s certain elements could be consistently detected in virtually all sex-exploitation films. For one thing, topical issues were reflected in the nevertheless trite plot lines. When the New York *Daily News*, for example, ran an exposé of white slavery in Manhattan, several astute producers immediately made films on the subject. More important, though, are evidently the constant erotic components of a communal sexual imagination—many of which are commonly found in written pornography.

One of the most common erotic elements is female masturbation, which seems to hold an endless fascination for the male viewer. The activity, filmed with attention to gesture and nuance worthy of Kabuki drama, generally occurs early in the soft-core film, when the young, sexually innocent woman is either very much alone or extremely aroused by a passion to which she as yet dares not give in. In most cases, the young woman steps out of her bath or clothes, slowly undressing before her mirror, where she admires her figure and massages her breasts. She then retires to her bed and slowly moves her hands down her body, suggestively out of range of the camera. There are close-ups of her passionate face (with licking of the lips, closed eyes, and heavy breathing), and a few intercut shots of her body, until she noisily achieves orgasm. Often a man watches through a window, his voyeurism sometimes leading to rape or seduction.

A second erotic component of sex-exploitation films is the lovemaking of the hero and heroine. With the men clothed in their tight underwear (to avoid seizure and censorship of the film), this scene is generally a lot less interesting to watch than the others. Again, the lovemaking is accompanied by a great deal of panting and puffing, shots of hands clutching sheets and feet at odd angles, and a lot of close-ups of the woman's face in sustained if contrived ecstasy. A fade-out sometimes rescues the audience from having to hear the trite and trying post-coital dialogue of many of these movies.

Later, when the innocent heroine has been betrayed by the man who introduced her to the joys of sex, she is seduced by another woman, usually slightly older and more experienced, and, significantly, bisexual. There is a great deal more explicit activity in lesbian scenes than in the heterosexual ones, because it is much easier to fake sex between two women than between a woman and a man. Our heroine does not become a confirmed lesbian, however; the scene has been merely an illicit interlude. Except in films made expressly for gay audiences, male homosexual activity is very seldom shown, because the predominantly male audi- ence for sex-exploitation films would undoubtedly find such scenes distasteful.

The other erotic elements in sex-exploitation films are taken from among the more unusual forms of sexual activity: rape, group sex, wife-swapping. An orgy sequence with dance or strip-tease is an absolute essential, for that activity eventually con-vinces the heroine that she must reform and settle down with the man she truly loves. Most sex-exploitation movies end with some sort of moral, and a woman who does not repent her carnal life usually meets with a violent death.

Dave Friedman has commented that sex-exploitation films were all "gesture and tease," but several directors, among them Joe Sarno, Lee Frost, Barry Mahon, and Bob Cresse, became quite expert within the genre. Although they did not show the viewer what he wanted to see, the audience kept coming back. The con-stant shifting between concealment and display, between expecta-tion and surprise was stimulating, and as nudity and sexual activ-ity in these films became more explicit, their success was assured. Two reviews in the periodical *Artisex* indicate what the audience was interested in. *Kiss Me Mate* features "an attractive, though tough-looking blonde nymphomaniac with lovely, responsive-nippled breasts, which come in for copious mauling and occa-sional nibbling in an imaginative variety of positions. Intercourse is reasonably realistic and there is a plot (largely narrated), trite as it may be." In *Monique, My Love*, "a narrator describes the experiences of her ambitious roommate in breaking into the sex-ploitation movie actress profession. That theme is the justification for showing several dances, a shower scene, a girl masturbating and a clumsy rape with lots of rope and stocking action for the fetishists."

By 1966 the American sex-exploitation film reached another point of stasis, and the impetus for change was once again foreign films. Among those imports released between 1966 and 1970 were *Dear John; Persona; Blow-Up; I, a Woman; I Am Curious (Yellow); Without a Stitch; The Libertine; Birds in Peru; Rela-tions; Juliette de Sade; Venus in Furs; I Am Curious (Blue); Danish Blue; Helga; Belle du Jour;* and the work of Isabel Sarli, including *Fuego* and *Muhair*.

I, A Woman, directed by Mac Ahlberg and starring Essy Pers-son, is one of the most intense, elegant, explicit, and erotic films ever released. Radley Metzger bought it for $20,000 and pared down certain sequences in the editing room to give the film a brighter pace. At the suggestion of Ava Leighton, he released a subtitled version to make the movie look like "art." The picture proved to be such a great success on the American market, grossing $4 million on Metzger's original investment, that it was even handled by several large, respectable old-line theater chains, including the Trans-Lux chain in New York.

The plot of *I, A Woman* is confined almost entirely to the erotic, following a young girl from first masturbation to the final realization that a somewhat promiscuous life has brought her to a point of great personal unhappiness. From early in the film it is clear that this girl is in love with her father, an accomplished amateur musician; during one sequence the father plays the violin in the living room, while the girl masturbates to climax in her bedroom. Shots of fingers on the violin, intercut with shots of fingers on flesh, are very arty and very effective. After her seduction by an older man, the girl has a series of affairs, finally realizing that she has not been able to form a lasting sexual relationship with anyone. The performance by Essy Persson is remarkable; the actress fully creates a portrait of a sensitive woman who is constantly betrayed by the strength of her erotic feelings.

The next landmark foreign film to be released in the United States was *I Am Curious (Yellow)*, shown in 1969, one of the three most widely known titles in the history of the erotic film (the other two are *The Immoral Mr. Teas* and *Deep Throat*). Produced by Sandrews Film Studios in Stockholm, it was written and directed by Vilgot Sjoman, a radical young Swedish director who had previously made *491*, a film about juvenile delinquency and (implied) bestiality that ran into trouble with both American Customs and censors. The troubles over *491* were only a mild prelude, however, to the difficulties faced by Grove Press in the importation and distribution of *I Am Curious (Yellow)*. The film was seized by U.S. Customs and after a lengthy trial in federal court—at which a number of eminent citizens, including critics Hollis Alpert, Paul D. Zimmerman, John Simon, Judith Crist, author Norman Mailer, and the Reverend Dr. Howard Moody, testified in favor of the film—the jury declared the film to be obscene. In the Circuit Court of Appeals, however, two of the three judges found to the contrary. The leading opinion in the case was cogently written by Judge Paul Hays who, in one remarkable footnote, condensed the testimony of thirteen experts who testified about the dominant theme of the film:

Some of their answers to questions as to the dominant theme of the film were: change, transition; the nature of reality or of "modern" reality; the New Left; the interrelationship of various aspects of human activity; the quest for values; the beliefs and commitments of the young; the younger generation; the generation gap; the relationship between fantasy and reality; young people's

search for identity and self-recognition; political, social and sexual
maturity; political responsibility; the use of ritual to establish
fundamental truth; the nature of politics; the complexity of modern reality.

Following this, Judge Hays delivered the opinion that

> . . . although sexual conduct is undeniably an important aspect of
> the picture and may be thought of as constituting one of its principal themes, it cannot be said that "the dominant theme of the
> material taken as a whole appeals to a prurient interest in sex."
> Whatever the dominant theme may be said to be it is certainly not
> sex. . . . *I Am Curious* does present ideas and does strive to present
> these ideas artistically. It falls within the ambit of intellectual effort that the First Amendment was designed to protect.

I Am Curious (Yellow) ran up high grosses, became a public
issue, and ran into trouble with the law from one end of the
country to the other. Most of the cases were won in court, however, and it was even licensed by the Maryland State Board of
Censors in 1972 after ten minutes of cuts were made. The ultimate importance of this sour, uncharitable movie about the quality
of contemporary Swedish life is that it changed the standards of
acceptability in an industry that was inching toward the presentation of explicit sex. The initial determination of obscenity was
based on the fact that the film showed the exposed, semi-erect penis
of one man and an oral sex scene in which genuine cunnilingus
may have taken place. (Not even the director knew for sure.)
These small but real differences separated the film from the American sex-exploitation product in general release in the United
States at that time. The success of *I Am Curious*, as it came to be
known, almost immediately pushed explicitness to a point where
the only illegal acts were those that showed intromission or
ejaculation.

The running time of *I Am Curious* is two hours, most of it spent
in seemingly endless interviews, discourses, excursions, digressions, and discussions. The occasional, seemingly salacious sex
scenes were shot in such a way as to deter prurient interest and
were meant to be comic. Lena and her boyfriend make (simulated)
love on the balustrade in front of the royal palace and later in the
uncomfortable branches of the largest tree in Europe. These two
brief love scenes, though explicit, are something of a bore. The
ultimate purpose of the film was to show the ways in which parental and public authority are challenged by sexual experiment and
sexual expression.

The artless, energetic, endearing performance of Lena Nyman
as the modern Swedish girl who, though not beautiful, has a rare

59

ability to project warmth, intellectual confusion, and basic goodness of character, probably accounted for much of the extraordinary success of *I Am Curious (Yellow)* and undoubtedly prompted Grove Press to release the companion piece called *I Am Curious (Blue)*. The second film went over some of the same ground, once again sending Lena Nyman into the streets to talk with common men and once again being openly critical of Swedish society, particularly emphasizing the shortcomings of the vaunted Swedish penal system. Because, despite a good press, the word of mouth on *Yellow* was not good, and because its sequel was also weak, *I Am Curious (Blue)* was released on a saturation-booking basis. The returns were so poor that there was a general restructuring at Grove Press.

The notice accorded to *Yellow* was not lost on the American distributors of art films, however, and a number of follow-up films were released—among them Grove Press's *Quiet Days in Clichy,* a pleasant, mildly amusing Danish film with English-language dialogue. Jens Jorgen Thorsen directed Louise White and Paul Valjean in a story loosely adapted from Henry Miller's classic memoir about sex and hunger during his down-and-out days in Paris. With frontal nudity, simulated sex, and "dirty" words, the film was faithful in spirit to Miller, but it lacked real style and conviction, going too often for the easy joke and the bared breast at the expense of character and erotic coherence. Grove Press also released the Kronhausen documentary *Freedom to Love,* and another Vilgot Sjoman film, *You're Lying,* which was yet another movie about the Swedish penal system.

One of the best of the new erotic European films was *Without a Stitch,* distributed in the United States by Jack Harris through VIP Productions. That Swedish film introduced a young woman (Anne Grete) who suffers from frigidity and is healed by her physician, who then sends the girl out into the world to experiment further with the nature and limits of her own sensuality. The success of *Without a Stitch* was due to the humor with which it mocked the stilted manufacture of stag films, the preposterous postures of extreme forms of sexuality, and the banal inanities of the "scientific" approach to sex.

Also released around this time was Cinemation's *The Female Animal,* starring Arlene Tiger in a story of a poor village girl who is used and abused by a wealthy count, his son, and a stray lesbian, and who ultimately becomes a prostitute. The film was successfully released on a first-run basis in Broadway movie houses. Similarly profitable was *Muhair,* one of the numerous sex dramas from Argentina directed by Armando Bo, who co-starred in the film with his wife, the wondrously constructed Isabel Sarli. Sarli is one of the greatest of the sex-exploitation stars and makes periodic trips to New York with Armondo to appear at the openings of her films, which are attended by a mixed audience of Anglo-Saxon fans and Latin American *aficionados. Muhair,* the story of a conflict between a father and son over the monumental Miss Sarli, is no better than or worse than most of her other films. There is nude swimming, simulated cunnilingus, intense dialogue, beatings, and so on, all happily resolved at the end.

Foreign films did not long hold their monopoly on American theater screens. By January 1971 a headline in *Variety* proclaimed, "YANKS OUT-EXPLOIT EUROPE," and Addison Verrill's story detailed the American market for the first time in history. As Verrill pointed out, the U.S. exploitation market had been "practically created and almost fully supplied by European producers." Yet there were no great European hits on the American screen in 1970 except for *Without a Stitch,* which grossed $2.2 million and placed forty-fourth among top-grossing films. The domestic American product was not necessarily more technically polished than the European, but it was a good deal more explicit. That same year the American-made *Sexual Freedom in Denmark* was one of the largest grossing films in the United States, showing a profit of $1.9 million in just the twenty-six cities covered by *Variety. Pornography in Denmark* was sixty-sixth on the chart, just ahead of Stanley Kramer's *Secret of Santa Vittoria,* making $1.3 million in the major cities. Other American sex films in the top hundred grossers of the year included *He and She,* a sex-education film, and *The Minx,* a Cambist release featuring Hollywood actress Jan Sterling.

The years between 1966 and 1970 that saw the fortunes of the foreign film go from good to bad were the same years that now can be considered to be the "classic" period of the American sex-exploitation film. A number of talented directors and producers working in the soft-core field had perfected a way to make good melodramas on low budgets and to sell them profitably and effectively.

The films produced by Russ Meyer in these key years were *Common Law Cabin* (also known as *How Much Loving Does a Normal Couple Need?* and *Conjugal Cabin*); *Good Morning . . . and Goodbye; Finders Keepers, Lovers Weepers; Vixen;* and *Cherry, Harry and Raquel. Common Law Cabin* and *Good Morning . . . and Goodbye,* further entries in the Meyer school of backwoods melodrama, are less violent and bizarre than the Roughies like *Lorna* that Meyer had made in previous years. *Good Morning . . . and Goodbye* was well cast (including Capri, Haji, and Karen Ciral), and the direction and cinematography were up to professional standards. Its only weakness was the endless bickering among the various characters—farmer, farmer's wife, farmer's daughter, construction-worker lover of wife, daughter's boy-friend, and sorceress.

Good Morning . . . and Goodbye was followed by *Finders Keepers, Lovers Weepers*, a gangster melodrama in the Don Siegel tradition of rough, realistic, understated melodrama about two small-time hoods who plan and almost pull off an after-hours robbery of a bar. It is the first film in which it becomes absolutely clear that Meyer is less interested in exposed nipples and hard-breathing sex scenes than he is in the exploration of the erotic tensions that compel people to commit rape and adultery. Its rough, endemic violence is the logical result of too many angry people thrown together in a narrow dramatic space. The limited number of sets and the small casts of Meyer's films were a neces-sity because of the low budgets with which he worked at the time, but he nevertheless used the claustrophobic spaces to advan-tage. Meyer's sophisticated use of timing and staging to create and sustain dramatic tension is perhaps most evident, however, in *Vixen*, which starred Erica Gavin and is concerned with incest, miscegenation, lesbianism, wife-swapping, draft-dodging, sexual dysfunction, nude bathing, hijacking, and the victory of democ-racy over communism. There is little overt violence, but once again Meyer exhibits his fascination with eroticism, large breasts, and the hostility and tensions between people on sexual, political, and racial grounds. "What is significant today that we can put in to give it a thread of a story?" Meyer recalls asking his partner, Jim Ryan. "The hijacking thing, the Cuba bit, the black man run-ning away to Canada. We'll get some real redneck broad who hates Negroes and get that confrontation going, and we'll have her make it with all sorts of people." The movie did enough busi-ness—$7.5 million gross—to get Meyer a contract with Twentieth Century-Fox for *Beyond the Valley of the Dolls*.

The move to a major studio was a cultural event of importance, a recognition by Hollywood that Meyer had the ability to make highly popular entertainment quickly, cheaply, and well, even though the films he made there, *Beyond the Valley of the Dolls* and *The Seven Minutes*, did not score at the box office as well as the Fox management had anticipated. Meyer's contract was ter-minated shortly after Richard Zanuck, the studio head who hired him, lost his own job.

Radley Metzger never made the move to Hollywood. Instead, he continued to import films, including *The Libertine* and *The Laughing Woman*, while gradually increasing the production costs of his own features so that they could compete with Hollywood movies. Metzger's *Thérèse and Isabelle*, one of Audubon's biggest grossers, was based on *La Bâtarde*, an autobiographical novel by Violette Leduc about a romance between two girls at a boarding

school. Metzger was impressed with the book, and before he began
filming he sought out Violette Leduc, who said to him, "Please
don't make a pornographic movie, that's all I ask." Even though
La Bâtarde, Metzger relates, "was rather explicit in the descriptions of eating Isabelle's pussy, I promised Leduc I wouldn't make
a pornographic movie. When she met Anna Gael, who played
Isabelle, it was a very poignant moment; she was terribly affected
by it. I saw Leduc several times after that, and I was very touched
by the fact that she was moved by the film itself."

Essy Persson, the star of *I, A Woman,* gave a sensitive, evoca-
tive performance as Thérèse, a difficult role that moves back and
forth between adolescence and middle age. The film is about memory, shot in long takes and tracking shots, with a final encounter
between the two girls that is highly suggestive, mixing explicit
narration with several elegantly composed shots of thighs and
mouths in proximity.

Metzger's next film, *Camille 2000,* a highly erotic and beautiful
work, was an updating of the classic French novel by Alexandre
Dumas, featuring Danielle Gaubert as the consumptive prostitute.
The set decoration by Enrico Sabbatini places Camille in a lifeless
milieu—she dresses only in black or white and lives in an apartment that is furnished in plastic and glass. Next, Metzger made
The Lickerish Quartet, an allegorical chamber film for four players
generally considered to be his most personal work. It opens as
the Man projects blue movies for the Woman (his wife) and the
Boy (stepson). They later go to a nearby town and become fascinated by the Girl, who rides a motorcycle in a wall-of-death circus
act. Sure that she is one of the performers they saw in the blue
movie, they ask her back to their home, where the Girl later
makes love to the Man in his library, to the Boy in an open field,
and to the Woman in the screening room. *The Lickerish Quartet*
is visually elegant, and the camerawork (by Hans Jura) and set
design (Sabbatini) are patterned after Alain Resnais's *Last Year
at Marienbad.* More recent Metzger releases are *Little Mother,*
based on the life of Eva Peron, and *Score,* another four-character
drama.

Like Metzger's later films David F. Friedman's are more polished than his early Nudies and Roughies. The EVI releases in the
late '60s and early '70s were distinguished by the Friedman trade-
marks: parody, pastiche, vaudeville humor, tight story construc-
tion, convincing action, and sex scenes that border on hard core.
Starlet, produced and written by Dave Friedman, directed by
Richard Kanter, and with music by William Allen Castleman, had
as its setting the sex-exploitation industry itself, and the location
scenes were shot on the EVI lot. This improbable saga featured
the adventures of a young Hollywood hopeful and was played

straight, but several of Friedman's later films are designed for laughs and thrills, such as *Trader Hornee*; *The Long, Swift Sword of Siegfried*; and *The Erotic Adventures of Zorro*—all adventure films that mock legendary heroes.

Other producers have turned out soft-core films that did well financially during the erotic cinema's classic period. Some of the better-known titles include *The Secret Sex Lives of Romeo and Juliet, Diamond Jim,* and *All the Loving Couples.* A series released by Derio Productions, the *Ginger* films—*Ginger, Girls Are for Loving,* and *The Abductors*—starred Cheri Caffaro as a secret agent who uses her hands and mouth in the service of the state. According to *Variety,* these films appealed to "mayhem freaks and femmes with rape fantasies."

One of the most remarkable soft-core films ever released was *The Stewardesses.* It grossed more than $25 million, despite the fact that it is not very well made and does not show much in the way of sexual activity. Originally, it was not even designed as a feature film. Director Alf Stillman, Jr., stitched together a series of 3-D loops shot in San Francisco and released the result in the summer of 1970. A staggering total of fifty-six girls are displayed in the film, and it has as many stories as *Grand Hotel,* all happening within the eighteen hours between the time an airliner lands in Los Angeles and leaves for Honolulu, and includes wild parties, lesbian scenes, rape, LSD trips, and a suicide. The lack of explicit sex did not hurt the film, for its combination of notorious plot (reaffirming every known stereotype about stewardesses) and gimmick (Magnavision) made the film into a hit.

The success of *The Stewardesses* represents a triumph of creative merchandising and clever promotion. The technical process used in the film was not without headaches for the exhibitor. It required the theater to have a silver or metallic screen, special lenses, masking, and aperture plates, and cold reflectors in the projector. The process required the viewer to wear glasses and gave the illusion of depth that, however, diminished the impact of the image. The film quickly became successful at such specialty theaters as the Lido East and the World cinemas in New York, but it was at first a disappointment on the sex-theater circuit. Only after Sherpix decided to change the ad campaign (compulsory for the exhibitor were radio spots and billboards) and to open at class downtown theaters—the Town in Washington, D.C., and the 4,400-seat Music Hall Theater in Boston—did the film take off.

The acceptability of soft-core films like *The Stewardesses* to most middle-class audiences accounts for the fact that a market still exists for films that do not show explicit sex. There is no erection, ejaculation, or penetration in *The Erotic Adventures of Zorro, The Toy Box,* or *The Godson,* but these films have nevertheless established acceptable grosses at a substantial number of theaters. Reliable figures are hard to come by, but Entertainment Ventures, in one of its annual reports, stated that its sixteen features in distribution (the EVI output since 1959) grossed $555,000 in rental fees, including those for *Starlet.* The EVI report also indicated that its biggest all-time money-maker was *The Notorious Daughter of Fanny Hill,* which in the four years from its release to 1969 had grossed $325,000.

The soft-core film itself has undergone few changes since the middle of the last decade. Sexual activity is still simulated, and the story still generally contains a socially acceptable moral, supported by highly developed codes of right and wrong behavior. What has been transformed, however, is the rest of the field of sex-exploitation films. In the '70s hard-core films have cornered, however tentatively, an important percentage of the erotic market.

6

TWICE AS ELEGANT

AN INTERVIEW WITH RADLEY METZGER

For Radley Metzger—called "Aristocrat of the Erotic" by as arcane a journal as *Film Comment*, honored by the Museum of Modern Art, a man whom David F. Friedman, eternal president of the Adult Film Association of America, calls "the only genius working in exploitation films, years ahead of his time"—for this man, it all started with a bad case of hay fever.

"It sounds absolutely ridiculous but it's quite true," he says, thinking back to his salad days in the Bronx. "I was a big sufferer and air conditioning gave you instant relief. They didn't have it in homes as widely as they do now, but they had it in movie theaters, and I used to go to two movies in the afternoon and two movies at night. I must have seen *Cross of Lorraine* eleven times, but it was the only place I could get relief."

You look at Radley Metzger and you figure there must be some mistake. Age forty-four, he has curly silver hair, classic features that could have come out of an ad for men's cologne, as well as a very cordial, mellow, self-assured way about him. Could this distinguished and charming gentleman who twirls a silver Star of David as he speaks, who lives in a tasteful East Side apartment right near the river, could this guy make sex films? Yes, he can, and very well, too, thank you.

In fact, the films Metzger makes, as well as the ones his company, Audubon Films, merely distributes, have been credited, by as august a source as the President's Commission on Obscenity and Pornography, with opening the conventional theatrical and art house market to well-made, though undeniably erotic, soft-core sex-exploitation films—things like the $4 million grossing *I, a Woman*, and the $3 million *Carmen, Baby*. They played regular theaters and regular people went to see them, which was a breakthrough at the time. But does Metzger feel like a pioneer? Not quite.

"I don't think anybody feels it," he counters. "It's like saying 'How does it feel to live before Christ?' Well if you were living before Christ you didn't know you were." In a field where modesty is as rare off the screen as on it, someone who shuns the opportunity to bang his own drum, someone who says he wants to be remembered only as "somebody that just practiced his craft as well as he could and perhaps made life a little easier for some people," someone like that is almost not to be believed. The reason, Metzger says with a small grin, is simply, "that's my style."

His style is a style that reeks of style, that has caused critics to call his films elegant erotic romances, sleek and expensive, sensual without being vulgar. "His movies were classier, more literate, better made, and blessed with women who looked as if they could communicate desire without carrying disease," wrote *Film Comment* editor Richard Corliss, which is not bad for someone who had an early film called "a City College student's sex fantasy" by the head of the New York State Board of Censors.

Nowadays Metzger's films are far from "that kind of seedy exploitation film that is sort of the soup kitchen of the erotic world. I happen to like pictures that look elegant, and I like pictures that have a gloss to them," he says, and his pictures follow suit to the point where "a friend always makes fun of them because every picture I make, sooner or later somebody shows up in a tuxedo. I don't know if that's from seeing too many William Powell pictures, but it's a way of subtly saying that you can relax and not worry about being offended by the picture.

"You don't want to create a climate of discomfort, 'cause who the hell wants to pay to be uncomfortable? I don't like to go to a thing and say, 'Well, what freak made this picture?' I think you have to be a little bit like BOAC and take care of your audience. You have a responsibility."

And if anything Metzger, who says Bertolucci's *The Conformist* is "the best film I've seen in fifteen years," feels more of a responsibility than most because he was there first, the first to try and make really quality out of what everyone considered trash. "It's like when you're the first Jew in the corporation, you have to have a cleaner shirt than anyone else, or the first black man, you have to be twice as elegant," he explains. "Perhaps that's why I try to get the pictures looking more elegant and being a little flashier. But in a sense it's not for me to say."

There it is again, this reluctance to discuss his own films, a feeling that "people shouldn't talk about their own pictures; I think people talk much too much about pictures as it is." Metzger's dislike of blowing his own horn makes him apt to preface even minimal defenses of his own work with "I'm not trying to say I'm an artistic director." And if he can't quite deny that his name is as well known in the exploitation field as that other R. M., Russ Meyer—"we can probably get our laundry mixed up very easily"—he has his own explanation for that. "I'm getting to be a much more important director now," he says, "because there's so much shit made today that all my pictures have gotten better by contrast. Not intrinsically, just relatively."

Yet if Metzger does not go out of his way to pump up his own work, he has a very low tolerance for people who go out of their way to deflate it. Just because he won't say he is without peer as a master of cinematic erotica doesn't mean he smiles with equanimity when his films are called well-photographed trash. Worst of all are those critics who persist in seeing him, no matter what he does, no matter how much class his movies exude, as just another dirty filmmaker. That grates, oh, does that grate.

"I decided to do a political film based loosely on the life of Eva Peron," he says by way of example. "And it had two sex scenes, which is a hell of a lot less than a lot of Hollywood pictures. And to show you how we are living in an era of robots, there was a critic who holds professorships in universities, and he saw this picture, and this Neanderthal, well, not Neanderthal, but that semihuman being reviewed *Little Mother* and called it another porno from Radley Metzger. That's the point to which people get programmed."

For Radley Metzger had become the unwilling prisoner of the people he calls "the maintitlers, these *Manchurian Candidate* reviewers," the people who look at his films and say, " 'Ho-hum, here we go, another tits and asses picture.' I think if you took main titles off pictures, ninety per cent of your critics would resign because they wouldn't know what to say about the pictures. We live in an era of 'give-it-to-me-fast' and 'what's-the-category' and anything beyond that, anything that might be ambivalent, like both erotic and witty, is somehow a little more than people could handle."

In his case the typecasting started back in 1964 when Metzger took a title off a film he was to distribute and put it on one he directed himself. The film was *The Dirty Girls*, and, says Metzger, "it really gave people the impression that I made dirty movies. I probably could have called it *Ma and Pa Kettle* and it would have done a certain amount of exploitation business, but I called it *The Dirty Girls*, and suddenly it was Radley Metzger, that dirty filmmaker. I'm not putting that down, I don't say it's wrong to make dirty movies, but I think people tended not to see the other values that were in the films.

"It depends again on the orientation. There are certain young French directors that will start with a brilliant movie and then for the next fifteen years they make brilliant movies that miss a little, instead of lousy movies with one good scene. I just happened to start with *The Dirty Girls,* so it's always a dirty film trying to fool the public into being something else, which is generally what they say."

"They" being people like "a rather erudite critic who said he wanted to talk film and then asked, 'What do you think about people who jerk off in the movies when they watch your pictures?' And I know why he said it, because this was the orientation, the guy that made a picture like *The Dirty Girls* would answer a question like that. Had the picture been called *Woman of the Year* he might've said something else."

And even later on, with films that Metzger considers quality productions, the typecasting didn't end. For instance, *Thérèse and Isabelle,* which by now "has played in every country in the world and to great success and great critical success, people like Brooks Atkinson wrote nice things about it, and it was sort of vindicated. But the people weren't ready for it here, and of course they weren't ready for it because the guy who made it made *The Dirty Girls.* A lot of people came up to me and they said, 'Hey, you want to know something, that really wasn't a bad picture, I mean, that was a good film,' as if, you know, 'What's happened, did they mix your film up in the lab and send you the wrong rushes because something came out that wasn't, you know, a fuck film.'

"I've never heard it better said than in *The Wizard of Oz,* when the wizard says to the scarecrow, 'You don't need a brain, you've got as much brain as anybody, what you need is a diploma.' And that's the way people tend to rate things."

So Metzger, in real life a ballet enthusiast and a collector of graphic art, is faced with a feeling that "it's more than people can handle to think that somebody that isn't the Marquis de Sade's illegitimate brother-in-law would make a sex film. What's my life-style like? I just rape thirteen-year-old girls and cut up butterflies when they're alive. I mean this is what anybody would do."

It's all very ironically said and puts one in mind of another incongruity—that out of all the people in the exploitation field, Metzger has had probably the most comprehensive and diversified film background, including being known as "Kubrick No. 2" when he occupied Stanley K.'s New York editing room and, like his predecessor, neglected to get haircuts.

Coming from "a typical Clifford Odets background, the hard-working parents on relief, the brother who went to night school and got into medical school," he survived his air-conditioned youth to get a job as a movie usher—"I had the distinction of seeing *The Treasure of Sierra Madre* 128 times"—and eventually join the film editors' union and work for two years as a cutter with the air force during the Korean war.

After a short, unprofitable postwar stint with RKO, Metzger got into "what was then kind of a budding industry that looked like it was just gonna break open." That happened to be foreign films, "pictures for Jewish intellectuals who wouldn't go to see anything unless it was either made in England or had subtitles." He worked as a dubber, was the synchronization editor for the Bardot-Vadim *And God Created Woman*, and ended up doing the trailers for all the Ingmar Bergman movies at Janus Films. "Bergman saw one of the trailers and paid it a great compliment, and I was very pleased," he says. "That was maybe the best compliment I've ever had." It was especially pleasing because the only foreign film of note that Metzger had dealt with before Bergman's was the pre-Korea *Bitter Rice*, where he had the unenviable job of going through 150 prints and making the appropriate cuts in each, so the movie would get a clean enough Legion of Decency rating to enable it to show on the RKO circuit. "That was really the first paying job I had," he says, "and the cuts we made you would not believe. There was a peddler, he wasn't even in the foreground, he was in the background of the scene, waving some brassieres and panties. Now, I mean, you think I'm joking, but that had to be cut out."

About the time of the Bergman work, Metzger set out to do a film of his own. Working with a partner over a period of two and a half years—"We would shoot the picture and then when we ran out of money we'd stop and be film editors"—and using a minimum of money—"We didn't have enough for a shoestring production"—he turned out *Dark Odyssey* in 1961. Though Metzger still thinks the story (a Greek man becomes a criminal in New York when he tries to uphold the old-country custom of avenging his sister's honor) is a good one, he takes unending, uncompromising delight in telling of its woes, both aesthetic and financial.

"I've heard an art film defined as a foreign film that nobody wants to see," he begins, "and this was an American art film. I wouldn't say it was arty, but I can guarantee nobody wanted to see it. I think you could give that story to a third-rate director today, and he'd come up with a fairly good film, but we had absolutely no conception of people having to pay their money to see it. I mean, you think your audience is the seven people that you go to parties with and go to the movies with, and you think that's the extent of the world movie-going population.

"Nobody wanted this film. You know how in death row you

look at the people in the cells and you have a certain expression on your face, like 'You're in there and I'm not.' That was the sort of expression we had from people when they'd come out of the screening room. They would look at you really like a condemned man, I mean, Ronald Reagan is the President and there's no pardons available."

So Metzger and his codirector, coproducer William Kyriakys decided to distribute it themselves, but "we couldn't get an opening on the picture until we dubbed it into Greek and opened it in Greek neighborhoods. And I think it still holds certain records around the United States for the most disastrous grosses a theater could possibly have. I often thought theaters should have booked this picture when they wanted to paint the ceiling or change the seats and not disturb anybody, but they didn't even do that."

And because that film was such a disaster—"I don't know if there's a word in English, in any language, that sums up the flop this thing was"—Metzger became "a celluloid orphan," wanted by no one, not even himself. "There's an old Russian expression," he says. "If you burn your tongue on tea, you'll blow on ice water after that. And I was in the stage of blowing on ice water."

But *Dark Odyssey* left debts to be paid, and Metzger, convinced he had the skills to take foreign films and recut and redub them so they'd be successful in American markets, founded Audubon Films and started buying up films that were considered racy but unsalable and turning them into money-makers. Over thirty have been distributed so far, quickly forgotten ones like *The Artful Penetration* and *Days of Sin and Nights of Nymphomania,* as well as films with underground reputations like *I Spit on Your Grave* and trendsetters like the first Elke Sommer pictures to hit the United States. "We call them house pictures or bread-and-butter pictures," Metzger explains. "We buy small, modest pictures and package them up and distribute them. And because of being able to cut out the middlemen, they don't all have to be *Birth of a Nation* to turn a profit."

Although amassing capital for his own films is a prime reason for distributing the other ones, Metzger admits that part of him feels "advertising can be very, very creative, trailers can be exciting, marketing can be exciting." He was especially drawn to ad campaigns, where he had the knack of creating classic lines for his films. *The Dirty Girls* became "the film that goes too far," *Carmen, Baby* was "The Total Female Animal," and *I Spit on Your Grave* ended up as "The film that defies every taboo! . . . He passed for white . . . And they loved it." Metzger, obviously, gets a kick out of it, too. "Words mean absolutely nothing in their denotation; it's only what they connote that has meaning," he says. "That's got nothing to do with eroticism, it's merchan-

71

dising and communication. I mean what does 'All the Way with LBJ' mean? It means absolutely nothing. We had a poster campaign once that said 'a sexual romance.' I really don't know what that means, but it strikes people. And people respond much more to what they feel than to what they see."

One of the films Audubon bought, a French film renamed *The Twilight Girls*, needed about a 5-minute insert to spice it up: "Some nudity, two girls actually kissing—I thought the projectionist was going to call the FBI when he ran it the first time." It was the first time Metzger had shot any film since the abortive *Dark Odyssey*, and he remembers preparing for it as carefully as for any of the full-length features that followed. And one of the girls who did those inserts a decade ago metamorphosed into Georgina Spelvin, the spicy star of *The Devil in Miss Jones*. "It was the first thing she'd ever done," Metzger says, "and only the second thing I had. She came by the other day, and it was kind of a warm reunion."

With his confidence and his finances finally rebuilt, Metzger directed his first solo feature, the infamous *Dirty Girls*, in 1964 but hedged a bit by making it a sketch film *à la* the then popular *Boccaccio 70*. His first "really full-length film" was *The Alley Cats*, done two years later and successful enough for Metzger to take his next big step, "doing a film in color. I know this stuff sounds semimoronic now, but it was a very big step at the time. This was 1966, and little people didn't do color pictures." That turned out to be the wildly popular *Carmen, Baby*, highlighted by a snazzy promotion photo of an unknown woman licking her lips. Lots of people said, " 'Well, gee, this isn't like the opera at all; this fuck must've just really changed it all around.' " Not true, says Metzger; the critics just weren't knowledgeable enough to realize that his source was not the Bizet opera but the original Prosper Merimée story. "When you don't have a literate critical population it's very difficult to do things like this, because you're working on a level of subtlety which just eludes them," he sniffs.

Right before this directorial success came Metzger's biggest coup as a distributor. Seeing a review of a likely film in *Variety*, he went all the way to Copenhagen to take a look. "They didn't even have a screening print; I had to go to a suburb to see it," he remembers. "I don't know that Admiral Byrd ever saw more snow than I did." He liked it and offered "a fortune of money— $20,000"—to get it, only to be told that someone else had bought the film and still had one payment to go before the sale was final. Well, that one payment never came through, and Metzger, after doing a bit of editing and rearranging of footage, had himself *I, a Woman*, his highest grosser to date and what he himself calls "kind of a breakthrough, a landmark film."

From here on things got fatter, with Metzger spending a quarter of a million dollars on *Thérèse and Isabelle* and twice that on *Camille 2000,* his most expensive item yet. His latest picture, *Score,* based on an off-Broadway play about a swinging couple that meets a nonswinging pair, is a change for Metzger, his first film with an all-American cast and his first situation comedy. And undeterred by the Supreme Court's anti-obscenity ruling, he announced yet another project, *The Picture,* based on a novel about sadomasochism that has been banned in its native France. This show, apparently, will go on and on and on.

And so the question is inevitable. Why does it go on? Why does a man who could be making whatever films he chose end up again and again with sex? "It's the bank I go to to borrow money," Metzger explains. "It gives one a little more surety that you'll be here next year making pictures. That's really what my goal is—I really want to make pictures. I don't want to get financed by a bank; I would like to be financed by the public."

And sex, it goes without saying, "seems to be an area in which people are interested. It's one of the fundamental aspects of our lives. I mean, when you do it well, people will respond all over the world in the same way. There are very few of the major countries in the world where, say, *Carmen, Baby, or Thérèse,* or *Camille* is not distributed. And the response does seem to be the same. I mean we are touching fundamental aspects of the personality."

Radley Metzger deals with sex in a way that seems to be unlike anyone else's. "The films I do are beauty films, erotic in atmosphere, not in anything explicit," says the man who adores Rita Hayworth's *Gilda* because "there is not one kiss in it and it is one of the sexiest films I have ever seen." He has nothing against hard core *per se* and says he might use it himself should the right subject surface, but it seems really to go against his basic tenets, his feeling that "if you handle it well, the unexplicit can get more juices flowing. Your thoughts might go to what you're gonna do Saturday night a lot faster."

For Metzger believes that "in an erotic film, when you get down to the fucking, it's already decided whether or not it's successful. It's in the preparation area that I think you tell the men from the boys. During the Olympics, for instance, when you watched a pole vaulter, you knew when he started out if he was going to hit that bar or not, anybody could see if he was going to make it. It's not whether he looks like Steve Stunning, it's the preparation, it's when you're running down that runway with the pole in your hand—that's when it's decided, not when you're up there trying to get over the bar. It's all done by then. And I think that my pictures are different because they dwell a little more in that area.

We worry about running down the road and not about getting over the bar."

And so Metzger gets miffed when critics say that people are going to see his films just because there are a couple of hot parts in them. "Everybody thought that *I, a Woman* made a lot of money because she fucked all through the movie, when of course there were so many fuck movies, much hotter pictures actually, around at the time. What happened was she touched women, there was something in this girl's personality, in her story, that touched an awful lot of women in the audience, and that's really, I believe, what caused the success of *I, a Woman*. And with something like *And God Created Woman,* it's equally wrong to say that the picture was successful because it was just a lot of cunt. I always say, 'Why didn't the seven other pictures playing across the street make as much money?' I mean, if that's it, if people were just looking for tits and asses ... But the fact is it had this atmosphere and this quality, this fabric that people were responding to."

Take, for instance, his *Thérèse and Isabelle,* which was subtitled "a love story" in the ads. "We meant that," Metzger says meaningfully, erotica's Last Angry Man. "It was really a story about two people that are in love; it had nothing to do with lesbianism or anything like that. I really tend to do love stories much more than sex stories. These were people that were very emotionally involved with each other. They're not there just to fuck."

The difference, as he sees it, is "the difference between a sex picture and a picture with sex, or a violent picture and a picture with violence. It's not a question of looking at a story and saying, 'All right, we're stuck with this, let's heat it up.' If you have a picture where they just go around killing a lot of people, I don't think you've got a successfully violent picture. I use the word atmosphere a lot, and I happen to think that's what movies are about. I think *The Maltese Falcon* is one of the most violent films ever made. There's a viscous solution of violence that runs through that thing; it doesn't matter if anybody hits anybody. You couldn't cut the violence out of *The Maltese Falcon,* and that's pretty much the way I approach eroticism."

So when Radley Metzger thinks of a successful erotic film, it's one where no censor could cut the hot parts out. "If you depend on the one left tit that you're exposing or if you're dependent on that one suck scene, then I don't think you've got a successful picture. I think you have to have a bridge where all the girders are in place, and some of the girders are sex girders. It's a question of whether you want to make a sex picture or take a feeling or an attitude or an emotion in which sex is involved. I think that might be the difference."

PART 2

GOING ALL THE WAY

7

ERECT MEN AND FALLEN WOMEN

BEAVERS AND HOW-TO'S

By the late '60s, the sex-exploitation film that featured simulated sex had gone about as far as it could go. Then, probably sometime around 1967, an unknown and very enterprising San Francisco exhibitor began to screen a type of film that was then doing good business in the mail-order houses and in some of the more daring peep-show arcades, where they were "looped" together in continuous shows. This was the "beaver" film, and it was to revolutionize the entire sex-exploitation industry. The first beaver movies—whose main attraction was the visible pubic region of the women (and later men) who posed for them— were nothing more than short loops, several loops making up a show, in which, for once, the stripper followed the request of the boys in the front row and actually took it all off. Films like *Beaver Bondage, Ruthless Shaved Beaver, Beaver's Night Off, Beaver's Pride, Beaver Valley, Bad Beaver, Beaver Madness, I Am Curious . . . Beaver,* and *Manchurian Beaver* were made with a staggering artlessness, and there was, at first, no overt sexual content. The performers were not strippers but rather young girls who were earning a little spare cash to put them through San Francisco State or Berkeley. It was easy money, and there were no strings attached: no sexual activity; no lines to remember; just fifteen minutes of slowly taking off clothes, parading about, and going through a series of suggestive gyrations on the nearest bed.

The simple beaver film soon developed two significant variations. In the first, which came to be known as the split beaver, the woman spread her legs and exhibited her vagina directly to the cameras, often pulling aside the labia in order to provide a better view of what everyone had come to see. Her fingers never penetrated into the vagina, however; for, according to a series of court rulings, that would have made these films obscene.

The action beaver, the next logical cinematic step, featured increasingly explicit sexual activity along with complete nudity. A number of these films showed lesbian activity—girls wrestling, being tied up, and stripped by other girls. Scenes of whippings, spankings, and some benign torture were all designed to present the maximum amount of female flesh in the largest variety of revealing and uncomfortable positions. *Robin Crusoe,* for example, produced by Fearless Productions, told the story of four lesbians stranded on a desert isle. This poorly made film was relatively explicit, but, as one commentator noted at the time, the erotic ambience of the film was greatly reduced by the fact that the women joked around with each other and talked to the cameraman. A second Fearless production, also lacking in technical finesse, was *Mimi La Douce,* which showed a quartet of bored lesbians going through their paces—kissing with open mouths, fondling breasts, simulating cunnilingus, and playing with fingers in and around vaginas.

Beaver films couldn't satisfy the San Francisco erotic-movie audience for long. Movies showing real—not simulated—sex were available behind the counter of hundreds of bookstores in the city; they were simply waiting for the theater exhibitor willing to risk arrest, court battles, public scrutiny, and community pressure to show them. Several people rose to the occasion, in late 1969, among them the Mitchell Brothers, owners of the O'Farrell Theater, and Alex de Renzy, a moderately talented filmmaker, who operated a theater called the Screening Room. De Renzy had been trained as an industrial cameraman, and, after opening the Screening Room, he began to shoot and exhibit five or six loops every week, progressing gradually from beaver films to hard-core loops. As De Renzy said in an interview with *Newsweek* in 1970, "There were certain things that everyone accepted you didn't do—and we did them." Unlike many of his competitors, De Renzy was willing to expend the time, energy, and money to make money. He once remarked that he was busted seventeen times in six months, winning some of his cases, and paying the nominal fines when he was found guilty under the local obscenity laws.

The Screening Room, a small, clean, well-lighted theater that was radically different from the average run-down sex-exploitation movie palace or storefront, first showed silent films in color;

music was provided by records played over the theater's PA system—an arrangement that could get disastrously out of sync as the projectionist played "Hearts and Flowers" during the frenzied orgasm of a trio of stoned lesbians. Many of the films were shown without titles or credits, and the overall quality was highly variable at first.

As De Renzy moved into hard core, however, the films gradually became better, with refinements in both form and content. Production values improved, color quality became adequate, and dialogue was added. This last was an important step; even rudimentary dialogue—timeless phrases like "That feels good" and "Gee, I never knew it could be like that"—was a vast improvement over canned music. At the same time there was an attempt to tailor the music track—preferably progressive rock but sometimes cannibalized classics, in particular the work of Bach—to the dramatic needs of the film.

Just what those dramatic needs were is illustrated in the following description of a 1970 hard-core film (similar to the work of De Renzy) contained in a study of the San Francisco erotic-film market that was part of the *Technical Reports* of the Commission on Obscenity and Pornography:

> [An older woman and a young girl] sit on the bed and kiss; they recline and continue. We are shown some close-ups of the oral sex that the woman performs on the girl. Then the younger one changes position and begins to kiss the elder's boots. She caresses the woman's inner thighs, and the older one feigns sexual excitement. The girl leaves our view for a moment, returning with a cup of coffee which she proceeds to spill on the older woman. This initiates the actual beating—which begins with some degree of vehemence but subsides into love taps. . . . We are shown close-ups of the younger girl's inner thighs and vagina—the area where she receives the lashes. The woman rolls the girl over and beats her on the bottom. End.

Even the best improvements by De Renzy, however, could not overcome the built-in limitations of working in a form where creative effort is circumscribed by length and the pressure of time. As a result, few of the films were very coherent. The plots—almost universally the search for and depiction of sexual climax—involved the standard randy housewife who tritely seduces the delivery boy or the robbers who force their victims to perform sex acts. Dramatic complications meant people changing partners and places and forming various sexual combinations to show or imply intercourse, fellatio, cunnilingus, analingus, anal intercourse, group sex, and sadism.

Male arousal and release in these hard-core loops are obvious:

Erections are very much in evidence, and all ejaculations take place in full sight of the camera. Female orgasm, however, is more difficult to determine. While some erotic films feature what appear to be frenzied, sustained, and multiple orgasms, actresses who perform in sex films claim in interviews that most of the time they do not achieve orgasm. Worrying about lights and camera angles and keeping fashionably long hair from obscuring the camera shot evidently preclude the kind of sustained erotic involvement that leads to orgasm.

San Francisco was the first city to get into hard core on a city-wide, nationally recognized basis. Approximately twenty-five theaters played hard-core films in 1969, and the city by the Golden Gate was used as a come-on to merchandise all kinds of films, including some made elsewhere. By 1970 theaters in Indianapolis, Dallas, Houston, and New York were advertising *Frisco Beaver Action*, *Frisco Girls*, and *Hot Frisco Shorts* and showing a considerable amount of oral sex, some mutual masturbation, and, occasionally, scenes of sexual intercourse.

By and large the sex-film theaters (most estimates place the number of these between one and four hundred) were marginal operations, but John Lamb, with *Sexual Freedom in Denmark*, and Alex de Renzy, with *Censorship in Denmark: A New Approach*, were to produce films that would move out of the grind-houses and play better and more profitable theaters that catered to a wider public, theaters similar to De Renzy's own Screening Room.

Released later than the Lamb film, but markedly greater in impact, *Censorship in Denmark: A New Approach* was produced, directed, and edited by De Renzy and distributed by Sherpix. Camerawork in Eastmancolor was the work of Paul Gerber, Jack Kerpan, and Michael Martin. Originally, the 90-minute film had been released under the title *Pornography in Denmark* and favorably received, but De Renzy was forced to change the name when major newspapers, particularly those in New York, would not accept advertisements for the film. The first title, moreover, was a red flag to any prosecutor who wanted to seize the film on the charge of pandering.

The film was, in fact, a documentary about pornography in that Scandinavian country, and De Renzy filmed it when he went to Copenhagen to visit "Sex '69," the first large trade show after the Danes legalized pornography in 1968, an event designed to show off new merchandise to buyers for the sex trade that attracted the curious public in such numbers that a thousand people were turned away each day. *Censorship in Denmark* opens with a few quaint establishing shots of the city, standard travel-ogue fare that shows birds in the park, the statue of the Little

Mermaid, and the changing of the palace guard. A sequence at the fair itself follows, where De Renzy interviews a number of visitors to get their reaction to the legalization of pornography and to the trade fair. (One woman quips, "Is this the line for Lenin's tomb?") Inside there are numerous shots of the exhibits, most of which feature either sex tools (vibrators, rubber novelties, whips, and two-headed dildos) or magazines such as *Triple Lesbian, Carnaby Kinks, TV Sex, Manner Klimaks, Color Sperma, Lesbian Orgasm,* and *Pan Sex.*

The magazines, showing the whole gamut of human sexual activity, are merely a preview, however, for the rest of the film, which soon tours sex shops, a fashion show at which ladies' undergarments are modeled, and a club that presents live lesbian sex shows. Also included is an interview with Tony, a young girl who makes a precarious living by acting in sex films with her boyfriend. Tony is nude during the interview with De Renzy, but she is completely dignified and unselfconscious about her nudity and the nature of her employment. She talks about herself (she is eighteen, she does not take drugs, she likes sex and rock music) and admits that she really enjoys working in sex films but only when she appears with her boyfriend. This highly personal, touching monologue is intercut with footage from a very hard-core film that Tony and her boyfriend had previously made with a bisexual, somewhat older prostitute as the third partner, and the impact of the words-and-action portrait is calculatedly powerful. De Renzy follows the sequence by a visit to a movie club where hard-core movies are shown, and he includes several examples in the film. Significantly, De Renzy photographed these films directly from the movie screens in the Danish clubs, rather than making duplicate negatives of the originals, and this was, of course, the legal pretext by which he was able to defend the film in court: He was not making a pornographic movie but a movie about the showing of pornographic movies.

Finally, in a refreshing and candid section, De Renzy photographed a group of Danish filmmakers in the process of making a sex film. A few scenes of peculiar authenticity stand out. A sailor who is called upon to perform a number of sex acts has occasional difficulty in sustaining an erection between scenes, and the woman in the film helps him excite himself with a vibrator. The extremely sexual act is rendered neutral by the fact that, at that point, she is only doing her job.

Censorship in Denmark was greeted with a great deal of public, press, and police notice when it first opened in San Francisco. In April 1970, *Variety* found it "highly interesting," well-paced, and technically correct, and Vincent Canby reviewed the film in the *New York Times* on June 17, the first time a major critic from a major newspaper took notice, much less sympathetic notice, of a film that graphically showed intercourse, fellatio, and cunnilingus. Canby discussed the movie with restraint and humor:

> It may boggle the mind, but only after it boggles, shakes up, and threatens a lot of other things that are more difficult—and less fashionable to talk about, including the puritan conscience and our traditional taboos. . . . In its favor is the fact that *Censorship in Denmark* is an impolite film that makes very little pretense of being anything else.

This was not Canby's last word on the film. Several days later he wrote a long article in which he covered not only the De Renzy film but also *Sexual Freedom in Denmark* and *Wide Open Copenhagen '70* (originally titled *Pornography in Copenhagen*). The study of Danish sex customs was obviously an idea whose time had come. In general, Canby found the films dull and a little heavy-handed, but he was ultimately sympathetic to the cause of screen freedom:

> My own experience is that some of the sequences in these new films are erotic, but it is a fleeting, certainly harmless kind of eroticism that depends largely on shock and curiosity which turn into an almost scholarly interest and then dwindle into a sort of arrogant boredom.

Censorship in Denmark eventually was shown throughout the New York area, playing boroughs and suburbs that previously had seen nothing more explicit than an occasional, quick glimpse of pubic hair in a couple of the more widely seen imports. Many middle-class people who did not realize that there were hard-core films on Eighth Avenue (and would not have gone in any case) were suddenly perfectly willing to go to a "nice" theater to see a film that was reviewed in the *New York Times*. Pornography was beginning to become more widely seen and even somewhat fashionable.

The other feature documentary released in the early part of 1970, *Sexual Freedom in Denmark*, was far less notorious and successful, probably because it confined itself to strictly educational material. Like *Censorship*, it examines the effects of very liberal Scandinavian attitudes toward sex, including interviews with people about the new Danish freedoms, a study of erotic art, a section on nudism, and a long sequence about sex education during which, for one shocking moment, there is a photograph of a penis in the advanced stages of syphilitic deterioration. The sex acts in the film are performed in an orderly and almost antiseptic manner: A man ejaculates into a test tube; a woman masturbates to orgasm (there are close shots of her muscular contractions); and a handsome couple demonstrate the various positions and techniques for making love. Only once, during the filming of a sex movie that features the oral activities of two lesbians, is there the suggestion of hard-breathing, prurient sex. Generally, the makers of *Sexual Freedom in Denmark* were very careful to keep the film within the documentary framework, and the tone of the narration is deadly serious. Besides citing statistics showing a drop in sex crimes following the legalization of pornography, there is an interesting interview with a physician who speaks of the positive value of sex education—including the use of pornographic material—in preventing crime and adding to human happiness.

Almost simultaneously with the Lamb and De Renzy films, a whole new subgenre of "educational" films were released—the so-called marriage manual films like *Man and Wife* and *101 Acts of Love*. The pattern of these films, which were successful, for the most part, both in finding audiences and in avoiding prosecution for violating the obscenity laws, was always the same. A doctor gave out advanced medical advice on sex, and several couples illustrated the benefits to be derived from doing what the doctor ordered. Since the only costume worn in these films was the standard white laboratory garment, they came to be known affectionately in the trade as "white coaters." Quite often the tone of advertising and promotion of these films was dignified and understated. For example, the advertising copy for *The Marriage Manual* was the epitome of sobriety:

THE ONLY THING THAT STANDS BETWEEN YOU AND COMPLETE SEXUAL FULFILLMENT ARE THE BARRIERS OF IGNORANCE. SEX IS THE CORNERSTONE OF YOUR MARRIAGE. IT IS OUR FIRM BELIEF THAT BOTH HUSBAND AND WIFE CAN BENEFIT GREATLY BY THE FRANK AND HONEST INSTRUCTION OF SEXUAL INTERCOURSE AS SHOWN IN "THE MARRIAGE MANUAL."

The frank come-on was obviously pitched at a new audience, the dating crowd and young marrieds who could respond without embarrassment to the clean sex and pristine ideological message of these movies.

One of the first filmmakers to work with this kind of material was Matt Cimber (Jayne Mansfield's last husband), who with $86,000 made *Man and Wife*, featuring two ostensibly married couples who take turns illustrating about forty different positions of intercourse. *Man and Wife* is a very dull film but it is competently made, with clear sound, good color photography, and attractive actors. The sex, both real and simulated, is handled with care. And the technical frigidity and erotic deadness of *Man and Wife* did not hurt it at the box office. Cimber claimed that the film grossed more than $2.5 million in the first year of its release in close to 100 cities, with relatively little trouble with the law. In Denver, where the film was busted, Judge John Bernard declared the film not obscene, ordered District Attorney Stanley Johnson to return the print to the theater, and dismissed the charges against the theater manager.

Matt Cimber followed the success of *Man and Wife* with *He and She*, a similar venture that showed more in the way of foreplay—mutual masturbation, cunnilingus, and fellatio. *He and She* is also somewhat more daring technically than Cimber's first sex film, occasionally moving away from graphic intercourse and including metaphoric sex scenes. As Joseph Slade writes in an article for *Transaction*, "As she reaches climax, a collage of images: a romp in a wheat field, a baby, a kiss, etc., creates a mood of tenderness but does not tell us anything."

Despite such lyricism, however, the formula quickly became dull—after all, there are only so many positions for intercourse and so many ways of expressing verbally certain platitudes about the relationship between an inventive sex life and a sound marriage—but these limitations did not seem to discourage other filmmakers. Rushed into release were *The Art of Marriage, Marital Fulfillment, Master's Degree, Lessons in Love, Sexual Education in Scandinavia,* and *101 Acts of Love. Marital Fulfillment* was perhaps the least interesting of these, seventy minutes of erotic poses and tepid couplings produced, directed, and photographed by Fred Sebastian, the filmmaker who had just produced a film for the federal government called *Oral Hygiene for the Handicapped.*

At the other end of the spectrum, *101 Acts of Love,* produced by Donn Greer, is one of the best white-coaters. Greer was an experienced producer who made more than five thousand commercials before going into the business of making 35mm soft-core films. As increased competition from Hollywood films and foreign products like *I Am Curious (Yellow)* caused Greer's business to drop off, he began making quality 16mm films that were less expensive, more explicit, and more profitable. The narrative of *101 Acts of Love* concerns a married couple—everyone in the film wears a wedding ring and little else—who go to see a doctor because the joy has gone out of their sex lives. The doctor (played with touching conviction by lovely Linda Guiness) explains to the couple that they should experiment with and vary the positions of intercourse and the techniques of foreplay. The couple enthusiastically follow her advice, and soon they are gamboling

Promotional material for Kroger Babb's *Mom and Dad*

Exploitation pioneer Louis Sonney

Union Films

Nudies: *Naked Island* (above and below); *The Secret of Venus* (facing page, above); and a Nudie-Cutie with its original ad caption (facing page, below)

Lewking Associates

Entertainment Ventures, Inc.

Starring
CONNIE MASON
PLAYBOY'S FAVORITE PLAYMATE
THOMAS WOOD
JEFFREY ALLEN

Box Office Spectaculars, Inc. presents a Friedman-Lewis Production
"TWO THOUSAND MANIACS!"
A TOWN OF MADMEN CRAZED WITH BLOOD LUST!
Produced by DAVID F. FRIEDMAN / Directed by HERSCHELL G. LEWIS

GRUESOME SLAUGHTER
STAINED IN BRUTAL BLOOD COLOR!
with SHELBY LIVINGSTON /
BEN MOORE / YVONNE GILBERT /
JEROME EDEN / LINDA COCHRAN

Entertainment Ventures, Inc.

Deek Stills (left) in *Trader Hornee,* another David F. Friedman film; and Friedman (facing page), photographed by Kenneth Turan

Entertainment Ventures, Inc.

Russ Meyer (above), photographed by Kenneth Turan; and two Meyer films (facing page), *The Immoral Mr. Teas* (above) and *Wild Gals of the Naked West* (below)

Eve Productions

Lorna Maitland in Russ Meyer's *Lorna*—"too much for one man"

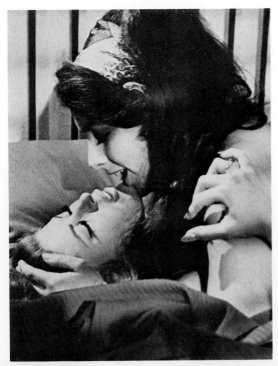

Russ Meyer's *Vixen:* Erica Gavin and Vincene Wallace (left), and Jon Evans and Erica Gavin (facing page)

Eve Productions

Eve Productions

Eve Productions

Essy Persson (above) as Thérèse in Radley Metzger's *Thérèse and Isabelle;* and Silvana Venturelli and Frank Wolff (below) in *The Lickerish Quartet,* also by Metzger

Radley Metzger directing Silvana Venturelli in *Camille 2000*

Audubon Films

The Laughing Woman

Audubon Films

Essy Persson in *I, A Woman*

Audubon Films

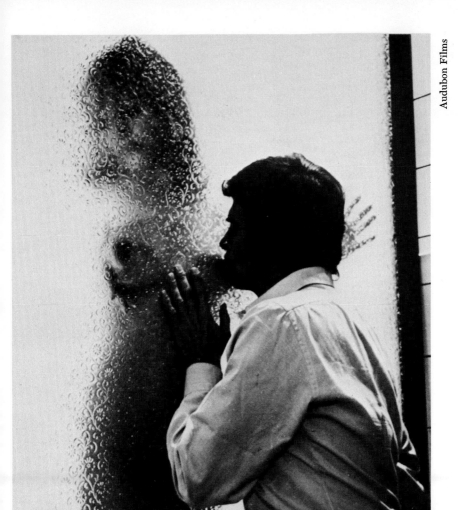

Mark Damon and Christiane Kruger in Radley Metzger's *Little Mother*

All the Loving Couples   Marie Liljedahl as *Inga*

Her and She and Him

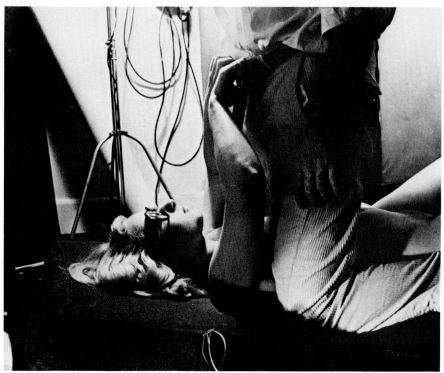

That Woman (above) and Gertie Jung in *Relations* (below)

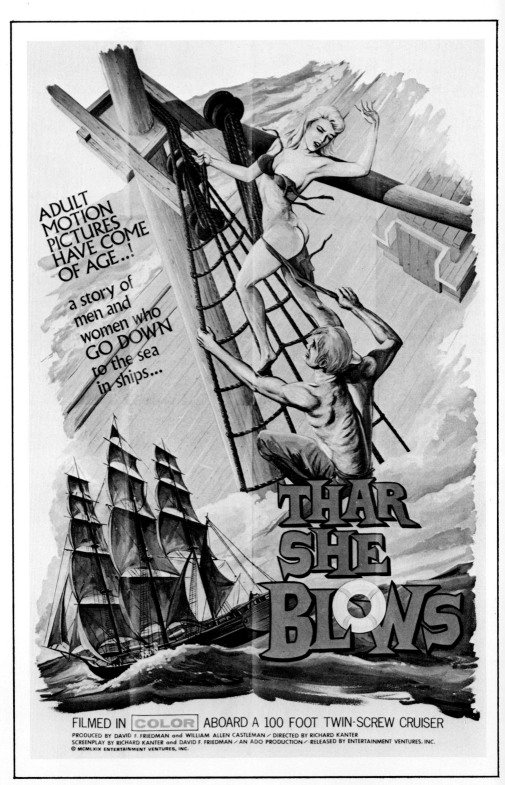

ADULT
MOTION
PICTURES
HAVE COME
OF AGE..!

a story of
men and
women who
GO DOWN
to the sea
in ships...

THAR
SHE
BLOWS

FILMED IN COLOR ABOARD A 100 FOOT TWIN-SCREW CRUISER

PRODUCED BY DAVID F. FRIEDMAN and WILLIAM ALLEN CASTLEMAN / DIRECTED BY RICHARD KANTER
SCREENPLAY BY RICHARD KANTER and DAVID F. FRIEDMAN / AN ADO PRODUCTION / RELEASED BY ENTERTAINMENT VENTURES, INC.
© MCMLXIX ENTERTAINMENT VENTURES, INC.

Entertainment Ventures, Inc.

gratefully in the woods and in bed. There are graphic scenes of intercourse but no ejaculation.

101 Acts of Love is one of the few "educational" films that is not shot like an army training movie. Director Eric Haims and his cinematographer, David Worth, set up a novel, intriguing way to photograph the several couples who took part in making the film by suspending a ½-inch-thick Plexiglas platform from the ceiling of the studio by six thin wires designed for aeronautical use. They then built catwalks around part of the Plexiglas and rigged it so that an operator could revolve the platform 360 degrees. This elaborate apparatus enabled the cameraman to shoot the love-making from every possible angle, including several previously available only to bedbugs. The platform was kept in constant motion during the film, making the 101 acts of love visually interesting. A variety of filters, optical effects, and lighting patterns were also used to jazz up the color photography, and the sound, universally the weakest and most irritating part of sex films, was far above the usual dim, fuzzy standard. The soundtrack made subtle use of songs (a musical score by Randy Scott) and poetry (the, in this case, ironic sonnet beginning "How do I love thee? Let me count the ways," by Elizabeth Barrett Browning).

Sex-education films became increasingly explicit until it was difficult to tell them from hard-core loops. One of the most graphic, *Sexual Communication*, depicts two sexually troubled young couples who attend a group-therapy session at Shangri-La Sex Clinic where they are counseled by a pair of doctors, one of whom was played by Sheila I. Rossi, Ph.D. Dr. Rossi, who believes in the educational value of this kind of movie, was both performer and technical adviser on *Sexual Communication*, which shows scenes of oral sex, mutual masturbation, and various positions of intercourse, shot in the close, prurient manner of hard-core loops. The producers defended the erotic activity in the film in their advertising:

The fact that the film presents extreme closeups of the genitals in function is not an attempt to insert random or unnecessary hard core into a quality film. It is our strong belief that these revelations are necessary for a true understanding and acceptance of each and every part of the body.

In their search for new formats with redeeming social value and significance for their nonfiction sex films, producers of hard core eventually hit on the idea of studies of the past history and present manufacture of stag films in the United States and Denmark. The first, best, and most popular of these films was Alex de Renzy's *A History of the Blue Movie*, a chronological

85

history of stag films tied together by a narration based on the excellent *Playboy* study of stag films written by Arthur Knight and Hollis Alpert. The opening sequence of the 1970 film is an extraordinary silent stag called *A Free Ride* (contained in the collection of the Kinsey Institute for Sex Research under the alternate title of *A Grass Sandwich*), identified by internal evidence as having been made sometime around 1915 by people familiar with the rudiments of cinematography and editing. Unlike many stag films from later years, the story is handled well: A man gives two women a ride in his car, flirts with them and offers them a drink out of his flask. Feeling the need to relieve himself, he stops the car and goes off into the woods. Out of curiosity the women follow him and are amused by the sight of him urinating. They soon follow suit, and the man spies on them. Aroused, he exposes himself and, after some abrupt foreplay, makes love first to one of the women and then the other. The sexual content (intercourse, fellatio, urination, and fleeting cunnilingus) is presented gracefully and with good humor. There is nothing dirty or smirking about the film, and the little incidents are developed not merely to show sexual activity, but to tell an amusing story.

The second stag film in the De Renzy compilation, *On the Beach* (circa 1925), is a dirty joke elaborated in visual terms. A young man daydreams on Idlewild Beach ("Where the men are idle and the women are wild") as three women appear and undress. The man steals their clothes and then propositions them. One girl agrees to make love to him, provided that intercourse takes place through a hole in the fence, and when the man obliges, she substitutes a goat for herself. Time passes. The young man is once again on the beach, and the women reappear. This time the woman who has tricked him stuffs a pillow under her dress and, accusing the hapless fellow of getting her in a family way, extorts money from him. There is relatively little sex in *On the Beach*, but the wry humor has several folkloric elements—the stolen clothes, the animal substituted for the woman, and the character of the deceitful woman—that are common to oral and written erotic stories and give this early stag film archetypal resonance.

These comedies are followed by an animated cartoon of unknown authorship called *Buried Treasure*. Made in the United States around 1930, it has a highly professional graphic style similar to that of the Krazy Kat cartoons of the same period. The protagonist of this bizarrely humorous episode is a randy little man who becomes involved in a series of erotic and horrific encounters. The film is full of sight gags, and the humor is derived entirely from the awkward, painful, and humiliating experiences of the hero, who wants to have sex in the worst way. He makes love to a cow and to a woman; he trips over his own penis, catches it in a cactus, and even loses it. It is a classic of its kind and remained unequaled until Ralph Bakshi's *Fritz the Cat* and *Heavy Traffic* about forty years later.

Next, *A History of the Blue Movie* is taken up with a number of sequences of varied quality and interest: *Keyhole Silhouettes* (circa 1930), in which a number of people in adjoining rooms crudely engage in sex, while the janitor watches through a series of keyholes; several tedious, interminable burlesque reels, including ten seconds of bumps and grinds in a grass skirt from *Hula Tease* (circa 1940); and a section from the classic *Smart Aleck*, with a hard-driving intercourse scene during which the crewcut and tattooed protagonist is quite obviously having the time of his life, while his partner, famed stripper Candy Barr, obviously is not.

The De Renzy film next shows *The Nun's Story* (sometimes called *The None Story* in deference to Catholic sensitivities), one of the few stag films produced in this country with an anticlerical theme and plot: A nun removes her habit and begins to fondle herself. A young man who watches through a crack in the venetian blind then boldly enters the nun's apartment and confronts her. They caress and then make love in a variety of positions. Satiated, the nun dons her habit again. While *The Nun's Story* is remarkable neither for the modest technical expertise with which it is made nor for its plot, standard stag stuff, the raven beauty of the woman, who looks a little like one of the sex goddesses of the '50s, has made the film a stag classic. The absolute, all-consuming passion with which the "nun" makes love, the physically greedy body movements with which she responds, result in one of the very few moments in erotic films in which the erotic involvement of the woman reaches the point of ecstatic abandon.

The final part of *A History of the Blue Movie* is composed of three movies originally filmed by De Renzy for exhibition in the Screening Room. The first of them, *The Masseuse*, is a beaver classic. A young, hip San Francisco man comes into a massage parlor with the obvious intention of getting a "local" massage. The masseuse, however, is interested only in doing her job. The dialogue is witty and low-keyed, poking fun at the naked man's growing frustration with the staid masseuse who will not respond to his subtle attempts at seduction. This is followed by a reel in which a pretty girl masturbates while narrating the most salacious and obscene descriptions of her love life, speaking of the things she has done, what turns her on, and even her own feelings at the time of being filmed for the segment. It is obviously an improvised put-on, but the suspicion still exists that the woman may be telling the truth or, at least, may be aroused by telling lies about herself. The power of this sequence confirms that people talking about making love may be as arousing as people actually making love. The final Screening Room portion recreates the adventures of a hippie couple from the time they answer an advertisement in the *Berkeley Barb* for sex-film performers until they complete the filming of the loop for which they were hired. It is an arty, self-conscious sequence that makes use of the photographic possibilities of shooting both straight-on and in mirrors. The patterns, pace, and natural predilections of the couple are not interfered with, and the loop is wholly free of the distracting, unnatural posings that are sometimes demanded by directors who get the lighting or angle right only by interrupting the flow of the erotic experience of the performers.

The success of *A History of the Blue Movie* spawned a number of imitators: *Hollywood Blue, Making the Blue Movie*, and certain sequences in *Personals* and *Sexual Liberty Now*. The first of these offshoots, *Hollywood Blue*, described by its maker Bill Osco as a "rip-off," is known primarily for the tacky audacity with which it exploits and possibly defames several revered Hollywood stars. *Hollywood Blue* purports to reveal the indiscretions committed by these stars before they became famous, but the material available to Osco (edited by Mike Light and Howard Ziehm) is scrappy and disappointing, and the resulting film is incoherent and, despite its relative short running time of ninety minutes, overlong. Its most notorious piece of footage is a grainy, hardcore homosexual loop featuring a love bout between a soldier and a sailor, unremarkable except for the fact that the sailor involved in fellatio and sodomy resembles one of the more popular television cowboy stars; it is an episode the man in question has neither confirmed nor denied.

The second well-known segment is called "Apple Knockers and Coke Bottle," a short Nudie loop featuring a woman said to be Marilyn Monroe. Several of Monroe's friends, however, have identified this starlet as Arline Hunter, a woman who, according to Arthur Knight, "enjoyed brief popularity in girlie magazines of the early Fifties as 'the poor man's Marilyn Monroe.'" Whatever the identity of the woman, the sequence is one of the saddest, least erotic pieces of film ever screened. The woman in the film strips down to her panties, rubs an apple between her breasts, gyrates suggestively, and pours Coke over herself as Osco tastelessly intercuts films of Monroe's funeral.

The rest of *Hollywood Blue* is strung together from marginal material: a parody of the Valentino picture *The Sheik*, showing what really went on in the tent after Valentino abducted Agnes Ayres; a clip from *Buried Treasure*; Hedy Lamarr's nude swimming sequence from *Ecstasy*; and a segment from the initial release version of *King Kong* in which Kong strips Fay Wray of some of her clothes and sniffs them appreciatively. There is also footage of Evelyn West, whose "Treasure Chest" was insured by Lloyd's of London for $1 million. To pad out the movie, Osco includes footage of Jayne Mansfield at an awards dinner, interviews with Mickey Rooney and June Wilkinson, both of whom knew and worked with Mansfield, man-on-the-street interviews, news clips of Shirley Temple and Ronald Reagan, and a couple of new hard-core sequences filmed for the occasion—one documenting the love of a young girl for her Saint Bernard. (This sequence was quickly cut out of the picture but not before it gave *Hollywood Blue* a notorious reputation that helped the box office.)

Making the Blue Movie, variously attributed to J. Nehemiah and Jeraldo Stuarti, similarly contains a number of old stag reels, but these are intercut with a considerable amount of new footage, including some revealing interviews shot by the director during the actual filming of several hard-core loops. One of the performers, Harry Reems, was then at the beginning of his long, distinguished hard-core career, and he is interviewed while reclining nude on a mattress. Reems complains that acting in sex films is harming his love life because he is professionally required to act out, and thus destroy, his wildest and most personal fantasies. Also interviewed are Tina Russell, author of a recent autobiography called *Porno Star*, and her husband, Jason Russell, with whom she made more than eighty hard-core films and worked live shows during the short months theatrical sex was tolerated in New York City. Russell openly admits that he does not mind Tina working with other men. His work with Tina in hard-core loops, he states, was the logical extension of an open, liberated life-style that embraced both bisexuality and group sex.

This theme is further elaborated upon by Tina and Jason Russell in *Personals*, directed by Armand Weston and Howard Winters and released by Distripix. The film consists of black-and-white interviews with real people—ranging from a sculptor who makes plaster casts of female genitalia to a young man whose greatest pleasure in life comes from being used and abused by other men and whose dearest memory is a weekend he once spent pretending to be a dog—who had at some time placed or answered sex advertisements in underground newspapers. There are also dialogues with a lesbian, a transvestite, a self-proclaimed nymphomaniac, three troilists, and finally with the Russells. The latter interview, intercut with explicit color footage of the Russells making love, is remarkable for the intelligence and candor with which Jason and Tina speak of their lives. "I am completely free," said **Tina,**

to make love to someone outside of my marriage, but it all depends upon the situation and the person. If it happens spontaneously with someone that I like, that's the way it happens. But it usually occurs only when I have really warm, loving feelings toward that person.

Later in the interview, Jason spoke of his and Tina's bisexuality, commenting:

I think that bisexuality would be what I personally would consider normal. By cutting off a realm of relationships with people simply because they are of our own sex, we are cheating ourselves of a realm of experience that we should be sharing. Love is love, and people are people, and sex is something that we should all be sharing. What your sex is should not matter. Physically, two people of the same sex can satisfy each other just as well as two people of the opposite sex.

Other interviews in *Personals* sustain the same level of interest, and the constant shifting back and forth between fantasy and reality, between people talking and other people acting out the experiences, provide a dreamy quality that sets it apart from other interview films.

Another sort of documentary approach to sex films capitalized on audience fascination with erotic rites and practices of various peoples of the world. Using a pop-sociology tone, these films were generally episodic, superficial, and inherently fictional accounts of the ways different—preferably "exotic"—peoples make love. In *Black Is Beautiful* (also known as *Africanus Sexualis*), for example, which was produced by Matt Cimber after his initial success with *Man and Wife*, the black men are portrayed as beings of legendary sexual prowess—rugged, childlike, sensual, sometimes savage, and closer to nature than whites. The heavy ad campaign for *Black Is Beautiful* described "the strange and erotic practices which have made the modern black man the happiest, best adjusted of all humans." Intercut with shots of an extremely handsome black couple making love is an "expert" on African affairs who delivers a not-so-learned dissertation on the sex lives and practices of African tribes, throwing in an occasional recipe for homemade aphrodisiacs as well as irrelevant footage of Africans at work and play. Despite its pseudo-anthropology, *Black Is Beautiful* was quite successful with black audiences, playing extended engagements in the ghetto theaters of cities with substantial black populations.

Blacks had been seen in sex films, but they always appeared in highly stereotyped roles, similar to those they portrayed in nonpornographic movies. In the stag films made before World War II, for example, blacks were included for humorous value—

the women as maids and the men as comic bellhops and inept
servants—and as passive observers of the erotic action. After
World War II blacks began to perform sexually in stag films, as
filmmakers took advantage of the shock value of interracial intercourse, but the themes almost invariably turned on the concept of
dominance and subservience based on the old characterizations
(proud, savage black men who lust after weak white women;
cruel white men who abuse black women) and the old situations
(black maids are seduced by white employers; black repairmen
come to fix the phone and fix the Vassar wife instead). A hard-
core loop from the late '60s is a classic example: The reel begins
as a beautiful blonde woman, a velvet halter around her neck and
white gloves on her hands, fellates a massively endowed black
man who does not reciprocate in any way. The man turns
around slowly, and the woman performs analingus on him. They
move to a bed, and the man takes her anally. She pulls away,
turns around, and fellates him to climax. There is no kissing, no
tenderness. The black man uses the white woman, and she does
not share in his pleasure, being very much the unequal partner
in their lovemaking. The film reverses the usual relationship
between the races in the United States, and the subservient role
of the white woman can be seen as an unusual expiation of guilt
or the enactment of a common fearful fantasy by white men.

In *Black and White*, a film by the Dakota Brothers, a white girl
taunts and teases her four black lovers until they confront her
simultaneously and cruelly and together force themselves on her,
enacting another stereotype of awesome black sexual appetite and
ability. (These persistent myths and stereotypes die hard. Even the
sex-film documentaries, the comparative "erotologies," use them,
and the stereotype reappears in such recent hard-core features as
Behind the Green Door and *Boys in the Sand*.)

Other films also dealt with the sexual customs of nonwhites,
for example, *Kama Sutra '71*, which combined illustrated readings
of that ancient compendium of sexual wisdom with a banal story
of a modern Indian couple with sex problems. The scenes devoted
to the explication of the *Kama Sutra* are done with a certain
charm, and the young Indian couple making love exhibit more
than a passing knowledge of the more arcane passages in the
book, particularly those requiring the stamina and balance of
trained gymnasts. The rest of the film, however, is unbearably
tedious.

Kama Sutra '71 was the work of Variety Films, a small New
York company that soon released another movie along the same
lines called *Worlds of Love*. Promising "a voyage into the eroticism of the entire world," the film delivered only the imaginative
recreation of certain sex practices around the world, including

the antics of two intoxicated prostitutes in a nineteenth-century French brothel; the precise, ritualized activities of a sedate Japanese geisha; an Arabian feast of gastronomic and erotic pleasures; and a self-conscious, staid orgy set in modern Scandinavia.

Not all of the pseudo-anthropological documentaries were devoted to alien lands and cultures. *Together*, produced and directed by Sean Cunningham and released at the end of 1971, studied American sex practices. Filmed in a soft-focus, highly romantic fashion (there is only the most fleeting of hard-core sequences), it was sold to the large middle-class audience—including the Saturday night date crowd—by means of a series of saturation radio spots and substantial newspaper coverage. After a strong beginning in Providence, Rhode Island, the movie became a national hit, grossing $5 million in the first year of its release, a financial success all out of proportion to the movie's merit. The setting for *Together* is a beautiful seaside retreat on the New England coast where a doctor conducts a program of sensitivity training that includes yoga exercises, the saying of dirty words, dabbling in the *Kama Sutra* (including advocacy of the rapid in-and-out motion known as "chasing the sparrow"), playing leapfrog and ring-around-the-rosy, meditating, and doing somersaults as part of foreplay.

The impossibly idyllic and simplistic gospel preached by the doctor is that masks are to be stripped away and roles no longer played. Most of the footage is taken up with harmless, naked encounters by handsome men and beautiful women (one, billed as Marilyn Briggs, was, as Marilyn Chambers, to achieve national fame after her startling appearance in *Behind the Green Door* and the subsequent revelation that she was the model pictured, babe-in-arms, on the box of Ivory Snow), but there is some sex in the film, including frank, energetic scenes of intercourse, oral sex, and masturbation.

If *Together* is a film about healthy, normal sex, the other end of the sexual spectrum is represented by films that deal with prostitution, pornography, and perversion, films like *Pornography— Are You Offended; Pornography in Hollywood; Pornography USA; Pornography—Prostitution USA; Changes; Sex USA; Red White and Blue; Freedom To Love; Erotikon; Open City '72; Sexual Liberty Now; Bizarre Sex Practices; Censorship USA; Sex Clinic Girls; Pornorama; and Anomalies. Sexual Liberty Now*, for example, contained footage from a Danish import called *Animal Lover*, detailing the sex life of a Danish farm woman who takes more than a casual interest in barnyard animals. *Animal Lover* featured scenes of the woman coupling with a horse, a dog, and a pig, but the only footage used in *Sexual Liberty Now* was a startling, graphic, and reportedly dangerous scene of bedroom intercourse with the rotund, bewildered porker. Other scenes in this cinematic jumble of statistics and statements about "the evil caused by restrictions and repressions of human sexuality" include man-on-the-street interviews about pornography, shots of Charles Keating giving his dissenting views on the recommendation by the Commission on Obscenity and Pornography that pornography be legalized, several old pornographic stag films and cartoons, and a discussion of the sex-education programs of the Glide Methodist Church in San Francisco.

Bizarre Sex Practices, Anomalies, and *Daughters of Anomaly*— "documentaries" involving homosexuality, lesbianism, orgies, transvestism, fetishism, masochism, and sadism—were explicit and rather successful. *Anomalies,* though not a famous title, made $2,136,842 in its first 128 engagements.

Of the films dealing with the nature and legalization of pornography in the United States, one of the earliest and most distinguished is Ferd Sebastian's *Red White and Blue,* a technically glossy and relatively intelligent treatment of the subject. *Pornography in Hollywood,* a documentary put together by John Kirkland and written by Ron Reego, had neither of those virtues but did include interviews with the owner of a topless bar, with four men engaged in the Gay Liberation movement, and with a defrocked homosexual minister, as well as scenes of naked male go-go dancers performing in a gay bar. The movie's most notable footage, a hard-core gay loop, is unusual in a film aimed primarily at a heterosexual audience.

Most of the "rites and practices" documentaries crudely exploit serious concepts of the nature of human sexual experience. These nonfiction films pretend to a legitimacy they do not have, hypocritically citing the work of serious students of both the erotic and the scientific aspects of sexuality in an attempt to provide justification for motion pictures actually designed to show hardcore sexual activity. The narrative is only pretext, and the hardcore sex scenes, devoid of the identifications and correspondences possible in filmic fantasies, are flat and stale. These documentaries were an erotic dead end; the next significant step in the development of hard-core genres had to be the invention of the explicit story film, combining the primal act with such stuff as dreams are made on.

THE HARD AND SOFT OF IT

FOUR INTERVIEWS

It may seem, as populist firebrand Tom Watson said of poor whites and blacks in the rural South, that hard- and soft-core pornographers are all in the ditch together. Those involved, however, don't see it quite that way, and in most cases a clear demarcation line can be drawn between the soft- and hard-core folk. The former view themselves as perfectly respectable, if a little risqué, and see hard core as far too clinical and explicit to be tasteful. The latter, meanwhile, feeling an Old Testament moral rectitude about what they do, dismiss the people who mess with soft-core sex as hypocritical, if not worse. You pays your money . . .

MARSHA JORDAN, QUEEN OF SOFT CORE

"Marsha is probably the one female star that has been developed in the exploitation business," says Dave Friedman. And out there in the great heartland, the little people remember. Linda Lovelace and the like may have captured the mass media, but the good people haven't forgotten Marsha Jordan, the Queen of Soft Core.

"I still have faithful fans," she says, happy at the thought. "They write me and tell me every little thing they're doing. One guy in Indiana, I know that every month I get a letter from him, whether I write him or not. He has a scrapbook and friends of his from different parts of the country, anytime they see anything in the paper when I've appeared at a theater or even just a movie, they send it to him. And I've got a standing invitation to their houses and all this." It's nice to be liked, very nice indeed.

A much shorter time ago than it seems—the middle '60s, in fact —blushingly frank theatrical hard-core films were still either a dream or a nightmare, depending on one's point of view. Since the only place you could see "it" actually being done was on some sheet tacked to the wall at the local firehouse or union hall, the fans mostly made do with simulated stuff performed by people who faked it with various degrees of artistry. People like Marsha Jordan.

A stewardess for Delta Airlines, tall, blonde, but hardly willowy, she came out to Hollywood for a vacation in 1960 and never left. "I got into exploitation films more or less by accident," she says. "But I really had fun." Someone who was making a movie asked her if she wanted to be in it. She said why not and someone on that set asked her if she wanted to be in another. Then a cameraman with a good eye asked if she'd ever done any X-rated films. "I said, 'What's an X-rated film?' and he said, 'There's nudity in it,' and I said, 'Oh, I don't have anything against nudity.' " And so it began.

When it ended there were something like twenty-five X-rated films in the can, films with coy titles like *Head Mistress, Brand of Shame, Office Love-In, Lady Godiva Rides, The Daisy Chain, The Divorcee,* and *The Golden Box.* And Marsha became the biggest star soft core ever had, featured in ads as "the incomparable," even getting the ultimate accolade of having a film—*Marsha, the Erotic Housewife*—named after her.

Drinking coffee in the paneled kitchen of her quiet brown ranch house on a quiet street in Hollywood, twice-married, twice-divorced thirty-four-year-old Marsha Jordan still doesn't seem to have quite figured out how or why it happened. Her films weren't that different from any other type of film, she says, except that "in exploitation films you have to have girls with pretty decent bodies. If you're gonna make nude films, you gotta have nudes."

And, no, the nudity didn't bother her at all, she says, surprised that someone might think it did. The thought that her acting ability might perhaps be inadequate disturbed her more than that. And all the adulation, well, that "tended to embarrass me a little bit," as did the director who insisted on treating her like an Important Person. "He gave me my own hairdresser and my own makeup man, and he would insist that everyone including the crew call me 'Miss Jordan.' Nobody was allowed to use profanity. He says, 'You're my star and you're gonna be treated like one.' Oh, now, things like that are embarrassing." For Marsha Jordan, a woman who calls John Wayne "my absolute hero" and sees

Gone With the Wind every time it's rereleased, is nothing if not just plain folks.

And it was precisely that open, warm, down-home quality that made Marsha Jordan a star. And not only the way she projected it on the screen, or the fact that the producers she worked for had the best distribution setup in the country, which didn't hurt either. Marsha Jordan became a sex star on a person-to-person basis—she humanized her films and her audiences by taking the unheard-of step of traveling from theater to theater on promotion tours, standing in lobbies from East to West and back again, adding the personal touch to what had been a cold, cruel world. And, oh, the people loved her for it. "Oh," she remembers, "it was absolutely fantastic."

Grand Rapids, Denver, Minneapolis, Memphis, New Orleans, Tampa, Jacksonville, Savannah, Nashville, Chattanooga, and even Canada—everywhere it was the same. "Maybe a little press conference and ads in the newspapers and TV saying I was going to be there signing or giving away 8 × 10 autographed pictures. And they would set up a little table with flowers on it in the lobby," and the people would come forth.

Sometimes there were so many people that in Indianapolis, for instance, she upstaged then Vice-President Agnew. "This guy got on TV, and he said, 'With our Vice-President coming to the airport, where do you think twenty-three newspaper reporters and umpteen number of TV reporters that were supposed to be at the airport interviewing him were? They were at the Art Theater interviewing Marsha Jordan, sexploitation queen.' It was funny."

And then there was that drive-in "right in the middle of the Amish country in a small, small town, I mean like they had one red blinker light. The show was to start about eight-thirty and we got there about six and it's pouring down rain, raining like crazy, and the place is packed. They've got cars in this way, cars behind the cars, cars over here in the fields with no speaker.

"They had set up a little table beside the snack bar, with a little awning, and they'd put a stool there for me to sit on and sign autographs. Now these were X-rated films, and here's this long line of people, two deep. There's women carrying babies, little kids, and"—she makes a stock face of amazement—"I can't believe it. Pouring down rain, absolutely pouring down rain. 'Well,' I said, 'they can't stand out there' but they did, coming up and saying 'Oh, hi, Marsha, gee I saw this picture,' and 'How're you doing' like we had known each other for ages. And I was like . . . " Amazed, maybe? "Yes, amazed."

There were other surprises, too. Someone who "always had in mind that the people who go to the theaters would be, you know, like sneaking in," she found places like a small town in Iowa where "90 per cent of the people who came in were couples, married couples and single couples. We said, 'Gee, this is weird,' and they said, 'Oh no, on the weekend people here don't have anyplace to go, so all the married people come to the sex theaters.' "

And most amazing of all was how warmly the people responded to someone actually coming to see *them*, what they said to her when at last face to face with the divinity. "I always had this thing in the back of my mind, I would think, 'Oh somebody's going to insult me or somebody's going to get nasty,' " she admitted, but the general reaction was more flabbergasted than disapproving. "They would say, 'Oh, you're the first real movie star I've met in my life.' And you'd want to laugh and know that you couldn't because most of them are real sincere. They'd say, 'It really is you, you look different, you're smaller,' and I'd say, 'No, I'm not smaller, I just look bigger on screen.' "

And after a while, after a tour or two, people started to feel "like they know you personally. They go see all your movies, and they ask about you and they write letters, 'What are you doing, are you interested in the Los Angeles Lakers this year?' They tell me, you know, little things about their lives. It's like they become kind of friends."

Sometimes, the personalization, the blending of movies and reality, could get out of hand, like when Marsha did a picture called *Diary of a Madam*, followed by the usual tour. "And so many people that I'd seen before would come up and say, 'I didn't know that you were a madam, I've seen all your pictures, but I didn't really know that you were a madam.' It happened so many times, I'd just break up laughing." It was not so funny, however, when they named another picture *Marsha, the Erotic Housewife* without her knowledge, "because I was more or less a housewife. Even though the story was absolutely foreign to what my private life was, I felt that maybe some people might associate it with my life." Perhaps not since the first days of the cinema when people ran out of the theater screaming when they saw trains moving on the screen had there been such a strong link between what people saw and how real they thought it was. For lots of people, Marsha Jordan was the realest thing they'd come across yet.

For the granddaughter of a minister, her childhood spent in a Catholic convent, this was all kind of daring. "But I guess in a way I'm a little rebellious about certain things," Marsha says, unable to understand, for instance, why "there's such a big deal made about sex. Sex has been happening for a million years, and it's just an average, normal thing." She is very open about what she does, speaking right up and saying, "I make nude movies" whenever anyone asks, as a sign that she isn't embarrassed in the least. And she tends to get upset with conventional morality of the type an old girlfriend exhibited when Marsha visited her hometown a while back.

"I said, 'Hey, let's get together.' But she says, 'Oh, my husband would be terribly upset. He doesn't want me to see you.' I said, 'Hey, that's cool, I knew there'd be a few people that would object to it.' Then she calls and asks if we can meet for coffee, and she sits down and tells me she's having an affair with this guy and she's really hung up on him but she can't let her husband know. And I can't believe it, she's putting me down for working in a movie where I'm nude and here she's having an affair with some guy and she's married. Now does that balance out and make sense? No. People's minds are just weird."

Marsha is always running into people she has to set straight about what she does, like the "Shakespearean theater critic" from a town in Oklahoma who "expected probably that I was going to be a dumb ignorant little girl" and ended up admitting he didn't know how much dedication was involved in exploitation films, that he'd thought "they were a bunch of people thrown together in a garage and shot." She was more worried about the reaction of her relatives, "real square people in Alabama who might really get uptight," especially her grandfather, the minister. She worried for nothing.

"He picked up a magazine that had a review of a movie I was in, it said there was nudity and this and that and the other. He took it on a train with him, and my mother said that between New Orleans and Dallas he was going through all the cars saying, 'This is my granddaughter, isn't she pretty? This is my granddaughter, isn't she pretty?' "

And in fact, Marsha's relatives have become her biggest fans, packing the theater in the small town of Atowa, population 2,500, outside of Gadsden to such an extent that "the film distributor in Atlanta called me up one morning like 4 A.M., he couldn't wait to tell me. 'I don't know how many relatives you have there,' he says, 'but every one of them had to go see that movie at least ten times, because we got over a $10,000 rental out of this one little theater in a week.'" And when one of her uncles said to her grandmother, " 'It was just a shame, it was a disgrace,' " and that Marsha should ask God's forgiveness for exploiting herself, her grandmother's reaction was " 'Well, if you're such a Christian, didn't God tell you you shouldn't throw stones?' " Nicely put, Marsha thought.

And if her family liked her job, her job had turned out to be like family. "Most of the people that have been making X-rated films started out together," she says. "It's like a close family thing; everybody's friends, and everybody knows each other. A lot of times you'll be working on the same films with more or less the same people, and it gives you a sense of being more relaxed because you know how they're gonna be.

"I have to say that in this particular field of the business, it's like fun. When you go on an interview, it's not like in the legit thing, where you go through all this hassle and the intrigue and all this. Any interview I've ever been on in sexploitation, and this goes from the very first one, it's conducted very businesslike. You read a script, and if you can act they might ask you to take off your clothes to see if you have any scars or anything like that. And they'll say, 'We'll let you know,' or 'We can't use you,' or 'Okay, you've got the part, here's the script, here's the time, this, that, and the other.' There's no bullshit, there's no hanky-panky."

And the pay was all right too, sometimes $100 or $125 a day, sometimes $1,000 a week. Mostly, as Marsha noted, the men in the industry treated her pretty straight, but on some occasions, "you do feel exploited. Like when a so-called friend calls you up and asks would you do this little part, and it'd probably be three days at $100 a day, and there wasn't much. And then they cram it in one 18-hour day and hand you a check for $100.

"Or people asked me would I do a little vignette, a little cameo thing in the film they were doing, as a favor to them, and I said okay. Well, I worked like a half-day or whatever for $100, and then when you get the calendar section of the *Los Angeles Times* and see a double-page ad saying 'starring Marsha Jordan,' you feel a little bit abused and a little bit upset."

Lately, however, since there has been almost no one at all around to put money into soft-core sex-exploitation films, Marsha has drifted into other fields: "real films," though ones that "don't get that much advertising"—items like *Hellcats*, a motorcycle epic, and *Count Yorga*, an underrated vampire movie; voice-overs, reading lines off-camera; TV shows—a bit part in the old "Star Trek" series and a guest spot in "Gunsmoke"; and a lot of Proctor and Gamble commercials for products like Gain and Gleem, and, perhaps most noticeably, as one of the devoted band of ladies who can be seen heroically "squeezing the Charmin" on TV sets everywhere. She has become fascinated by the idea of acting on the stage, and while she gets up her nerve to try something where there is no such thing as a retake, she has been sewing and reading about ancient history, mythology, and reincarnation.

One thing she is definitely not considering is making a hard-core film. Simulated sex was so far from reality that it was often a joke, so that "in the middle of a love scene you'd both be giggling at some silly little thing and then they'd have to cut." But with this new stuff, "I guess because of my upbringing, my personal feeling is that I just don't particularly feel like going to bed with anybody that I don't have a personal feeling for."

Although she doesn't like the vulgar stuff, the films made with "no creative attempt, nothing, just a piece of shit, excuse my language, that's what it is," she has no philosophical problem with hard core in general. She doesn't especially put it down, "it's, you know, part of human nature." But still there is the feeling that something vital is missing there, that the old days, if not necessarily good, were at least better.

"I think that what sexploitation films started out to do in the beginning was to give a certain section of people a way to fantasize and escape from their everyday lives," she says carefully, "where they could place themselves as the man or the woman in the film and they could become involved. But with hard core there's just no imagination and nothing to fantasize with. It's just a voyeur-type thing rather than being involved with it. I've seen some trailers and it's like a medical film, there's nothing left to the imagination. It takes away all the romance." And what, she wonders without asking, are all those good people going to do without their romance, anyway?

MARY REXROTH, POET'S CHILD

Her casual conversation covers an imposing range of subjects, from pre-Yahwistic religion, the Platonic idea of ideal forms and Brecht's Theater of Alienation all the way to the reason Aldous Huxley chose to die on LSD and why she doesn't like simulated sex with mechanical vibrators ("They make an incredible racket.") Her interests and occupations sometimes seem so diverse that people who would stereotype her don't have a chance. Mary Rexroth—daughter of Kenneth, old-worldly bohemian and father of San Francisco poetry—seems at once self-assured and droll, articulate and ironic, much older than her twenty-three years. She is very much the poet's child.

"A lot of people have a lot of trouble with me," she says with some satisfaction. "I don't behave like I'm supposed to behave. Say I've been talking to someone for a while, and they've established, 'Well, she's intelligent and she's well-read, she's read Proust twice, my God,' you know, and then you say something about 'when I was working for Leo Productions' and they go, 'Aarghh!' because that's not something somebody like that's supposed to do. If you're an intellectual they don't expect you to be a dirty-movie star, that's very disturbing to some people."

Mary Rexroth is very definitely a former pornographic movie queen, though "Joe Shmo meeting me, it would never occur to him." Currently a belly dancer at a San Francisco club as well as a poet—"poets are most unphysical people generally speaking. I mean, it's hard to think of Eliot doing anything, so they don't expect you to be doing anything like making dirty movies"—she was at one time one of the best-known female hard-core stars, though she made no more than twenty films. The stuff she did—mostly low-class loops for mail-order distribution and peep shows and a few generally forgotten features like *Intersection, Cozy Cool,* and *The Nurses*—is still considered a pornographic benchmark. Though she laughs and says, "I had no intention of changing the dirty-movie industry when I started," Mary Rexroth, by being one of the first women to be given star billing under her own name, and a famous name at that, did just that.

Sitting among the plants, Indian masks, records, and all the rest of the comfortable clutter of her San Francisco apartment, her longish brown hair surrounding dark eyes and an enormous Cheshire cat grin, Mary can hardly believe what has happened to her old stomping grounds. "It's funny, it's become very accepted now, which when I was making it it wasn't," she says in her extremely animated way. "Like people didn't say that they had gone to see a dirty movie. I mean, you didn't do that, you didn't arrive at a cocktail party and say, 'Oh we just saw *Deep Throat*,' which is the kind of thing that's happening now."

Not only are people seeing them, the darndest people are making them. "This editor I've worked with at a publishing company, she's the associate editor, second in command, right, she's telling me about how she was in a pornographic film once. She's telling me what a wonderful liberating experience it was and all of this. And I thought, 'God, what is the world coming to.' It struck me as very strange. The people who used to make them, they all needed the money, and they lived a very different kind of life than the average movie star. And they were not associate editors of a publishing company, you know."

Mary Rexroth has never been doing what everyone else was doing. Born in San Francisco, her early years were interspersed with trips to Europe with her father. In junior high school she was "the weirdo" in "a very straight school where everybody's very busy looking like they came out of *Seventeen* magazine." Instead of going to an academically prestigious high school, she "created a furor" by choosing Polytechnic, a yeastier, 75 per cent black school where, she believes, "I managed to learn more." She went to the University of California at Santa Barbara for a while, and was a dancer at the San Francisco Ballet School, "very skinny and very unkempt, very pale and kind of black coffee and cigarettes, you know," when she began making hard-core films.

It was a time before porno chic, before anyone in the business had any pretensions of any kind. The way she remembers it, "it was very sleazy, a very kind of fly-by-night, warehouse-room" operation, where some filmmakers would refuse to pay the couple if the man couldn't ejaculate, and others would fake it with some Jergens hand lotion. Filmmakers would come from the film departments of the Bay Area's colleges wanting to "play around with the camera and not have to spend eight years loading magazines in a television station," eager for the opportunity to "shoot twice as much footage as Fellini." Sometimes they came with the idea of making "THE definitive good pornographic film," but everyone would just smile. "You're a student at State studying film, right? You've made the surrealistic short, right? You think you're top dog. You see this film and it's out of focus and blah, blah, blah, and you can see the microphone over in the corner, and you think 'God, I can do better than that!' And you probably could too, but once you get into the business the whole atmosphere begins to wear, and you decide, 'Why should I bother? The sex will sell it, it's just a dirty movie.' "

All was usually quiet on the set "in terror of somebody losing an erection," but sometimes a couple would be so nervous, "the director had to tell them how to fuck. One director was telling me, 'I don't understand, I think everybody, you know, should know how to do that.' " And since a lot of people found it understandably hard to perform with "the light meter up your asshole, 'One, two, three, go,' " a kind of star system arose. "They discovered if you just took two people off the street, it was kind of a 50-50 chance you'd come out with a film," Mary explains. "People might get very upset—'Let me out, what am I doing here, let me out.' You never know with somebody who's new, where if you called George McDonald and Mary David you're sure to have a film. The surety is not that you're sure it'll sell, because the star system doesn't work on the box-office level: It works in terms of you're sure that you're gonna have an erection and nobody's gonna freak out."

Mary herself has worked in all kinds of situations—with hidden cameras, outdoors in the middle of winter, even on a waterbed inside a houseboat with a mirror above the bed. "So the houseboat's rocking one way, I'm rocking another way, and the mirror's going another way, and I'm watching the mirror and I'm getting so seasick, it was incredible. When I finished I had the most awful headache, my whole equilibrium got totally fucked up, really completely. That was the greatest complication I ever ran into making sex films."

Before a job started, she says, "they ask you will you do oral sex with the opposite sex, oral sex with the same sex, anal sex, mechanical devices, and the answer was basically yes, yes, yes,

yes, yes, yes." The only noes were for sadomasochism—"evil,
mad, blah, blah, blah, blah"—and bestiality—"it's okay for two
consenting adults, but I don't know, maybe this dog doesn't want
to fuck me, maybe he's not a consenting adult, you know."

The actors, who often met weekly at midnight at the Sutter
Theater to share wine and food and watch previews of their new
films, tended, once the one-shot weirdos were sorted out, to be
"really incredibly well-adjusted and very calm about the whole
trip." There were all kinds of women, but the men, Mary feels,
were "of a type, basically pretty straight guys. Like he was busy
being the all-American boy and discovered America didn't want
him."

Who you worked with was basically a given, though Mary
fondly remembers one film where the director showed her "this
immense file of large index cards and on each one there's a Polar-
oid nude photograph and a mug shot and a brief description of
name, age, height, weight, what they will do and will not do,
the sun sign, and acting experience, and the guy says, 'Pick
your own.' " And after the film was made, there was no telling
what happened to it. "If it was a good erection or a good come
shot, they'd save it," she says. "So if the guy couldn't get an erection or there wasn't anyone and they needed a come shot, they'd
splice it in. So for all I know I'm in like three hundred films, right,
in little pieces, and how can you tell?"

It was an atmosphere where unscrupulousness often prevailed,
where the producers "sort of hope that you will let yourself be
ripped off, they kind of count on it." And people often acquiesce,
like a girl Mary knows who described a movie she'd made with
"a guy that she'd known before, she used to go with a long time
ago, blah, blah, blah, blah, he was freaked out and she was
freaked out and he couldn't get an erection. And she spent something like twelve hours going down on him, massaging him. I
mean, I said, 'Well, did it ever occur to you that, you know, it
might get numb after a while? You should give it a rest.' Things
like that will happen occasionally and the trip is you can let yourself be ripped off, and a lot of people do. It's funny, somehow by
agreeing to make a sex film, they seem to lose their will." Mary
was not one of those people.

For *Cozy Cool*, for instance, "they hired two Hollywood actors.
Oh, they were bad. The one guy wouldn't fuck, and after I finished the sex scene, he happened to appear and he spent some ten
minutes trying to tell me this was not a dirty movie, this was not
a sex film. I said, 'What do you think I just got through doing?'
And he said, 'It's not, it's not, it's different.' Well, the trip was
they were paying them union scale. I raised hell. I said, 'So you're
going to pay them union scale and they're not even going to fuck?'

So they paid me, the producer hemmed and hawed and bit his nails, but he came through. The thing is nobody else did that. The thing that puzzles me about a lot of people making pornographic films is if it's a bad scene, they'll stay. That's where the rip-off is."

The pay was not tremendous—anywhere from $50 to $75 for a couple of hours work on a loop to twice that for a feature. But on the other hand, for what was involved, or more precisely, what wasn't involved, it was very good indeed. "It's really easy, you walk in, and you walk out, and there's no extra trip, you know," Mary says. "The people that were doing it at the time when it became a big thing, I figure that almost none of them gave it any particular thought. It was just there."

The justifications, the theories about revolt and new freedoms, tended to come later, "after people started running around asking everybody questions." After she was in *Intersection*, for instance, Mary and the director decided to call it "a nonlinear religious rite" just to have something to say to all the interviewers. "I'm making it up, right there," she says, pleased at the memory. "The seriousness came from the other people."

To the people in it at the beginning, hard-core films were nothing more than one of "the things one can do to make money easily in order to survive, if you don't want to make a whole lot of money. You're gonna do it once or twice a month and that's it." At one point a man might do a pornographic film, at another he might be a longshoreman or a peeler and scaler on a boat. A woman might be a topless dancer or a cocktail waitress, but the idea is to make "the most money for the least amount of emotional hassle." And to Mary Rexroth, who is unsympathetic to people who don't have an identity outside of their occupations—"It really bugs me when I'm marked by what I do"—working in a pornographic film once a week is "less an emotional hassle than working nine to five in an office where the boss is constantly trying to seduce you."

There were, of course, other reasons operative too, because one doesn't have to turn to pornography to make a quick and easy dollar. For Mary, part of it is her view of herself as "somebody who's been performing in one form or another all of her life, since you know, a tiny little girl. I was into costumes and dress-up, there are all kinds of photographs of me. I've always been into that. And the whole trip about performing is a very weird kind of trip. It's like a compulsion—once you get into it you've got to do it."

And not to be discounted either is the element of sexual fantasy. Some women Mary has known like "the fantasy of someone watching. They tend to project more of a kind of third person, a former lover they want to get back at." Then there are those with prostitution fantasies, like the woman who told Mary "she was too scared to actually work as a prostitute, but that this was a risk-free way to do it. I mean there's sex and you're being paid for it and therefore you can add all the attendant details very easily. You can fantasize all the rest into it without too much problem." Though Mary basically feels that people who are doing it solely to work out their fantasies aren't going to make very many films—"The more of them you make the less important it is; the fantasy has been thoroughly taken care of, it's been actualized"— she has had a fantasy or two herself. Her favorite is that "in your terms, not in terms of the guy sitting in the theater but in your own terms, you're spending an hour being a sex goddess, you know, and that's nice to do. I mean, my God, I was in *Playboy,* you know, and in *Cosmopolitan,* one after the other—*Cosmopolitan* twice, no less. To have that, that's an awful compelling fantasy."

There is, obviously, a different morality about sex operative here than would warm the heart of the little old lady from Dubuque. Yet, what Mary's done doesn't seem any big deal to her. It had no particular effect on her life, she says, adding drolly, "Isn't that terrible? I can't give you any intricate psychological problems." She makes it all seem so normal, the most natural thing in the world, that you wonder what you're doing there asking questions in the first place. In her mind the real taboo of our society is not sex but death, and it's a little hard for her to figure out "what it is about hard-core films that makes it such a subject of controversy, of speculation, of analysis. I mean some girl showed up from some school back East and she was writing her master's thesis on pornographic films. I mean it's something that seems to affect people, I'm not sure where."

Social pressure, though, obviously plays a big part, especially "the incredible amount of conditioning in this society about sex and what's right. You only do it at night, you know, when it's dark with the lights out and under the covers." But while some people claim that it's just plain unnatural for animals of any kind, especially people, to make it in public, Mary feels it's just a question of "the social milieu where that's something that's all right. There are some wonderful Japanese prints of here's daddy and mommy fucking and daddy's playing with a rattle with the little kid over here. That kind of thing seems to come very easily to human beings."

With a background admittedly different than most people's, coming from a family where "the whole attitude was more open and sex was something you were supposed to know about," Mary finds that what is repellent to her is not sex itself but the tease that sometimes goes with it. In the club she works at she sees women from the audience attempting belly dancing, and often the result horrifies her. "There's something very sick about them," she says. "They do the most incredible things that I could never do. There is no way that I could do them. I couldn't do them with all the shades drawn and the lights out. I can't, I can't, because there's something, it's the taunting and the lewdness and the striptease— I can't understand it." And as a corollary to this, Mary feels that for her "there is a kind of morality" about making a hard-core film as opposed to a soft-core film. "I won't do a soft-core film, and I won't do sort of standard beaver films because, as I said, I don't understand the tease trip. I think there's something lewd and dirty and sick and so on and so forth about soft-core films, I really do. You gotta know how to do that. I mean, I know how to fuck, I don't know how to do that. And it all seems rather silly, that's what I think it boils down to, it's silly."

Despite her view of hard-core films as healthy, Mary believes that acting in them can sometimes have strange effects on an actor's private sex life. Mary knows one man who makes a lot of sex films and who fanatically "goes through the house, he turns out every light, every light in the house" before indulging at home. Or another fellow, who in personal life uses "all the really tight, closed positions he can't use on film" because "when you're fucking in films you have to be up and apart enough so that they can get the camera in and get a nice clear shot and it can be well-lighted and so on." For Mary, working in hard core is "not to be equated with other varieties of sex. It's not a promiscuous trip, because it's only every so often. I mean you can't make a film every day; there aren't that many films to be made. It's not something that if somebody wanted to get laid I'd recommend that they do. It's very different. You're not choosing the person, you have less control, and, really, if you're looking for any kind of sexual satisfaction, it's touch and go."

So Mary Rexroth, after "reaching a point at which what is interesting about the whole process ceases to be interesting, there's nothing you're headed towards as a performer," became tired of hard core, left the field, and turned instead to belly dancing, six hours a night, five nights a week under an alluring Persian stage name. "I wanted to start dancing again," she explains. "I decided ballet is not the thing. And modern dance doesn't appeal to me— I always think of Feiffer cartoons whenever I see it. It's a great kind of dancing, the same way folk dancing is a great kind of dancing, because it's very open and it's fun to do." Plus you get to wear a lot of fancy fabric and jewelry and two different veils and chains and bangles and scarves and there you are. "I go to work and I'm exotic," Mary says, pleased. "I mean, what more could you want."

Now that it is all well into her past, what fascinates Mary Rexroth most about hard core is not what she did but the way other people reacted to it. For herself it was only "an image on a piece of celluloid that really has very little to do with you. It's got to do with a kind of point in time at which you were doing this, and it's hard to really think about that any more than thinking about some guy who whips his head around and gives you a whistle when you walk down the street. It really has nothing to do with you personally."

Some of the reactions people had were predictable, like the antagonism of the straight housewife who asked Mary at a party what kind of advice she could give her about her daughter, because "I don't want her to end up like you." Then there were the self-proclaimed hip guys. "Ugh, they're so hip, right? 'What do you mean you won't fuck me? You make pornographic movies!' Like they can't understand that, well, maybe I don't feel like fucking them." On the other hand, she found that her work sometimes tended to make men uneasy, "because it's 'Oh, she makes dirty movies, wow, she must know what she's doing and I don't and I can't get it up. My God, how can I deal with that?' Anything that threatens male security in that way can create some kind of problem." And as for her parents, her father "seems to have taken it in stride," and her mother went so far as to see one of her films, concluding not unreasonably that "sex gets awfully dull seen close up for ten minutes." And after Mary's undraped photo came out in *Playboy*, her mother called up with only one anguished comment: "Mary, you wore your glasses!"

Most puzzling of all were the people who couldn't seem to believe that an honest-to-God flesh-and-blood person would indulge him- or herself in a blue movie. Though she often visited the theaters where her films were shown, she rarely got as much as a second glance, because "people don't associate that person up there on the screen with somebody who walks around." And if she did chance to be spotted, "they're always super polite and kind of nervous. 'Can I buy you a cup of coffee and talk to you for a minute?' That's as far as they would ever dream of carrying it. It's just kind of a reassurance thing. 'Here you are, you're real and, good heavens, my God!' "

Mary ran into the same feeling when she guest-lectured in psychology classes at Stanford, "where they think they're very hip and very sophisticated because they go to Stanford, and they've got a good education and they come from good families. But actually, all that means is that they are incredibly naïve." For them, "pornographic films only exist in movies," and whenever she would walk into a class, "they're expecting bleached blonde hair and the whole bit and they couldn't quite fathom me. It was like, 'Real people don't do that kind of thing.' "

Someone who also found it hard to understand was a San Francisco critic who had been a friend of hers and her family's for years. And when the newspaper stories came out about "Mary Rexroth, San Francisco's newest pornographic film star, blah, blah, blah, blah," he called up for an interview. The conversation was strained for a while, until Mary felt she understood what he really wanted to know. "It was like, 'Are you weird somehow?' or 'Are you some sort of deviant in some strange way?' And that's what all the questions mean. I think what they're asking is not, 'Why do you do it?' but, 'Please reassure me that you're all there, please reassure me that, you know, you're still a human being.' "

PAT ROCCO, MOVIES A MOTHER COULD LOVE

Behind a seven-foot, yellow-and-turquoise striped corrugated metal fence, past a "Beware of Dog" sign, past the dog itself, an intimidating but ultimately friendly black German Shepherd named Venus, is the Hollywood cottage of Pat Rocco, a humble monument to eclecticism gone wild.

Inside the door, a startling collection of goodies presents itself. A 1939 jukebox, a player piano, a couple of hundred piano rolls, a director's chair, a small copy of Michelangelo's "David" with what appears to be an Imperial Margarine crown on the top, a banana on a painted backdrop, an oil painting of Clark Gable, a very tastefully photographed male nude, a water cooler, a bunch of old movie stills, Snoopy and Uncle Sam dolls, knickknacks and gewgaws without apparent end. There is more in a back room, too, including a "thousands of dollars' worth" collection of movie sound tracks, featuring *Raintree County, The Seventh Voyage of Sinbad*—most of the rare ones." The most impressive sight of all, however, is on a nearby table where more than a dozen gold-plated trophies sit in elegant repose. All were presented to Pat Rocco by an organization named SPREE. So the question is, what is SPREE?

"The Society of Pat Rocco Enlightened Enthusiasts," Mr. Rocco answers, happy to be asked. "It's a cult of well-wishers and followers, a fan club going for me for four years. It's people who have stuck together and liked the films I made before and would rather see them again than go and see what's going on now. There are five hundred members—we meet once a month—and it's a growing and important organization here in Southern California. It's very appreciated. It's a very pleasant thing to know

108

that you've got so many people that are for you and with you. It just gives you an overwhelming glow to know that this thing still exists."

The minions of SPREE notwithstanding, Pat Rocco is an interesting example of almost instant obsolescence in the erotic film world. Four years ago, when his male films were first shown, they were considered so daring, so hot, you could have fried an egg on the sidewalk outside the theater. *Esquire* called him "the Cecil B. De Mille of male films." He was making upwards of $40,000 a year and attracting so much personal attention he had to put up that yellow and turquoise fence. Then came hard core, and Mr. Rocco suddenly wasn't so hot anymore.

For Pat Rocco, who is more than pleased to be referred to as a most sensitive filmmaker, does not believe in getting too technical. "There was lots of nudity but no pornography. Sex was implied but never shown, occasionally simulated but never seen," he says of his films, the result being that a lot of people now think of Pat Rocco as too timid, too squeamish, someone time has passed by. They got tired, the critics say, of lovely boys forever holding hands, walking through glades, being photographed through chiffon, never doing anything more risqué than kissing. "People don't relate to his rather anachronistic attitude toward young love. Things don't happen like the Loretta Young show," says one West Coast critic. "He is a very gifted man, but Pat Rocco is sort of living in the past." Gorton Hall, who went on to make hard-core gay movies of his own, commented, "He was like the Walt Disney of the homosexual. Everything was wonderful; people were all like you would love them to be. It was gorgeous, it was fantasy, it wasn't guts, it wasn't real."

Pat Rocco, who knows what they're saying out there in movie-land, takes it all with amiable equanimity. "A lot of people have put me down, have categorized me and put me in their own slot," he says, "and, occasionally, I meet these people and I find out that they haven't seen any of my films." He is aware that his films "are no longer the kind of films that are in demand," that they are shown theatrically only "once in a great, great while." He is comforted by his fans' continuing allegiance, by what he considers his films' timelessness—"stories that could happen fifty years ago or fifty years from now, anytime"—and by the fact that he is a real live pioneer. "I started a whole new revolution in films, and other people jumped on the bandwagon, started making films with male nudity. Mine were the first to be shown theatrically right out in the open. The films have had quite a bit of play. For several years certain theaters would play the same films over and over again and they would do that in response to audience reaction to my films. So the films have had their day and done what was necessary for them to do. I hate to think that they were a stepping-stone to hard core, but obviously they were. Somebody had to get the ball rolling."

Pat Rocco says all this in a regular, well-modulated voice that might belong to a TV newscaster. With his boyish smile and slightly receding pompadour, he might be almost any age at all, and that's the way he likes it. "Let's not get into that; we don't need to go into that," he says, begging off. "Most everybody is a little vain about their age, and I'm no exception."

Born in New York, he came to Los Angeles with his parents at age eleven and never left. His background is mostly in music, starting at age fifteen when he had his own radio program. A professional singer for years, he had done television, stage, and nightclub work, including "three years as a regular on the Ford show on television, in nightclubs with people like Phyllis Diller, I did a touring show as a featured singer with Marge and Gower Champion. Oh, gee, what more can I tell you?"

His entrance into the film business was totally unexpected. "It was quite a fluke. I was running a psychedelic shop called the Bizarre Bazaar when psychedelic shops were very, very, very big, and it was the only one in Hollywood and very popular," he says. The shop sold lots of underground papers, including the *Los Angeles Free Press*, in which an ad caught Rocco's eye one day. "Somebody wanted a photographer to shoot male nudes, and I thought well, I'll try it, just for the heck of it. So I went to see the people, and they handed me a camera and a model and a roll of film and said, 'Go ahead, we'll see what you can come out with.' And they liked the results, so they handed me more models and more film and it went on and on."

With all these models at his disposal, Rocco began shooting modest 8mm vignettes—"I'd create little story lines"—and after forming a company, Bizarre Productions, named after the shop that started it all, began selling a few by mail. About this time, in late 1968, Los Angeles's Park Theater, "the first theater to show films with extensive male nudity, particularly with gay themes," was getting ready to open and expressed an interest in Pat's little films. "They said, 'These don't belong in a private collection, these belong on the screen. They're good enough to show, and we'd like to start the Park Theater with them.' So they did, and the films were very successful and it just went on from there. It was something I never expected to get into, but there I was caught in the middle of it."

All told, Pat thinks he made somewhere between 100 and 150 films, ranging from minute-and-a-half things to about half a dozen features of an hour or more. The costs were minimal, no higher than $1,500 for the longest of the films, because Pat did everything on them himself, "wrote and directed and filmed and edited and soundtracked, did the whole ball of wax." Most of the shorts were gathered into more than a dozen film programs of approximately two hours' length with titles like *The Original Pat Rocco Male Film Festival, Sex and the Single Gay, Mondo Rocco,* and *Pat Rocco Dares.* "I found it easier to do it that way," Rocco says, "because then I could use more of a variety of actors and models and put them in different situations so that somebody wouldn't have to sit for two hours and get tired of a couple of people."

A typical Pat Rocco, one of his favorites in fact, was "a little innocent film" called *Discovery,* running time twenty-five minutes, released in 1968 and shot entirely in Disneyland. "We see two young men meeting in Disneyland, going on rides together, enjoying each other's company and finally ending up on Tom Sawyer's Island and going through a nude kissing relationship. Then they walk off out of Disneyland hand in hand together with brighter things to come. A very romantic film that somehow seemed to strike me, and also the public, nicely—it's been shown in churches, even. That film has a lot of warmth."

Though now it all sounds tamer than Smokey the Bear, Rocco claims, and rightly so, that at the time they came out "there was a certain shock value" to such films. "People couldn't believe it was happening, the so-called girlie theaters had split-beaver films and things like that, but I guess nobody thought that anybody would go into male films," he says. They were considered so daring that when Rocco first showed two males kissing—"It was unheard of, nobody had ever tried that"—the theater went so far as having lawyers present on opening night. "Everybody was waiting to be closed down," Pat says, because previously "no one had dared to put a foot forward, to put your name up there and say 'Gay films' right there on the marquee." And why did Pat Rocco dare? "Well, my thought was 'Why not?' It hasn't been done, so why not? If they liked it, and they did, then we'll just go on from there."

A big fan of the Hollywood movies of the '40s and someone who feels "more great films came out in 1939 than any other year," Rocco's own efforts quite naturally tended toward romanticism and what he calls "themes that were open. I tended to take a very positive point of view in the story lines in that everything is OK. By that I mean there was no discrimination against a gay person in the film. If we saw two people who were gay in a crowd, the crowd wasn't booing them, they were just going about their business. When you express gay love or a gay story theme, it just has to be done honestly. People have to be able to relate to that and be able to say, 'Yes, I've been through that kind of

111

situation' or 'Yes, I understand it' or 'Yes I would like to be in that situation.' " This all may be taken for granted now, but, at the time, Pat Rocco felt the need to be a proselytizer, to tell his audiences "let yourself get into it and be an open and honest person about it, it's not dirty," to extol over and again what he calls in his favorite phrase, "the beauty of male love."

And perhaps because they sensed that "love goes into each production," audiences responded. "People lined up at the box office, the reaction was tremendous," Pat reports. "When *Funny Girl* was released, I remember there was a report in *Variety* that my films were outgrossing *Funny Girl*, so if that's any measure of popularity, they were popular." So popular that Rocco found "I could use the same actor many times and thereby create young stars. Many of them told me that they couldn't walk down the street without being approached: 'Oh, I saw you in such and such' or 'Can I have your autograph?' It was a whole new thing to them; they suddenly found themselves the center of attention." And, quite naturally, the same thing happened to Pat Rocco himself.

"There was such an enormous upsurge of popularity," he says, looking momentarily afraid it was about to start again. "All of a sudden the doorbell was ringing constantly, and mail was coming in, and the phone wouldn't stop. Men would come up and say, 'I've got several young men that I know that I'd like you to meet' —that's very common. In a couple of cases I had fathers come and say, 'I'd like you to use my son in a film.' And you can imagine the mail, amazing kinds of mail. I never got any hate mail, but strange mail, mail from very lonely people, sometimes not even in the United States but out of the country. I tried to answer everything, but it was quite something.

"As far as having problems casting for films, there was never any because it was a matter of 'Keep them away, brush them away from the doorstep.' They found me, it was a matter of how to weed through and get the best ones and disappoint a lot of people. At the beginning, particularly, it seemed as if the whole world wanted to take off their clothes and act, that's what it seemed like." And when one day he did run "a little tiny ad in *Variety*, like a one-inch ad, 'Audition for Pat Rocco film,' we were mobbed. We had people all day. The fire department came, they had to clear out the building. They said, 'You have to wait on the sidewalk, there's too many people in the building.' We went till one o'clock the next morning with auditions. It was amazing, just amazing."

The instant notoriety has had other repercussions that have not been as pleasant. He has often had to deal with people who have the wrong idea about him. "They expect to come to this house and find hot and cold running boys running around naked, having constant orgies," Rocco says, finding even the mental image hard to take. "They also think I'm a millionaire, which is another thing that's not true. I just plod along and work just like everyone else. They also think I've got to be the world's worst dirty old man, which is simply not true." While he has come across film-makers whom he "would consider that, quote, dirty-old-man, un-quote, type of person, because they're in a situation where they get to hire and fire lots of models, and they take advantage of the situation," Rocco himself will have none of it. "I don't do that and even the models are sometimes surprised," he says. "They expect to be exploited, and when they're not, quite often they're surprised."

Despite the minor woes, Pat Rocco displays some nostalgia for the old days, when his films had big openings, "with champagne parties and limousines driving up in front and spotlights and the whole Hollywood type of film premiere." Even his mother would proudly show up at them, Rocco says. "They were fun, they were fun, they don't do that anymore now."

For though he says he has nothing against hard core *per se*, it's obvious that he finds it personally distasteful. No longer do stars meet their adoring public at fancy previews; instead, "if the stars show up at the theater when the vice happens to be there, they get arrested." Much of what's shown is, to his taste, "very gross," and he only wishes that "there could be more quality in the films, so that while they're having this outburst of interest the films could also be something of value. Unfortunately, most of the films are not. It's nothing you'd want to take your mother to."

What it is instead, with certain exceptions, is "simply hard core for hard core's sake. They do little except for a certain kind of audience to get a certain kind of release from seeing this." And in doing so, Rocco feels, "we've gotten away from the beauty of male love. It's difficult to show a hard-core scene where you see everything going and make it so beautiful that it would be pleas-ing to the rest of the story. You can't get away with doing a long story line building up to one hard-core scene at the end, mainly because the people who go to see hard-core films want to see lots of hard core within a film. They won't stand for that, they just wouldn't have it. It just had to be lots and lots of sex, and I wasn't interested in showing that. I felt as if that got away a great deal from the tenderness that's necessary in evolving an emotional relationship between people. Sex is fine and it's got its place, but for me personally, to show it on the screen so vividly is unnecessary and not my interest."

He could have stayed on and played the hard-core game, but he decided to go in another direction. He spent a comparatively large amount of money, some $50,000, on a feature he hopes will have general audience appeal. Called *Drifter*, it tells of a young man from Phoenix who comes to Hollywood "and gets involved with all kinds of strange people and gets involved in strange situations, both male and female." The sex is simulated, and Rocco, who is looking for someone to distribute it, is hoping for an R rating. "I think it's got a lot going for it, and I hope that the public will get something out of it," he says. "I'd like it to be appreciated by everyone."

Until that happens, Rocco, a self-described homebody, spends much of his time working with a theater group—"the only repertory gay theater group in the world"—that is an offshoot of the SPREE organization. The audience his films reached, he is aware, was largely "lonely people, particularly those who are so-called closety people who are afraid to come out in the open. Or the person who feels that he is not attractive and therefore can't get anyone to enjoy a relationship with him—he will relate to people on the screen and just live vicariously that way." Yet, overall, he feels his films have helped exactly these people, the ones who "kept thinking that not only gay life but they themselves are dirty for being what they are. I've tried to present in many of the films that it's not so. You're a human being like everybody else, and you've a right to enjoy life in your own life-style as you please. And I have a number of letters from people who have had their own lives changed by the films. It's very rewarding.

JOHN C. HOLMES (LONG JOHNNY WADD), SO BIG

In California, where hyperbole is a way of life, he is known simply as "Supercock." *Variety* has called him "a performer of lengthy credentials in the hard-core field . . . a wonder of nature . . . quite literally has to be seen to be believed." "This man, I must have," says Linda Lovelace. And walk into any El Sleazo dirty book emporium in New York City, mention his name, and chances are the acne-ridden cashier will smile behind his smudged glasses. Yeah, Long Johnny Wadd, the one with the longest you-know-what in the known world, a whole *foot* long. That guy. Oh yeah.

The real name is John C. Holmes. Age twenty-seven, he is one of the endless displaced New Yorkers now living in Los Angeles. He made his hard-core debut ten years ago, took some time off, and has been working steadily "for five, five and a half years now. And there's been a constant steady demand, no hiatus. I went for two and a half years and didn't take a vacation, man, it was just one straight steady shooting schedule, unfuckingbelievable. It's constant work, it's constant phone calls. Calls from agents, producers, directors, distributors, other actors and models, fans, people I know. I'll average eighty to ninety phone calls a day. It's been dynamic, it's been a hell of a life-style. I'm only sorry I'm not two people who can both enjoy it."

John Holmes is a genuine porno veteran, having been in the hard-core field since almost before it was hard core. He can remember when men actually had to wear pants, followed by a time when "they'd get a little risqué, you were allowed to take off your pants but you had to leave on your underwear—there were some ugly-looking boxer-shorts films back then." When the underwear came off, the back still had to be to the camera, until "finally, by just slight turns, the guy just showing a little bit of penis, they got to the point where you can see everything. It was really a milestone, a milestone of cock voyeurism."

Now a man with a half-dozen agents pulling in work for him, Holmes started by answering ads in underground newspapers. "The first thing I ever did was a crummy boy-girl beaver layout in a magazine," he says. "You should see me, I look like a fucking pimply faced little high school kid, it's sickening. I see it and I go, 'Oh my God, maybe all the copies are burned.' It's weird."

But from these low-rent beginnings came an inexhaustible gusher of erotica. How many films have you made, John? "Two thousand, seven hundred and six," he says with off-handed exactitude. "I keep track."

And he runs the whole gamut, too, from loops and 8mm stuff to 16mm and theatrical 35, not to mention stills and magazines and the nude modern-jazz-ballet-type dancing he's done in New York, Hawaii, Las Vegas, and God only knows where else. He works almost endlessly but has no complaints. "It's just my life-style," he repeats, "and I dig the shit out of it."

It is hard to say what is more amazing about John Holmes, the staggering profligacy of his work, the easygoing way he treats it all, or how very candid and well-adjusted he is about the whole thing. Expressions like "I can only be and do what I am . . . I am me, I can't not be me . . . That's who I am, that's why I do it" constantly punctuate his speech, and he just about dares you to find anything wrong, either morally or otherwise, with what he is about.

"It's a natural thing, it's a turn-on thing," he says, amazed that anyone might think otherwise. "While you're here, man, you're here to fuck, to dig life, enjoy it, do your thing, work, become somebody or not become somebody. To do your thing in life."

It's not an act of defiance, then? "I don't think in the back of my mind, 'Well, sock it to her again and just watch granny have a heart attack, man, when she sees it.'" And he can't understand why anyone might think he should be ashamed of what he **does**. "I've never seen a girl on a set that shouldn't be there," he says. "Whether she's greedy for bread, she's got an old man to pay for, she's trying to be an actress, she's there for a reason. I've never fucked a chick who's drunk, never fucked a chick who's high on dope, never fucked a chick who didn't know what she was doing."

And not to forget all those wonderful people out there in the dark who like pornography enough to lap it up as fast as it's produced. "It sells billions," Holmes says with satisfaction. "Six point four billion dollars in pornography was sold last year. That's according to the FBI survey. That outgrosses Twentieth Century-Fox and Seven Arts and CBS Film Productions together. I mean Seven Arts would shit if they hit a half a billion dollar year. And where's it going? I mean people don't buy it and then burn it; it's not, 'I'm gonna buy this film just to destroy it.' It's going somewhere, you know. Somebody's using this film."

Not that he has illusions about its importance. "I don't want to take over the fucking government, I don't want to be senator from Massachusetts because I make fuck films. It's not a big revolutionary thing," he says, while quickly adding, "But it is freedom. It's the right to say, 'Goddamn it, I'm a human being, let me think what I want to, be what I want to be, let me read what I want to read, let me view what I want to view, leave me alone. I pay my fucking taxes. I keep the United States government existing. So get off my fucking ass and let me blow my bread on what I want to blow it on.'"

As should be apparent, by his own lights John Holmes is a very moral person. He will rarely give his word on something because "it's a life and death thing with me, when I give it, it sticks. You've got a moral obligation to do what you've said you're gonna do." And he has a personal code that others might envy: "Don't hurt anybody physically or mentally in your whole entire lifetime, and you've had a damn good life. You're cool." And especially, "Don't fuck with children."

He is ironically aware that because of what he does, "a lot of people get into this weird thing about trusting you with their children," which saddens him. "I mean kids are beautiful, like the essence of innocence and beauty and happiness and well-adjustedness." In fact, the only time he can remember breaking his code and hurting someone was an incident involving a father and his child. It was some years back, while John was an ambulance driver. "I delivered thirteen babies, two sets of twins," he says. "And I had three or four hundred people die on me, freeway accidents and shit. It blows you up the first few times you have somebody die in the back of your ambulance." But it was the child-abuse cases that got him angry, especially "one little Mexican kid. The father was grinding cigarettes out on him. All over his chest and back, cigarette butts ground out. So the guy shows up at the hospital and says, 'Bullshit, I never laid a fucking finger on him.' I can't remember what happened for about five minutes. I just blacked out for a minute, I went insane. Finally, they got me off the guy. I mean you should have seen the kid laying there, he was past crying and past hysterics and he was just laying there trembling with his eyes big as saucers and those fucking burns. So I just beat the fuck out of the guy. But I didn't kill him. I regret that. I did not kill him."

As he tells the story, John Holmes is even more animated than usual. "I just can't sit still, man," he says, and he really can't. He fidgets, licks his lips, rolls his eyes, chews his gum, runs his long fingernails down the side of the chair he seems constantly on the verge of leaping out of. He is so exuberant that "everybody says, 'Are you on uppers, are you on speed?' And I say, 'No, man, I've just got this natural kick-in-the-ass energy level.'"

Constantly searching for new outlets for his energy, Holmes even does all the stunt work for his films—"scuba diving, flying, sky diving, jumping from building to building, crashing motorcycles." Spectator sports bore him because "I don't like anything unless I can participate." He likes to tinker with explosives, once blowing an English double-decker bus into "about 90 million pieces" for a film, and has a small gun collection, which, in line with his feelings about hurting things, he uses only on target ranges. He does endless odd jobs on movie sets, including mundane tasks like holding boom mikes and driving trucks, just so he won't be bored.

And he does all this without benefit of artificial stimulants. As a rule, he never takes "any type of narcotic, dope, no pills, not even aspirin, not even Rolaids. I don't drink alcohol, wine, nothing. The hardest thing I drink is coffee. Nothing, man, it's no good for you."

Holmes does smoke cigarettes, however, because "I've got to be slowed down. I could drink to slow me down, but I won't drink. I know what I'm doing constantly, but I'll do it with so much vigor that people just can't keep up with it. I'll completely blow people out of my way."

Appropriately, for someone with so much energy, Holmes has a thin, almost angular body. He wears a silver pinkie ring and has a weakness for solid gold pocket watches—he owns more than a hundred. And his boyish face, framed by curly hair and a goatee, has started one of the most persistent rumors in the pornography business, that as a teenager he played the role of Eddie Haskell in the "Leave It to Beaver" TV series. Universal Studios reports, however, that the actor who did that part was named Ken Osmond and is currently happily married and a member of the Los Angeles Police Department. Holmes has heard the rumor "constantly" and characterizes it as "a complete lie. I don't know where it came from, but it's not true." And though a comparison of current photographs shows the two men looking remarkably alike, it is also obvious that they are indeed two different people.

Unusual as it might seem, it was the idea of acting that drew John Holmes to pornography in the first place. "It was ready," he says in his intense way. "I mean there it is, right now, you don't have to wait, go to acting school. You learn as you go and you get paid for it too." If he's bad in a film, he feels "bad for a month. I feel like going back and giving the director back his money. I feel like an ass." And to people who would blanch at calling what he does acting, he has an interesting if not particularly conventional reply:

"You can go to a theater and if it is well done with terrific actors and actresses, then you'll cry, half the audience will break down and cry," he says. "And then for six months you'll look back and think 'Gee, that was pretty good' whenever someone discusses it. But if you go see a hard-core flick, for five years you'll remember everything about that goddamn movie, everything.

"I mean crying is an emotion, hating someone on the screen is an emotion, but no emotion is stronger than fuck, than screw, than an erection. When you make a fuck flick, if it's done well people go home and fuck. It's a deep thing. And a guy, two years from now a guy will think back to that dirty movie he went to and it's something to jack off to. It's a lasting thing, it's one of the strongest emotions there is."

And so John Holmes wants no part of any acting where people's visceral reaction is close to catatonic, where the ho-hum is a way of life. "I want people to enjoy what I do, to get some emotion other than killing time. You know how many fucking people watch television just to kill time? They watch three hours of TV and only blink; they show no fucking emotion. If I was an actor like for TV soap operas and shit like that, I'd go right out of my mind. I couldn't do it, because it's putting no emotion into a person."

And lest anybody think that the kind of performing Holmes does is as easy as falling out of bed, so to speak, he admits, "I'm nervous every time I do it. It's not something you get accustomed to. It never gets like driving a taxi or working in a Sears lawnmower assembly line. It's nothing like that. There's always that kick of excitement, you know, that chance of danger." For what he does is patently illegal in most parts of the country. "Everybody

takes a bust, you know, and this might be mine," he says, looking
around a rather plain hotel suite in semiserious consternation.
"Right this minute, you might have cops in the bedroom. It's a
constant thing, and it's a pain in the ass. Because when you're
on a set, it's hard to get your mind into giving a good performance when in the back of your mind you know there might be
cops pulling up in the driveway any second, right?"

And people who like their privacy have to consider that
"they've got a still man, a cameraman, two sound men, a couple
of grips, three or four actors and actresses on the set, and a money
backer who comes in because it's his money, and he always
brings a friend, plus five or six other people who watch to see
how it's going. So sometimes on some sets I fuck in front of as
many as twenty-five to thirty-five people." Not, of course, that he
minds at all. "I can fuck in front of anybody," he says, very
businesslike. "I go to orgies, fifty-couple orgies, fifty couples,
naked, fucking. Nobody drinks, they just go up and fuck in
groups of ten or more. That relaxes me."

And if the crowd on the set doesn't get to you, the heat will.
"I mean you use twenty-four-cam lights and nineteen-cam lights
and forty-two-cam lights and it's pure white, blue-white light, right
in your face," John notes. "The heat, the heat is terrific. It's so hot
that you drip constantly. And the headaches are a bad thing, too.
You know, if you're underneath the lights for three or four
hours you're gonna have headaches. You always have to think
about keeping up, keeping bright, keeping alert, keeping the best
you can perform."

If you think that the combination of all the above would in-
hibit most fellows' performance, you couldn't be more right. "I've
seen sets close down because it was a Saturday or Sunday and
the guy on the set couldn't get a hard-on, couldn't climax, and
they couldn't get another guy," John says. "Many's a set I've
gone on and had four guys with leads in it, three of them couldn't
climax and the other one could climax once or twice, so I had to
do five come shots, give close-up come shots because the other
guys couldn't handle it." Which, he adds parenthetically, "is a
pain in the ass when you've got a heavy date that night."

Now let's say you're not so inhibited that you can't perform,
but can you do it all on command, like it was the latest precision
movement the Radio City Music Hall Rockettes have to get
down just so? "With a lot of guys, the director will say, 'Okay,
please don't come. If you feel like you're gonna come, and you
can't hold it, tell us, and we'll shoot it somehow.' And so the
guy'll say"—and here John's voice gets appropriately frantic—
" 'Okay, I can't hold it, I'm gonna come.' And the director yells,
'Hold that motherfucker out'; and the guys with the camera are

trying to focus. Oh, it's strange. And some come shots you've seen are always out of focus and fucked up—that's because the guy said, 'I can't hold it.' "

With John Holmes, one understands, things are different. "With me, it's a mind thing," he says, not bragging but simply stating the facts. "I think *on* and I get a hard-on, I think *off* and I can't get a hard-on. If I say, 'No,' you can have chicks suck me off, a chick lick my ass, anything, I can't get a hard-on. If I say 'No,' I won't. But if I say 'Do it' then I fuck all night. Like I fuck chicks for like four or five hours at a time without losing a hard-on. I'll have five or six comes and just keep fucking."

It is a talent that has not been lost on most porno producers. "He knows he can shoot all of his fucking film and leave the come shot to the last thing. He says, 'I'll tell you when I've got a minute and ten seconds left, and I'll want it when I have a minute of film left.' And he'll say 'Okay' and I'll come. It's a mechanical thing, an *on-off* thing. I think *come*, I think *hard*, I think *soft* . . ."

Despite his openness and his amiability, there are some things John Holmes will not do, and he is quite definite about them. He will not do films involving real sadomasochism where people get hurt. He will not work with animals and has turned down offers from "chicks who are like married to a Great Dane, and they want me to come over and do a number with them and their dog." He won't do homosexual films where he has to touch another man, though he has done something called *The Homosexual Bible*, a series of 8 × 10 full-color pictures of John posing by himself against different backdrops, photographed in one long session with "a chick to give me head all day to keep me with an erection."

And although he generally has no qualms about whom he works with—"I just don't want 'em 612 pounds with warts, you know"—he can, on occasion, be particular if he sees the need. "There are chicks who'll shoot these films and their old men are pimps, dopers, I mean heavy into skag or something, and they'll say, 'Okay, get out there and fuck because I need a fix, we gotta pay the rent.' And this chick's been fucking everything—squirrels, chipmunks, dogs, neighbors, rats, anything she can fuck. She's weird, 'cause she's fucked up on dope or something. And she'll come in and get naked underneath those lights, and if she doesn't look right or doesn't smell good, I say, 'Whoa, I'm not gonna work with this one.' Because if a chick smells, they don't take care of themselves. And I've never had VD, never had the crabs, no syphilis, clap, gonorrhea, nothing. It's because some people I'll work with, some people I won't."

Despite these modest strictures, John Holmes has worked himself into just about a pre-eminent position in pornography, and he knows it. "I've got a direct-line following. I know a lot of distributors and producers and they tell me I'm still the biggest seller they've had in five years. Other guys come out here and shoot—fantastic bodies, good-looking faces, and they'll last three or four months and photographers will start telling them, 'Hey, you're overexposed, we just can't use you anymore.' But they keep calling me back up. With me in a film it's like 98 per cent guaranteed you're at least gonna get your basic investment back, which is more than anybody else can guarantee. It's just a fact, it's statistics. If I'm in a film, it sells. There is that certain amount of people who will go and see John Wadd or John Holmes."

Like the just plain folks who write the fan letters he gets all the time. Not even the bad ones bother him, like the man who wrote to say, " 'I think all your goddamn films are disgusting. I've seen every goddamn film, and every one of them that you make is rotten. I think you're the most rotten, filthy, you shouldn't even call yourself an American, you're so filthy.' "

This type of "freako stuff" doesn't get to John, at least partly because he can balance it out against a wall of adulation that extends even beyond America's borders. He had to turn down an invitation to a pornography exposition in Japan because of a schedule conflict, but he did go to one in Sweden as a guest of the Swedish Government, all expenses paid, "like the Olympics or something. It was in this gigantic auditorium and everyone had their own kind of cubicle. All I had to do was stand there completely dressed with suit and tie. People'd come in, and they'd look at all the pictures of me, and they'd look at me, and they'd look at the pictures again, and they'd look at me again, and they'd come over and really shake my hand. Autographs, man, I must've signed 50 million autographs."

Even in the good old U.S. of A. people know and love John. "I'll go to a restaurant, nice restaurant, thirty bucks for a meal for two, and the waiter brings over a fourteen-pound chopped-up fruit compote on ice. And I say, 'I think you've got the wrong table.' He says, 'No, this is compliments of the house.' Or a big liter of champagne will come over on ice. And they'll say, 'Someone asked us to send it over, but they'd rather not be pointed out.' That blows my mind, you know? I didn't know that many people were into pornography."

And just the other day, right on Hollywood Boulevard, John was stopped by a nice young couple. "The guy said to me, 'Will you step back in this alley and write your signature on my old lady's titty?' She had no bra, just a low-cut evening gown, and I did it. She pulled her whole titty out, and I wrote my signature on it with a ballpoint. And I asked, 'What the fuck you gonna do with it?' He says, 'We're in a swing club, and I'm gonna show it

121

to everybody I know. I'm gonna take ten Polaroids of it.' It was weird; it was fun. You run into shit like that all the time."

Then there are the people who want more from John than a signature or a handshake. "They buy a film from somebody. They'll buy it in a dirty book store, and they'll say to the proprietor, 'I want the guy's address and phone number. It's important to me, get it for me, I'll give you fifty bucks.' And it'll go back through the chain of command, and it may take months, but he'll finally get my number. And he'll call me up and say, 'I know your time is pretty well taken, and you can't get around as much as people want you to, so name a price and I'll make it worth your while to come over and fuck my old lady.' It's a real money trip with a lot of people. I get it all the time, constantly."

And, perhaps surprisingly, probably not, John Holmes accepts a lot of these offers. Like the guy with the indoor pool from Manhasset, New York, who wrote, " 'My wife's very beautiful and I'm very old and very ugly' " and who paid him $200 a day plus expenses for a week. Or a couple in Texas, with, "are you ready? oil wells and cattle, sounds like a 1946 Jane Wyman movie. It's weird, he's got oil wells going 'kachuck, kachuck,' right outside of his mansion, the whole fucking thing. Anyway, I go down there two times a year, and I stay for two weeks at a time. And I use one of their cars, and they buy me clothes and jewelry. As I get on the jet the guy hands me a check and says, 'It was terrific, be sure and come back.' They want me to live down there, and I said, 'Are you kidding? I'd go out of my mind having to fuck the same chick all the time.' "

Being in the business he's in, John Holmes doesn't have to. He admits to "six or eight" steady girlfriends, including a couple of serious types who don't know who he is or what he does. "That's my making love," he says. "I fuck, ball, and screw; I go to orgies and swing parties and do things. Then as a kind of a counterbalance to my own personality, I go to these girls who are very quiet and sincere. It balances my mind. I don't become completely wicked and tainted on a steady basis. I have a lapse of being a farmer in Iowa type thing. It balances out my mind."

Besides that, that is all John will say about his personal life. Aside from refusing to say how much money he makes, it is the only other taboo he observes. He will not say one word about his parents or other family, will not give out a phone number other than an answering service, will not tell you where he lives or even what kind of a house it is. John Holmes, who has what so many men think they want, doesn't have the only thing he could use right now: a little bit of time to himself.

"Private-life-wise, I can't have a private life. Very difficult, very difficult," he says, more resigned than angry. "I do have a

122

little bit, a place out of state that I go where nobody knows what I do and it's very quiet, very relaxing. It isn't that it embarrasses me that my neighbor knows that I fuck on film, that doesn't bother me. It's the constant 'Oh look, I want to shake your hand.' Everybody knows me."

And no one will leave him alone. Holmes used to have a phone number like everyone else, albeit a private one, but a crank caller put an end even to that. "He was a homosexual. Must've worked for the phone company, because I had a girl there who was working with me, and she'd change it every day for thirteen running days, and every day this bugger would get it. He was calling me for years, four-thirty in the morning, stoned on his ass. So I just said, 'Fuck it.' "

He used to have a nice apartment too, in a building where "everybody was over sixty years old, they had a pool nobody would use because they'd have drowned, they were so old." He got kicked out of there, however, because eager fans would not let him be.

"People would come up and knock on my neighbor's door saying, 'John isn't home. You know where he's at—would you tell him that Carol called or Jeanette called or Fred called.' I didn't know who the fuck those people were, it was just a steady stream. I'd have twenty-five people a day knocking on my door. It got so I'd sleep at my girlfriends' houses and only go to my apartment to change clothes. I had to have a place to get away, man, where I could sleep. I mean from one o'clock in the morning on to dawn I would get ten people. RING. It was weird. I finally had the janitor disconnect my doorbell, so it was BAM BAM BAM, beat on the door. I mean a good-looking twenty-three-year-old, fantastic, beautiful girl comes up and knocks on my door and says, 'I got your address from a friend of yours.' 'Oh yeah, who's that?' 'Well, they'd rather not say, but I'd love to take you to bed.' What are you gonna do, you got a chick in bed you're fucking, and there's one knocking on your door. So I finally gave up that fucking apartment. What are you gonna do?"

You can hold those messages of moral support right there, folks, for despite the kind of woes that Julie Andrews never had to deal with, John Holmes is not forsaking the industry. To a man who has always hated saying, 'Yes, sir,' the wonder of being self-employed and in control is really the fulfillment of a dream as strong as the dream of rampant sexuality. "How long do I want to do this type of thing?" he echoes. "Until I'm dead."

9

SWEET 16'S

THE FIRST HARD-CORE FEATURES

When Bill Osco produced *Mona: The Virgin Nymph* sometime
in 1970, the 16mm hard-core fiction feature sprang into life. And
if the film was not the first 60-minute feature of its kind to be
made or shown—such statistics are hard to come by—it was certainly the first to be known by name and promoted nationwide.
Osco and his co-workers, Mike Light and Howard Ziehm, some
of the most experienced loop manufacturers on the West Coast,
were likely candidates to be involved with the breakthrough
into quality pornographic features. Osco had made fifteen to
twenty loops a week—most of them split beavers with good
color, clear sound, and pretty girls—that were known for relative
excellence within the field, and had gone on to make two features with simulated sex. The first, *Whatever Happened to Stud
Flame?* was a financial and aesthetic bomb whose $7,000 pro-
duction cost was recouped only by selling prints of the film outright. The second, *The Virgin Runaway*, was slightly more successful and gave Osco the technical and marketing experience
to turn his attention to *Mona*.

The most remarkable thing about *Mona* is not the hard-core
sex but the film's recognizable dramatic structure. From the opening conversation between Mona (played by the charming Fifi
Watson) and her fiancé, the actors are able to develop their characterizations through dialogue, the relationships between people
are clear and credible, and Mona's psychological motivation is

fully developed. The action grows out of Mona's refusal to have intercourse with her fiancé until her wedding night. The heroine is not wholly without a sex life, however. She is more than willing to perform fellatio on her fiancé or any other man to whom she is attracted. When her fiancé first tries to persuade her to sleep with him, for example, she performs oral sex instead, on the spot, in the middle of a field with the whole world watching. (It is typical of Osco's Graffiti Productions that a lot of chances were taken in order to shoot in the open air, thus providing both a variety of settings and the added kick of showing forbidden behavior in forbidden places.) Subsequent scenes of explicit action include Mona fellating a young man in a Los Angeles alley (ending with one of the first oral come shots in hard-core features) and Mona making love to another woman in a lyrical indoor scene illuminated by sunlight coming through an open window. And, of course, there is a final "orgy" scene during which Mona is bound and forced to perform fellatio on two men at the same time, while others are performing cunnilingus on her and variously caressing her body.

Mona's mother (played by the remarkable Judy Angel, a woman of forty in a craft where it is unusual for a performer to be much beyond adolescence) is also a focus for some of the erotic action. In one key scene she is dressed in a garter belt and fur-collared gown and is masturbating with a vibrator fitted with a French tickler. Shot in extreme close-up, it is an episode that is vulgar, clinical, and ultimately unpleasant.

To ensure its having redeeming social value, *Mona* has a moral: Distorted sexuality is often the product of repression and hypocrisy, and the rigid, unrealistic Victorian standards under which women must wait for marriage to have intercourse are false and harmful. But there is little question that it is pornographic in intention and execution. Following the classic pattern of erotic scenes—from a little dalliance to a sadistic orgy—the movie also contains many of the significant thematic elements of traditional pornography: seduction, incest, a permissive-seductive parent figure, dirty words, nymphomania, lesbianism, masturbation, orgies, oral sex, oral fixation, bondage, sadomasochism, and sex toys.

The success of *Mona* on the hard-core circuit prompted Graffiti Productions to make *Harlot* as its second hard-core story film. Produced by Osco, and directed by the team of Mike Light and Howard Ziehm, who shared the cinematography and editing chores between them, the result is fast-paced, funny, and technically well-made. The dialogue scenes are shot with live sound, the music is good, the performers are attractive, and the sex is inventive and varied. The humor of *Harlot* is evident from the opening shot of the Graffiti logo, a small airplane jerkily circling the earth (a parody of the Universal logo of the '30s).

Harlot opens on the campus of Hollywood High, where Mary, the heroine of the film, persuades her girlfriend, Melody, to cut school and make a little spare change by hustling on the streets of Los Angeles. The girls hitchhike around the city and sell themselves to several of the men who give them rides. Back in school, Mary seduces one of her teachers, and the female principal blackmails the pair into having an orgy in her office. Melody, meanwhile, has fallen in love with a Hell's Angel who has raped her, and the two are later killed in a motorcycle accident. In a final scene, Mary goes to the cemetery to pay her last respects to her friend, vowing to remain celibate for the rest of her life. Attracted to the handsome driver of the hearse, however, she decides to break her vow—immediately.

Most of *Harlot* was shot on the streets and in the buildings of Los Angeles. There is sex in moving cars and stuck elevators and a passionate scene between the two girls and a man on the roof of the Federal Bank Building. The episode, striking in its audacity, is scored to music by Bach and end with a sweeping, lyrical helicopter shot that radically changes the viewer's perspective and reduces the actors to a jumble of flesh on a rooftop. This kind of creativity is also evident as Melody (played by Patty Alexon) and her biker boyfriend run gaily through a shopping center stark naked. The scene is shot in slow motion, capturing the delicate, graceful beauty of the girl, the rotund bulk of the biker, and the amazement and horror of the housewives who have been interrupted in their midday shopping.

Not all of *Harlot* is lyrical and pleasant, but *Harlot* lacked the false moralizing of the soft-core films, substituting an awareness that sex could be as much of a power trip as any other endeavor.

Bill Osco was unusual among the producer-directors of hard-core features. He made only a few, he made them well, and he saw to it that he received the maximum return on his investment. He handled the initial distribution of *Mona*, for example, before selling the rights outright to Sherpix for an undisclosed sum. He also handled the distribution of *Harlot*, and, at one point, he even got into the theater business, operating by his own estimate about twenty-five theaters. "There was a lot of money there," Osco said. "I'd open up *Mona* in Denver; I'm pulling $20,000 in a sixty-seat house, and we spend a thousand bucks on advertising. In Phoenix, Arizona, three years ago, we paid four hundred bucks a month rent, forty-two seats. We opened up *Mona* there and did something like $25,000. No advertising—you don't advertise there—it was all word of mouth."

Other Los Angeles directors lost no time in following Osco's lead. Richard Robinson, for example, a sometime actor, produced and directed *Adultery for Fun and Profit*, a 66-minute Sherpix release in color that won first prize in the First Wet Dream Film Festival, sponsored by *Suck* magazine in Amsterdam. The plot tells the sad story of a good-looking young man who makes a disreputable living doing some undercover work for a divorce lawyer, seducing the wives of the lawyer's clients in order to obtain compromising evidence on the women. His duplicity is finally discovered, and, rather than face a jail sentence for blackmail, he makes his services available to all of the women all of the time. *Adultery for Fun and Profit* is technically adequate and features a number of attractive women. There are scenes of intercourse and fellatio, but Robinson avoids meat shots and wet shots in preference to fleeting glimpses of the real thing, including a soapy scene in the shower.

Although Robinson did not attempt to capitalize on the success of *Adultery*, other directors did. Phillip and Merrill Dakota released a number of films through Signatures Films, including *I Am Curious but Not Yellow*, the gangster opus *Ripoff*, and the interracial fantasy *Black and White*. One of the directors who worked for the pair, Clay McCord, turned out *She Did What He Wanted*, *Midnight Hard*, and *Wet Lips*, the latter a film that, according to veteran porno director William Rotsler, is "practically the definitive film about young girls coming to Hollywood and getting the fast bed-shuffle from people in the motion-picture business."

Of course, several old-line exploitation producers also got into the hard-core feature business. Don Davis of Hollywood Cinema Associates came up with *Dial-A-Degenerate*, which is little more than a series of hard-core loops demonstrating voyeurism, masturbation, flagellation, and obscene phone calls, intercut with new footage to give the film some coherent framework. The new material was written by and starred Ann Myers, a Nudie actress-producer-director-writer who was featured in several of the better soft-core films (such as *The Golden Box*, co-starring Marsha Jordan; *The Toy Box*; *Kama Sutra '71*; and *Peggy, the Suburban Nymph*) and who has also produced eleven films for her own company, Diana Films. Myers appeared in *Dial-A-Degenerate* fully clothed, giving a winning performance as an operator who answers telephone requests for descriptions of deviant sexual behavior. And around this same time, Carlos Tobalina of Hollywood International wrote and directed *Refinements in Love*, an 88-minute Eastmancolor paean to heterosexuality.

The considerable financial and even critical success of films like *Harlot* and *Adultery for Fun and Profit* were not typical of most 16mm hard-core features. "A large portion of the hard-core movies are done by amateurs," writes William Rotsler. "These are the fast-buck operators. Grab a camera, some film, two people and a bed. 'Get it up, get it on, and let's get it over with!' This is where a lot of schlock comes from." In general, the 16mm hard-core feature is art at its most anonymous, almost a folk art or a cottage industry. Stories are written on matchbook covers, and dialogue is made up by performers more noted for looks than for talent. Filming takes place on a single day, and the results are sometimes little more than records of sexual activity framed by the collective sexual fantasies of the people who film and edit one film a week, every week of the year.

Collecting information about the films and the industry as a whole is not made easier by the belief on the part of many of the manufacturers that they are engaged in illegal activity. This is substantiated by Captain Jack Wilson, head of the Los Angeles Police Department's Division of Administrative Vice, who said, "You cannot make a hard-core film without violating the prostitution laws. When you pay actors to engage in sex or oral copulation, you've violated laws. You've solicited individuals to engage in prostitution by asking them to exchange sex for money. We direct our efforts against those violating the laws while making these films." It is also against the law to transport and exhibit obscene films. All of these prohibitions contribute to a desire for anonymity so strong that films may be released without credits and, in some instances, without titles, sometimes making it impossible to know what film is being shown on the screen.

Typical of the less carefully produced hard-core films are those made by Flaming Productions, an underground company located in Los Angeles. One of their early ventures was *Strangers When They Mate,* about an encounter session that is little more than a nonstop orgy, starring Long Johnny Wadd (John C. Holmes). Other Johnny Wadd vehicles from the same company include *You Are Invited to a Masked Costume Ball* and *Ride a Cock Horse.* The first is notable only for its kinkier aspects—Johnny Wadd's black leather costume (one of the key iconographic elements in hard-core pornography), a masturbation contest to see who can ejaculate first, and a transvestite seduction; but the second film, which has a fairly complicated plot and distinct characterizations, presents a stereographic view of human behavior, part fantasy and part nightmarish reality.

The action of *Ride a Cock Horse* embodies the infantile erotic fantasies of hurt and humiliation: Two couples vacationing at a ski lodge pick up a young female hitchhiker, abduct her, and subject her to various sexual abuses. She escapes from this rough foursome and goes to her brother (Johnny Wadd) for help. Wadd dons his leather jacket, pockets his gun, rounds up a buddy to help him, and makes his way back to the ski lodge, where he takes his revenge on the two couples. Wadd's swaggering, bad-talking performance is excellent as he ad-libs a script of abuse, threat, and obscenity for most of the sixty-two minutes of the film. He occasionally becomes too involved in his role, hits a little too hard, and pushes a little too far, something the other performers obviously do not like. But they take their cues from him, and he controls the flow and pace of the action.

Los Angeles did not have a monopoly on the production of hard-core features. San Francisco directors who had been active in the sex-exploitation business—and whose films, on the whole, have an interesting, iconoclastic, funky attitude even when the plots are chaotic or dull—were quick to move into the new market. One of the most prominent of these, Alex de Renzy, made *Powder Burns,* a porno western starring George McDonald and shot partly on location in Arizona, and *Sexual Encounter Group,* filmed in a single day at the minimal cost of $10,000.

More than a year went by before De Renzy followed these with one of the better hard-core fantasies, a pleasant fable called *Little Sisters.* This erotic fairy tale turns on the adventures of two adolescent girls who live in the woods with their mother and are kidnapped first by a gang of cutthroats and then by a band of lesbians. After two episodes featuring their mother's encounters with some randy clerics and a band of transvestites (played by the Cockettes), the girls are rescued by Derek, Guardian of the Forest Morals, who enforces peace among the warring factions in the woods. Despite the relative absence of hard-core action in it—some oral sex and an occasional discreet meat shot—*Little Sisters* ran into some legal trouble, partly because of the prominence of De Renzy's name in the advertising and partly because the film broke the taboo (generally observed by even hard-core filmmakers) on depicting underage sex.

Another important San Francisco hard-core director was Lowell Pickett, who learned his trade turning out Nudie-Cutie loops and then established his own chain of theaters to reap the profits to be had from showing sex films as well as making them. Pickett put $8,000 into *Love, Yolanda,* a two-handkerchief movie that relates in graphic detail how a cast-off, middle-aged actress stage-manages the career of her young niece by arranging for the girl to make love to a succession of men who can make her a star. Pickett later made a gangster film about the San Francisco protection rackets called *Cozy Cool* that starred Maria Arnold, Michael Clark, and Mary Rexroth and cost $30,000. Although the original version of the film had hard-core sequences and a running time of just under two hours, Pickett later recut, reshot, and retitled the film, releasing it in an R-rated version under several titles, including *Losers Weepers* and *The Hit Miss.*

Similarly, the Mitchell Brothers, who had exhibited their own loops in their O'Farrell Theater, began to make short features, including such titles as *Wild Campus, Rampaging Nurses, Flesh Factory, Scrimshaw Woman,* and *Rabin's Revenge,* many of which featured the Mitchell Brothers stock company—George McDonald, Jeff Hamlet, Felicia Mallery, and Cindy Spittler, among others.

Among the newer San Francisco sex-film directors, one of the best is Paul Gerber (a former cameraman with Alex de Renzy) whose first feature, *School Girl,* appeared in 1971. His heroine is a young sociology student, Debra, investigating the sexual underground by answering a series of sexual advertisements in the *Berkeley Barb.* What she discovers—troilism, lesbianism, orgies, masturbation, and a father-and-son team—thus forms the dramatic action of the film and the basis for her oral classroom report, which she prefaces with this statement: "These people are really lonely. They hate what they're doing, their sex lives are perverted and twisted in a frantic search for sexual fulfillment that they never seem to find." Those conclusions contrast oddly, however, with the joyful variety of the sexual episodes of the movie. The "establishment" world, moreover, is represented by a group of sterile, hypocritical professors and students. Debra's instructor mouths foolish platitudes and ineptly seduces Debra's roommate, and the rest of the students are cynical and lazy.

There is a long love scene between Debra and her student boyfriend (George McDonald) remarkable for its improvised dialogue (George makes love wearing his heavy white socks and claims he wears them because "I'm trying to bring them back— even Spiro Agnew wears 'em") and for its hard-driving finale. Also particularly well done is a sequence with Debra and a married couple in which the wife watches Debra and her husband make love. She eventually joins them on the bed, and as the three explore a number of sexual possibilities the erotic tension is heightened by the skill with which the scene is photographed and edited. Slow dissolves provide a dreamy elegance, and the music is scored to underline the rising emotional excitement.

The promise of *School Girl* is more than fulfilled in Gerber's second feature, *Bad Barbara,* the story of a woman whose inner life is being stifled in a conventional sexual relationship but who cannot find any truer sense of herself in casual promiscuity. As Peter Michaelson has noted, Barbara is afraid that "her love for a man will subsume self-identity, and the loss of that love will leave her without reason to be."

Gerber is more interested in erotic realism than in rank eroticism, but *Bad Barbara* is highly erotic, and the plot is arranged to vary the circumstances with regard to the complexity, intensity, normality, and number of persons in each successive sex act. As the movie begins, it is early morning. Barbara and her lover awake and begin to make love. The scene is genuine, passionate, and unmediated by directorial demands for arbitrary changes in position and levels of passion, and the two cameras Gerber uses provide a variety of shots without disturbing the intimacy and fervor of the performing couple.

Gerber is most fascinated, however, by what happens after the sex act. Although physically satisfied, Barbara realizes that there are other problems with the relationship, and she provokes an argument with her lover, who walks out on her. Unused to being without a steady man in the house, and ostensibly in search of liberation and identity, Barbara then drifts into a life of aimless promiscuity. There is a dream sequence in which Barbara's sexual confusion and anxiety are realized in disturbing and contradictory images as she is approached by a naked and aroused girlfriend who suddenly turns into an aroused man. Her girlfriend reappears, and both of the women separately perform fellatio on featureless men. This fantastic dream awakens Barbara, who then masturbates to climax.

In a final scene, a hippie couple, mouthing a belief in liberation and freedom from convention, seduce Barbara, but the heroine feels badly used, becomes angry, and goes off to look for the nearest telephone. The film closes with Barbara standing in a telephone booth, listening to the endless ringing of the phone in the apartment of her old boyfriend. It is a realistic and downbeat ending, quite suitable for a film that explores some of the consequences of human sexuality.

Most of the hard-core features shown in the United States were made on the West Coast until late in 1970, when the first wave of films made in New York City, including *All About Sex of All Nations*, *Sex USA*, and *The Healers*, was released. One of the first put into distribution, by Grove Press, was Fred Baker's *Events*, a film about two underground filmmakers who attempt to raise money to produce a movie about Lenny Bruce by making a sex film. The dialogue is all improvised, and the awkward performances are not helped by the poor technical quality of the sound recording.

A somewhat better movie, and an early solid hit, was *The Nurses*, a comedy that made full use of trite humor concerning young women who tend the sick. The movie, more amusing than arousing, is, in fact, an extended joke about medical malpractice in which a series of cardboard characters are placed in embarrassing, compromising, or humiliating positions: A man gives a sperm sample by masturbating to climax between the breasts of a nurse, a doctor performs intercourse with a patient as part of a medical examination, and a lusty nurse seduces a not-too-bright fellow only to discover that he is an out-patient suffering from venereal disease.

Perhaps the most interesting film made in the first years of New York hard-core production was *Dark Dreams*, a bizarre sex-and-horror fantasy directed by Roger Guermontes, written and produced by his wife, Candida Ference, and starring Harry Reems and Tina Russell. The couple portray virgin newlyweds whose wedding night is stage-managed by a group of satanic characters to whom they have innocently turned for help after their car breaks down. The technical quality of *Dark Dreams* is excellent, featuring an original soundtrack and convincing special effects. And Reems and Russell, reading their lines with conviction, have sex with the appearance of real pleasure and involvement.

By the end of 1971 distributors and exhibitors around the country found themselves in hard times. Too many theaters were playing hard core, and the public was no longer interested in a routine product. What the porno moguls needed was a hit film that would do well at the box office and renew public interest in sex films. The answer would come from Miami, where director Gerard Damiano was shooting a film with the working title *The Doctor Makes a House Call*.

10

"BOY KING OF L.A. PORNO"

AN INTERVIEW WITH BILL OSCO

It is hot in Los Angeles, and Bill Osco, wearing worn jeans, cowboy boots, and a ragged T-shirt under his black fur coat, is not feeling too good. "I get different moods on me every day," he explains. "One day I'm like king of the world, nobody can get near me. I get up another day and I feel like shit. It's just really bad." He pauses now, his deep-set eyes under tousled brown hair flicking around like a rattlesnake's tongue. "I hate depressing days like this."

That is not all Bill Osco doesn't like. To him Hollywood is "a sick, cold town. Everybody's after everybody; it's dog eat dog here." Of the major studios he says, "I think they suck. I'd like to see Fox go, Columbia just fold up. If I can take them to the cleaners I sure would; I'd soak the shit out of them." And as for humanity itself, "I don't like people that much. To me friends cost money, and I've supported a lot of fucking people the last couple of years. I like to be alone a lot. I don't like crowds anymore. I don't really have any use for people anymore."

And many people tend to feel the same way about him. "I got a lot of enemies that'd love to see me just fold up and fucking die," he admits with something resembling satisfaction before adding the final cut, "Those people are going nowhere."

Bill Osco, age twenty-six, self-proclaimed former minor league ballplayer and Hell's Angel, is one of hard core's millionaires. When just barely old enough to legally see his product, he established himself as the biggest 16mm loop supplier in the country,

133

earning the *Variety* sobriquet "Boy King of L.A. Porno." Then, in 1970, came *Mona,* generally considered to be the very first pornographic feature ever made, "the hard-core equivalent of *Birth of a Nation*" the trade papers claimed. New York's *Village Voice* predicted Osco might wind up as the porno medium's Federico Fellini and credited *Mona* with "the same combination of fascination and revulsion that characterized *La Dolce Vita.*"

Osco says, "I've got everything I've ever wanted," mentioning a ranch for his parents in Idaho, a house in Arizona, and a hilltop house in Beverly Hills. His chocolate brown Rolls Royce is only one of a small fleet of cars, including a Corvette, a Mark IV, and an Eldorado. As for women, "my looking days are over. Can't wait to get me in the sack to find out do I do what I do in my movies. In fact, I've gotten choosier because of the business, super choosy." Even Raquel Welch, it turns out, isn't quite good enough.

"I took her out once. That's as far as we got. We went to McDonald's, and that ended it right there. She says, 'You pull out of this place right now or I'm getting out and walking. I will not eat here.' And people started gathering around the car, 'cause a Rolls Royce is an attention-tracker right there, and with her in it, everybody started looking. After that I called her the most untalented actress I ever fucking met. I wouldn't even use her in a skin flick I was making. So we're not talking much anymore."

Yet, somehow, living in the material world has not quite been as advertised. The $35,000 Rolls is "a piece of shit; it falls apart every month." And he left the five-acre mansion he had rented in Encino because someone stole his two German shepherds. "I mean when they steal your fucking guard dogs, that's a hint, you know. That's bad." And he has, in general, stopped being "out to impress people how successful I was. I got money, here's my Rolls Royce, here's my house, here's my five hundred dollar suit. I figured what the fuck am I doing, you know? I'm just impressing myself really. And that's an expensive way to go around living."

And Osco is finished with pornography too. "I hate to be limited in what I do, and we were limited there," he says. "You can't get the people you want, you can't get decent people. You can't do nothing in hard core. It's people fucking and sucking, you know? That's about it. I made money; I got publicity and experience out of it. I've got nothing against it, but I'm not gonna pursue it. What can I say?"

For to Bill Osco, hard core was just a vehicle, just a way for him to get a toehold in the film business. "Our main concern was breaking into legitimate movies somehow, and without the money and the experience it's impossible," he says. "We weren't living for today; we were living for the future. Get some bucks in the bank, get new experiences, and go out and do a legitimate movie, that's what we kept on thinking. I'm not thinking about making money anymore; I made a lot of money. You know, if you get too greedy you go down the fucking drain. I want to do my own thing right now. That's why we're here. Nobody's ever made the transition yet from sex to legitimate. We'll probably be the first.

"I want to be known as a really creative filmmaker," he says simply, but there is more to it than that. Making it in Hollywood has been a dream, an obsession with Osco for almost as long as he can remember, a ambition that has harassed and driven him for so long that he absolutely refuses to believe it can't happen.

"There's nothing impossible. I don't believe in that word," he says. "I even feel if a guy wants to walk through that fucking wall there's a way to do it. That's why it's so easy to make money today. There's so many unambitious people—they sit there and wait for it to happen. I think I'm more ambitious than most people because I carry mine out. I'm getting my goals when most people can't. I've talked to a lot of people that said, 'Yeah, man, I want to be big; I want to be rich and famous.' I've heard them say it since I met them, five, six, seven years ago, and here they are still living in a fucking ten-dollar-a-week apartment. They haven't really made the big step yet."

For Bill Osco, it has been all one track since he was a kid in Akron, Ohio. "I've lived this all my life. Since I was nine I wanted to be rich and famous," he says, his low flat voice somehow conveying his urgency. "I used to live back in Ohio thinking, 'When the fuck can I go out there?' I asked my parents to take me out here when I was nine or ten. 'Let me go to Hollywood; I'm gonna make it.'"

Finally, after graduating high school at age seventeen, he made the trip. "I have a very strong family background. I was the first one in the family to break away and leave in like three generations," he says. "I took off, and it shocked everybody. They couldn't believe it. I couldn't believe it, but I knew I wanted it. My life was out here, and I couldn't stand Ohio. I knew I'd make it. I used to get so fucking depressed, but I just knew I'd make it. I fucking knew it."

Out on the Coast Osco says he contacted a scout for the Los Angeles Dodgers, a friend of his high school coach, who gave him a shot at minor league baseball. "I was good; I aced out the shortstop in like two weeks. I would've made pro ball easy," he says with typical offhand brashness, "but it was too long a process." Other short-lived enterprises followed, including a stint with the Venice branch of the Hell's Angels. "In Ohio, all you do

135

is fight. I was in a rough neighborhood; we'd fight every weekend. And I brought that attitude out here with me. I was the bad guy with a big chopper and the fucking Angels' colors, all that." He tried college, too—Cal State, Los Angeles—and all the time "I lived and dreamed of what I wanted and went out and hustled and broke my fucking ass and everything else."

All in all, he says, "I blew about four years out here living in cars, you know, bumming around, and fucking waiting. I'd go steal some food, a lot of stealing food, eating oranges and apples while you walk around. I had fun in those days, but out of those four years, I wouldn't say I had more than twenty days of fun. Those were a long four years. Not having any money, picking up a job here and there—it's not exactly easy. I would say that most people think the way I think but wouldn't have enough guts to do what I did, what I went through."

In the late '60s, Osco met Howard Ziehm and began a partnership in Graffiti Productions that still stands. "We had about eighty bucks between us, and we started knocking out these little single-girl, Nudie-Cutie things, a lot of them, fifteen or twenty a week to raise money," he remembers. This was before hard core, in the days of split beaver. Usually they cost a buyer $75 a throw, but Osco developed such a reputation for quality and technical superiority that his work went for twice that much. Like Owsley acid, another West Coast product, Osco loops became a status symbol of the California culture, and his name on a film was among the first to mean something to porno audiences.

"We were always proud of our work," Osco says. "I've always been proud of everything I've done—I wasn't just cranking out sleazy stuff. I've put my name on it, you know." And he did it, he says, by "having the camera work for the person. Instead of just a tripod sitting and watching somebody, instead of having the person work to the camera, your camera angles are all over the place, to bring more out of the person. That's a technique."

Still trying to get more experience, Osco and company shot two extended 40-minute loops, both with simulated sex, called *Whatever Happened to Stud Flame* and *The Virgin Runaway*. The first "turned out to be a total fucking piece of shit," Osco says. "It was an experience that cost us a couple of bucks." But out of those two films came *Mona*, a three-day, $7,000 wonder that Osco wryly calls "our classic."

And yes, when the film hit the screen, the fans did go wild. "A landmark," said *Variety*, "the long-awaited link between the stag loops and conventional theatrical fare." And though Osco says, "We knew it was better because there was nothing else out to compare it with," he had so little idea of the film's potential—it still plays and has hit the $2 million gross mark—that he would've sold it outright for $10,000.

"You had to have guts to see it three or four years ago. You had to sneak in the fucking door," Osco says. "It was still pretty well hidden; people were scared to come in, you got your dirty old men walking in there. Now everybody says, 'Did you see *Deep Throat* yet?' Three years ago they couldn't say, 'I've seen *Mona*,' you know, because it made them look sort of weird. See, we started everything—names on the movies and reviews and all that, you know. We tried to present our movies as legitimate movies, and people bought 'em like that." They bought them so well, in fact, that Osco is continually troubled by films turning up with names like *Monica, Daughter of Mona*, that claim for little or no reason to be made by Bill Osco. "New York sucks as far as I'm concerned, because they start sticking my name on shit films I had nothing to do with," he says, irritated. "There's a lot of idiots in New York. We're suing a couple of them now."

There are only two other legitimate Osco films. The first is *Hollywood Blue,* which Osco calls a quick rip-off of Alex de Renzy's *History of the Blue Movie.* The other feature, *Harlot,* which tells the tale of a fifteen-year-old tart who uses her body to improve her marks at school, opened as a big klieg-lit benefit, complete with celebrities, for Los Angeles's Free Clinic. "It hit the news that night. They're saying, 'What's this country coming to?' " Osco remembers. "I did it to slap people in the face. I can make a movie for $15,000 and make $3, maybe $4, million on it compared to a major studio that spends $3 million on a movie and can't even fucking break even. That's a laugh, you know. It's really a fucking joke. That shows how stupid they are."

Harlot is Osco's personal favorite and he claims to have been told that Henry Kissinger likes it too. It seems Robert Evans of Paramount called him up one day to ask for a copy to show at a party and reported back the next morning that " 'Henry just busted his fucking gut.' Who the hell's gonna believe it? I couldn't believe it. Nixon's fucking right-hand man sitting there watching a fuck movie!"

Directing films is not on Bill Osco's mind these days. In fact, he says, he didn't really direct any of the three that bear his name; he was more of a supervising co-director-producer. "I hate directing. I have no use for it. It's just too much of a fucking hassle. I just don't have the patience. I move fast, I gotta move fast. I got to move around and go out and do it."

What he wants to do now, among other things, is act. He's already made one movie, *Sweet, Mean and Deadly,* a blood-and-guts epic he calls "a $60,000 screen test for myself," that probably will not do a great deal of business. But Osco, involved in acting lessons, is as undisturbed by that as he is by his own admission that "I'm by far no great actor, but I'm not going out as an actor. I'm going to be a star, not an actor. I'll probably be a superstar I'd say within the next three years." How will he do it? With money, what else?

"I'll buy the best," he says with the usual hard-driving assurance. "There's only a handful of writers around, and that's who we gotta hit. It all depends on the material. It's gotta be the right thing, because I'm gonna hit like that. I'll go to any top writers I can get ahold of, and I'll offer 'em a fucking deal they can't refuse. I'll offer 'em money, cash money, percentage of the movie, which they never had before. They'll write, they'll write their fucking ass off."

But that is still in the future. For now Osco is occupied with a project that has occupied him for the past three years, a little number called *Flesh Gordon*. Not so little really, says Osco, calling it the biggest animated movie in the last fifteen years, using, among others, the art director of "Star Trek" and the man who did *When Dinosaurs Ruled the Earth*. Replete with names like Emperor Wang, the planet Porno, Dale Ardor, and the spaceship Penisourous, *Flesh* was originally going to be a sci-fi porno extravaganza, but when things got too extravagant—like the budget running to $2 million—*Flesh* was recut to get an R rating, hopefully to insure at least an even return on its investment. Osco, as usual, has no doubts.

"*Flesh Gordon's* got the potential of doing anywhere from $20 to $50 million dollars," he says, adding later, "If it doesn't do $20 million I'm going to quit the business. Even if it goes bad, it would be $10 million on it." For "we got the best special effects. We made *The Poseidon Adventure* look like nothing; we made *Silent Running* look like a fucking kids' show. This is big."

Flesh kicked up a big storm at the time of the 1972 Academy Awards when Osco claimed it was to be nominated for the award in special effects, only to have the Academy chicken out and designate *The Poseidon Adventure* the winner out of competition because his film was too racy. A large story in the *Hollywood Reporter* resulted, the Academy denied it all, but Osco was adamant, even going so far as picketing the Awards ceremony. "We were aced out," he says, and he does not smile when he says it.

Yet, when the release date comes, Osco is sure everything will work out, and that all his anguished dreams will start to be realized. "I've only done half of what I actually want to do so far," he says. "I'm more than half way up the ladder right now, and *Flesh Gordon*, if it does even a fifth of what I think it's gonna do, it's gonna put us right on top of the ladder. We can call our own shots. Everybody's watching us right now—all the studios, all the big people, writers, everybody. They're watching to see if we're gonna hit or not. And once we hit, the fucking doors are open all the way. The movie hits, we're home. I've done it. *Flesh* is gonna show people what we can do. And it's gonna happen, I see it happening. I feel it."

He can feel it, he says, because "I have control of my mind. That's why I don't mess with dope. I hate booze. I hate beer. I hate liquor. The strongest thing I take is aspirin. I feel I have about 95 . . . 96 per cent control of my own mind. I can control myself from flipping off and going crazy, from being involved in too much pressure. I really have control. I call my shots."

What Osco can't control is those nasty things people say about him, a nastiness he admits he seems to encourage. "Here I am, twenty-six, I'm doing it, getting all this publicity. There are people fifty years old in this town that have been spending their fucking life here trying, and my age kills them. They say, 'How the fuck can he do it at that fucking age?' They hate that. And then I'm arrogant about it, saying, 'Well I'm what's happening, you know.' I say it just to irritate people—I'm the greatest,' like the Cassius Clay of the porno business. It pisses people off."

Of course not everybody dislikes him. Columnist Joyce Haber thinks he's swell and even featured him as the subject of one of her full-page stories in the Sunday *Los Angeles Times,* a coup he never tires of gloating over. "That sort of put me up in the ranks of Hollywood, because she only writes about *the* people," he says, pleased. "A lot of your big-time people that've been in Hollywood for twenty, thirty years—they can't even get that kind of publicity. You can't even buy your way in there, you know. But she came to me and said, 'I want to do a thing on you.' We did it at the Beverly Hills Hotel, and all the big people are walking by and saying, 'Who the fuck's she talking to?' I was probably the first really unknown, underground guy to get in her column. It got us into the open."

And his parents, especially his mother, are "proud as hell of me. When I first told her what I was doing she said, 'Son, fucking money is green. When it comes to money you don't have any pride, just take it. I don't give a fuck where you get it from. If it's fucking green, take it.' "

So Bill Osco keeps driving for the big bucks, sharpening himself against the hard edge of everyone else's outrage. "It's an ego thing," he admits. "Because people say you can't do that. They've been saying all your life you can't do it. Well, here I am, you know? They're laughing at me now. They're saying 'No, no,' but I'll have the last laugh. Like always, I'll have the last laugh."

139

Bill Osco is determined that he will have what he wants, what he has always wanted. "I swear I lived for three years out here trying to break in some way, any way, and I got nowhere," he remembers, his voice getting harder. "I used to go home at night and dream what it would be like, and I really believed in it. I had my house picked out in Beverly Hills. I had my car picked out. My life didn't really begin until I went to bed at night. I'd dream I'd be driving down the street, I was known by everybody, and I was really a super guy, you know. I used to live my life in dreams."

And now, now that the dream seems to have some chance of taking solid form, what goes through Bill Osco's mind? "I dream about the old days," he says, not really sad. "You know, how good it was not to have any responsibilities and just to fucking bum around. I tell you, it's reversed all the way. I even go back once in a great while, go borrow a friend's car, an old beat-up piece of shit, pile in and drive into Hollywood, and rent me a place for two bucks a night just to get back in the atmosphere. You know, make sure I'm really living."

11

THE DEEP THROAT EXPERIENCE

A STAR IS MADE

Miami Beach, January 1972. Across town the Miami Dolphins and the Dallas Cowboys are playing in the Super Bowl. A woman appears, steps into a Cadillac, and drives off down Collins Avenue. The woman is Linda Lovelace, and this is the opening shot of *Deep Throat*, perhaps the most famous pornographic movie ever made. The titles flash on the screen, including the credit line "And Introducing Linda Lovelace as Herself." This offhand note is the key to the film, for Miss Lovelace is its *star* and the picaresque narrative—one woman in search of orgasm— exploits her now-legendary gifts as a fellatrice through a series of sexual adventures.

The plot is based on a simple problem. Linda, though excited by sex, has been unable to reach orgasm in conventional inter- course. Even an orgy with a dozen men leaves the heroine unable to climax. In despair, Linda turns to Doctor Young (Harry Reems), a demented psychiatrist who discovers that the patient's clitoris is not in its accustomed place but at the base of her throat instead. Volunteering his body to the cause of science, Dr. Young has Linda perform fellatio on him in order to test his strange hypothesis. The doctor is a generously endowed man, and his experiment works. The heroine reaches the first orgasm of her life, signified by shots of fireworks exploding, bells ringing, and a Saturn rocket being launched.

To take advantage of Linda's cure, Dr. Young engages her as a physical therapist for three of his patients, all of whom appreciate her services, which are wittily and imaginatively—and explicitly—portrayed. One elderly widower, who has not had sex since the death of his wife, tells Linda not to worry about the cost of his treatments—he has Blue Cross. Another home consultation ends with the patient sipping Coke from a glass dildo in the heroine's vagina, while on the soundtrack the audience hears "I'd Like To Teach the World To Screw," a parody of the famous Coca-Cola advertising jingle. The film ends as Linda Lovelace finds "true love" with a sinister masked man who sneaks into her apartment and acts out his sadistic fantasies in a spoof of stag films.

Deep Throat is an explicit hard-core film showing seven acts of fellatio and four of cunnilingus, as well as instances of both vaginal and anal intercourse—but it is not degrading or ugly. It is, rather, expertly made, funny, and almost unique among sex films in its celebration of individual response. The plot is more than just a pretext for a series of compulsive sexual encounters, and women are not portrayed as objects of sexual hatred and perversion, a perspective that is scored—or perhaps shaped—by Linda Lovelace's extraordinary erotic talent. She appears to be genuinely turned on by what she is doing, with the result that her performance shows none of the boredom, inadvertent laughter, or undisguised disgust that breaks the sensual reality of many films.

The genesis of *Deep Throat* is fast becoming the stuff of myth. One story has it that the director of the film, Gerard Damiano, first met Linda Lovelace and her husband-manager, photographer Chuck Traynor, at a party in Manhattan, and that Damiano, intrigued by Linda's unique capacity to take a penis deep into her throat by willfully suppressing the natural reflex to gag and by breathing at odd intervals, conceived the whole story of *Deep Throat* in a flash as he was driving home over the 59th Street Bridge. Now Damiano hedges a bit, saying, "Well, let's. say I found her, and I saw her doing what she was doing, and this so intrigued me that that weekend I wrote the premise for *Throat*." Linda Lovelace has a different version of events, claiming that she originally signed onto a Damiano film as a script girl to be with Chuck Traynor, who was to be the cameraman, and that Traynor had a hand in changing the original idea to *Deep Throat*. In any case, Damiano found backing from two New York acquaintances, Phil Parisi and Lou Perry. The total cost for the negative on the film, shot in Miami, Fort Lauderdale, and Coral Gables in six days, was $24,000; editing and sound mixing took several months. Damiano persuaded his partners that the film should be released under the present title of *Deep Throat* rather than *The Doctor Makes a House Call*, and it premiered in June

1972 at the New World Theater on Forty-ninth Street in the tenderloin district of Manhattan. A good review in *Screw* produced grosses of $33,033 the first week, and the movie soon had patrons lining up at the box office.

The technical quality and slapstick humor of *Deep Throat* are wholly the product of the skill with which Damiano manipulates the performers and shoots footage. He is an experienced craftsman who learned his trade making television commercials and several better-than-average sex-exploitation films. What really accounted for *Deep Throat*'s success, however, was the unprecedented media coverage of the film and its subsequent obscenity trial. The first press story, entitled "Gulp!" was an enthusiastic notice in *Screw*, written by Al Goldstein after the film had been previewed for him by Bob Sumner, the manager of the New World Theater. Goldstein was greatly taken with the film, claiming it showed "the greatest on-screen fellatio since the birth of Christ," and, flinging caution to the winds, gave it a rating of 100 on the Peter Meter (an honor previously accorded only to *Mona* and *School Girl*).

After that, the press and the public went wild. The film was reviewed by Judith Crist, Vincent Canby, Andrew Sarris, and critics and reporters for every conceivable publication from *Playboy* and *Women's Wear Daily* to the London *Times*, creating so much notoriety that the visiting Russian basketball team tried to see it in Albuquerque, New Mexico, only to bail out at the last minute because the price was too steep. Mike Nichols felt no such compunction, allegedly seeing it three times and recommending it to Truman Capote, while the *Los Angeles Free Press* claimed that Frank Sinatra showed it to then Vice-President Agnew.

A garbage collector in Lansing, Michigan, however, refused to service a theater where it played, and certainly there were critics as well who did not like the film. Ellen Willis wrote in the *New York Review of Books* that she found the film to be "witless, exploitative, and about as erotic as a tonsillectomy." She confessed that the film did not turn her on and then speculated about the nature of its appeal to men.

"Everybody" knows that men divorce sex from emotion because they can't afford to face their real emotions about women . . . Nevertheless, it baffles and angers women that men can get it off on all those bodies methodically humping away, their faces sweatless and passionless, their consummation so automatic that they never get a chance to experience desire.

A similar note of disgust and dissatisfaction appears in a column Nora Ephron wrote for *Esquire* in which she called *Deep Throat*

143

"one of the most unpleasant, disturbing films I have ever seen—
it is not just anti-female but anti-sex, as well . . . I came out of the
theater a quivering fanatic. Give me the goriest Peckinpah any
day."

As the focus of all this critical attention, *Deep Throat* was also
"reviewed" by patrolman Michael Sullivan of the Public Morals
Division, who, on August 17, saw the film in the company of
Judge Ernest Rosenberger of the New York County Criminal
Court. Judge Rosenberger immediately signed a warrant for the
seizure of the film, and patrolman Sullivan confiscated the theater's print. Under a previous New York State ruling, however, it
was necessary to hold an adversary hearing before seizing a film,
and the print was returned. Twelve days later another police
officer arrested Bob Sumner and charged him, as the owner of
Mature Enterprises, Inc., with exhibiting obscene material. Nevertheless, the film continued at the theater for the six months until
the trial (delayed by a crowded court schedule), and the publicity
during that time certainly did not hurt at the gate.

When the trial finally did begin on December 19, 1972, it
grew into an eleven-day national event. Among the several reporters covering the trial for local papers and national media was
Ralph Blumenthal of the *New York Times*, who gave a full and
accurate account of the controversial, sometimes ludicrous court-
room events as defense lawyer Herbert Kassner, Assistant District Attorney William Purcell, and Judge Joel E. Tyler put the
several "expert" witnesses through the painful paces of testifying
about the problematical issues of redeeming social value, prurient
interest, and contemporary community standards. The testimony,
by such people as psychiatrist Edward J. Hornick, CCNY psy-
chologist Charles Winnick, and Kenneth Lindsay, chairman of the
Art Department of Harpur College, came to more than one thousand pages of trial transcripts. And judgments ranged:

From the favorable

> I find in [*Deep Throat*] a kind of attractiveness about the peo-
> ple. . . . I found in it a very real attempt to use humor in depicting
> a sexual situation as to underlie that with some insight. . . . I think
> there was a kind of sophisticated fooling with the sexual content.
> It was not deep-breathing sex, you know. [Arthur Knight, motion-
> picture historian.]

To the unfavorable

> The presentation of sex, divorced from emotional relationships,
> . . . as an act of mutual exploitation, as it were, in which it permits
> the personalities of the participants to be totally disregarded and
> they themselves are, if I may speak symbolically, bearers of the

sexual organ and not human beings who are ends in themselves, I not only regard as being without redeeming social value; I regard it as highly antisocial. [Ernest van den Haag, sociologist and author of *Passion and Social Constraint.*]

From the sublime

It indicates that women have a right to a sex life of their own, and they are not simply an instrumentality of men's sex life which is the way things used to be chiefly in the Victorian era. For example, there is a theme in the film which implies that women should get sexual satisfaction and sexual gratification. [Dr. John Money, Professor of Medical Psychology at Johns Hopkins University Medical School.]

To the patently ridiculous

There were a couple of other films on the program and I'm not quite sure where the other films ended and [*Deep Throat*] began. There was plenty of normal intercourse and I think there was some in this particular film.... Was it all one film? It ran more than an hour and fifty-five minutes. [Dr. Max Levin, neurologist and psychiatrist.]

Judge Tyler's decision, however—based on the judgment that the experts had not shown that 51 per cent of the movie had redeeming social value—did not reflect any confusion. He punitively fined the theater a startling $3 million (twice the estimated gross), writing that the film was

. . . a feast of carrion and squalor . . . a Sodom and Gomorrah gone wild before the fire . . . one throat that deserves to be cut . . . a nadir of decadence—it is indisputably obscene by any legal measurement. . . . It does, in fact, demean and pervert the sexual experience, and insults it, shamelessly, without tenderness and without understanding of its roles as a concomitant of the human condition.

Bob Summer summed it up on his New World Theater marquee as he immediately booked a new film: JUDGE CUTS THROAT, WORLD MOURNS.

Despite the legal problems of *Deep Throat*, it eventually played in seventy cities and grossed $3.2 million by January 1973 (and an estimated $5 million by six months later). An important factor in this phenomenal success was the growing stardom of Linda Lovelace. She was mentioned in gossip columns, guested on talk shows, and made the television evening news after her public appearance at the film's premiere in Los Angeles. Richard Hill

145

interviewed her for an article in *Oui,* in which she explained why she appears in sex films: "I'm an exhibitionist. I dig doing it. I want everybody to see it. And I make good money." And in a telephone interview with Nora Ephron, the actress commented, "I don't have any inhibitions about sex. . . . I just hope everybody who goes to see the film enjoys it and maybe learns something from it." Perhaps the most lucid interview with the new star was one of the earliest, in which Al Goldstein asked her the inevitable question, "Do you come even though your clit isn't being worked on?" To which she answered, "I have an orgasm every time I get screwed in the throat." Of such candor was the legend of Linda Lovelace made.

It is a legend that several people have contributed to. As far as her name, for example, Gerard Damiano says, "Linda Lovelace is not Linda Lovelace. I gave her that name, which she carries today. Her name was Linda, and Lovelace was sort of like the American dream of putting love and old lace together and making it a sweet young thing. I was probably the only one that understood that if I could keep her young and innocent and have her emerge like the girl next door, we would have something very important."

For Linda, 1973 was a very good year. She was featured on the cover of *Esquire* and was the subject of a photographic essay in *Playboy.* To make her acceptable to the men who read that magazine, Hugh Hefner, a genius at mechanizing sex, presented a soft-focus, romantic version of the star. By means of gauzy photos and some crafty editorializing, she is characterized as having "a shy innocence combined with sexual enthusiasm and an utter absence of inhibitions." Several carefully chosen quotes from Linda herself follow. In one she modestly claims, "I'm not out to be actress of the year. . . . *Deep Throat* is just me, acting naturally." In another she lists her erotic preferences: "Everything turns me on, actually; my preference depends on my mood . . . but I'd say right now that I like throat, ass, cunt, one, two, three, in that order."

All this publicity eventually soured. Al Goldstein of *Screw,* one of her first fans, ran a series of articles presenting the dark past of the bright new porno star, a past that included work in a number of 8mm films intended for the home market and peep shows. At least seven films have come to light: *M-65, M-66, M-81, M-82, D-1, D-2* and *DT-LL.* One of the more unusual of these features Linda's adventures with the foot of a petite lesbian, but also in this series are the notorious *D-1* and *D-2.* The latter, according to *Screw,* which printed a still from the loop, is also called *Dog-Fuck,* a title that accurately describes the action. In her autobiography, *Inside Linda Lovelace,* Linda takes great

pains to deny the story and accuses Goldstein of faking the photo-
graph. Goldstein countered by running the photo a second time and insisting on its legitimacy:

> Linda *is* in the photos and *has* been fucked by dogs. In fact, this newest photo, which I'm running in this issue, shows Linda in her pre–*Deep Throat* days being pissed upon. Linda is a star and a real super-duper porn pro, and in that environment she will do anything her director wants her to. This makes her a fine thespian but a poor plaintiff in a libel action. For Linda to sue me would be as absurd as a madman trying to have the headshrink at a sanitarium arrested for mental aberration.

The controversy about Linda Lovelace and man's best friend is only one small part of the star's autobiography. The book, for which she received a $100,000 advance from Pinnacle Books, in many ways resembles old-fashioned Hollywood studio biographies. There is a little information about her life—and what there is is mostly inaccurate—but there are also instructions on how to "deep throat" and how to have painless anal intercourse, just as Bette Davis might once have given out her favorite recipe for baked Alaska. The inclusion of pornographic asides to the reader seemingly fulfills an audience need to know the guilty secrets of the stars and to be assured that their erotic fantasies about them are correct.

The publication of *Inside Linda Lovelace* is only one of the creative and money-making schemes the actress has been involved with since her emergence as the Garbo of hard core. She has made a sequel to *Deep Throat* called *Deep Throat II* that was directed in both an X and R version by porno veteran Joe Sarno. The film has not yet been widely shown—producer Phil Parisi is waiting until the effects of the recent Supreme Court rulings tightening the obscenity guidelines become clear—but the R version was unsuccessfully released in Manhattan. Lovelace's devout following, used to seeing the real thing, evidently was not content to watch her "deep throat" a foot-long hot dog.

Future plans for the star at one point included a stage show on a bill with Sammy Davis, Jr., and a film with a million-dollar budget. But things have not worked out well. Lovelace's marriage to Chuck Traynor broke up, and her scheduled nightclub appearance was canceled when she underwent surgery after an automobile accident. Just before Christmas she did make it onto the boards of the Locust Theater in Philadelphia starring in the '50s farce *Pajama Tops*, a "naughty" bedroom romp that once starred June Wilkinson and Barbara Eden, but the show bombed. Critics hated it, and the opening night audience walked out. On top of that, Lovelace was sued by her present manager for breach of contract. Then, on January 31, 1974, she was arrested in the Dunes Hotel in Las Vegas for illegal possession of cocaine and amphetamines, an event that did nothing to impede the announcement of yet another book, *The Intimate Diary of Linda Lovelace*, which promises "the shocking truth about her first marriage; the wild parties and love games of Hollywood, New York, and Las Vegas; the true stories behind the headline-making rumors of her affairs with the famous," and, if at all possible, more.

In the face of the notoriety of this biggest of all porno stars, it is sometimes difficult to keep in mind those few qualities that first made her famous: the fresh carnality, the air of thoroughly debauched innocence, the sense of a woman exploring the limits of sexual expression and feeling. Linda Lovelace is the girl next door grown up into a shameless, voracious woman. Her entire attitude to life and love is summed up in a few remarks she made to a *Variety* staffer:

> I'm not going to sit here and say I'll never do another hard-core film because I was forced into this one, that I needed the money or something like that. I did it because I loved it. It was something I believed in. And if, when I'm sixty-five years old, they're making an X-rated movie and they need a little old lady to be in it, I'm gonna say, hey, I'm right here.

And it is a sure thing that those of her fans who are still alive in 2006 will spend part of their Social Security check to see her.

Phil Heffernan, Mitchell Brothers Film Group

Marilyn Chambers

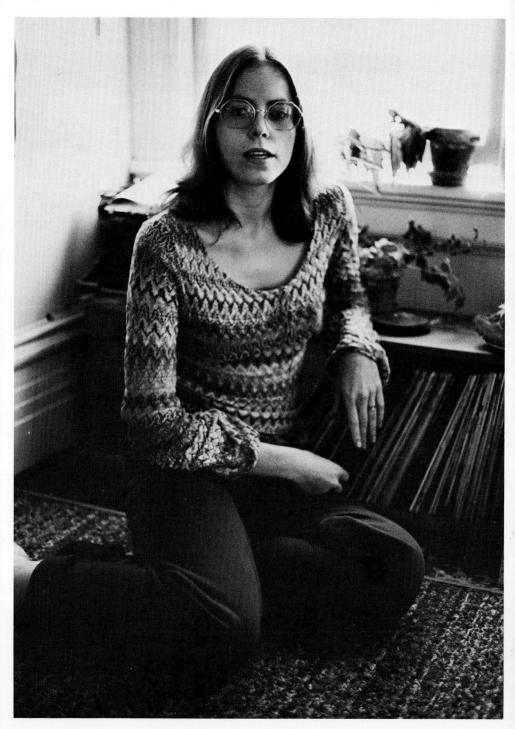

Mary Rexroth, photographed by Kenneth Turan

Marsha Jordan, photographed by
Kenneth Turan and (below) in
Head Mistress

Entertainment Ventures, Inc.

Pat Rocco (above, left), photographed by Kenneth Turan; and Bob Nelson and John Helr (above, right), in Rocco's *Autumn Nocturne*

John C. Holmes (left), photographed by Kenneth Turan

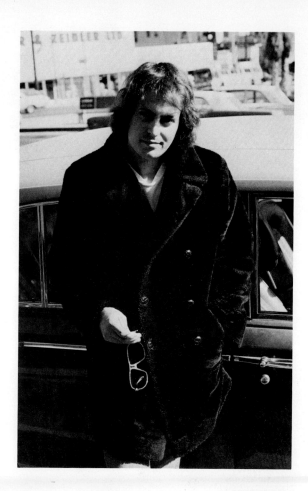

Right: Bill Osco, photographed by Kenneth Turan

Below: Fifi Watson in Bill Osco's *Mona*

Sherpix

Gerard Damiano, photographed by Kenneth Turan

Linda Lovelace   Ken Feil

Georgina Spelvin (above) and with Gerard Damiano (below) in *The Devil in Miss Jones,* written, produced, and directed by Damiano

Mitchell Brothers Film Group

Johnnie Keyes (facing camera) and Marilyn Chambers (with back to camera) in *Behind the Green Door*

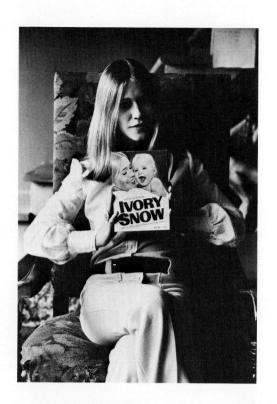

Marilyn Chambers (left), photographed by Kenneth Turan and (below) in *Behind the Green Door*

Art and Jim Mitchell, photographed by Kenneth Turan

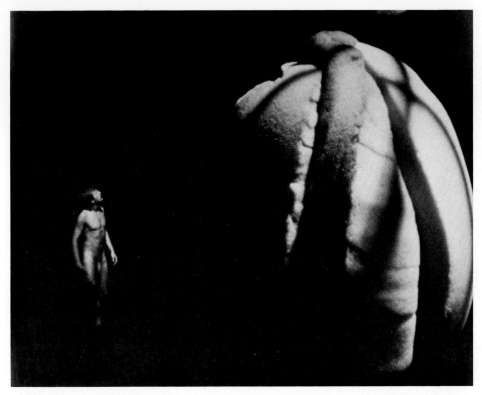

Bill Harrison, in Wakefield Poole's *Bijou*   Poolemar Productions

Wakefield Poole (facing page) and
Cal Culver (right), photographed
by Kenneth Turan

Gorton Hall, photographed by
Kenneth Turan

Mike Stevens and Joey Daniels
in Gorton Hall's *The Experiment*

Jaguar Productions

Barry Kinn, Poolemar Productions

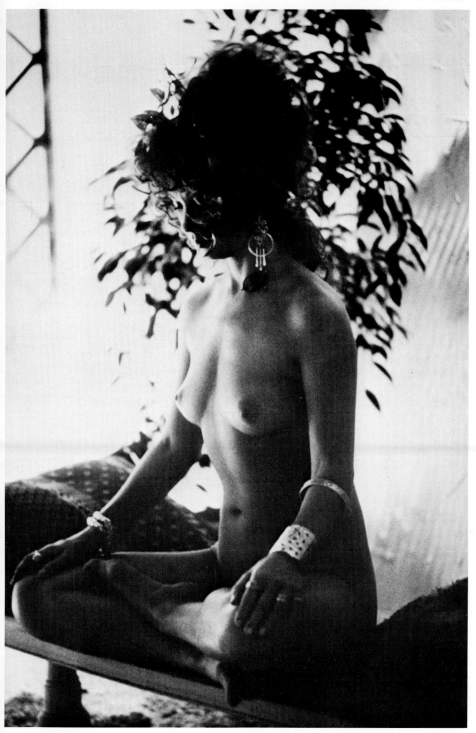

Georgina Spelvin in the David and Bathsheba sequence from *Wakefield Poole's Scandals*

Harry Reems, photographed by Kenneth Turan

12

THE AMERICAN DREAMER

AN INTERVIEW WITH GERARD DAMIANO

Gerard Damiano just can't believe it. "It keeps knocking me on the head every time I turn around," he says with the slight Brooklyn accent he is slightly embarrassed about. "Being recognized in public places, my phone never stops ringing—this whole interest in me and my films, it's sort of staggering. I think I'm the one that believes it least of all. It really hasn't caught up with me."

And with a bashful grin he relates how "it was a trip being interviewed at *Newsweek* right after the guy interviewed Bertolucci and talking about *Last Tango* and my films in the same breath." Not to mention that night in a restaurant in California when "the owner came over and said, 'Mr. John Cassavetes would like to meet you.' Now here's a man that I've admired for many, many years, for his *Faces,* his acting, just for himself, and for him to want to meet me was probably one of the biggest thrills."

It even happened at a party not too long ago, where "a young lady found out who I was, and before I left she says, 'I should get your autograph.' I said, 'Why?' She said, 'Well, I never met a celebrity before.' That was kind of nice. It's sort of amazing at times to be taken for a celebrity. So she wanted my autograph for that, and I said I'd give it to her for a dollar. And as famous as I was, I wasn't that famous."

If Jerry Damiano is prone to be just a trifle disbelieving and

149

cynical about his new fame, it is not hard to understand. He is a forty-five-year-old high school graduate who has been working since he was fourteen and can never remember collecting an unemployment check. Seven years ago he was a happily married hairdresser who owned a couple of beauty salons in Queens named "Living Doll" and "Fantasticks." He is still happily married, but the salons are gone and he has become America's preeminent director of pornography. He is the man who wrote, directed, and edited both *The Devil in Miss Jones* (called "the most ambitious blue movie yet made" by the *New Yorker's* Brendan Gill) as well as the film that needs no introduction, *Deep Throat.*

What is left to say about that film? Well, the man who made it says this: "I enjoyed making the film. I thought it would be a good film. I felt very happy about it. I had enough experience to know when I had something unique, but I had no idea it would reach the proportion that it did. For it to be the main topic of discussion in the United States of America at any particular point, that is ludicrous."

And the reason it happened, he is quick to point out with more scorn than anything else, is "because of some asshole idiots trying to legislate morality. You cannot legislate morality. There's so much talk about trying to stamp out pornography. They don't have to stamp it out. All they have to do is leave it alone, and it will die a natural death in a very short time. It is only when they try and restrict it that, in effect, what they're doing is perpetuating it.

"The American public is adult enough, intelligent enough, to know what they'd like to do and what they'd like to see. I mean, they're tired of people raising their guilt complexes by saying, 'You can do this and you can't do this.' Only pain can come from that, only anxiety can come from that. And the American public is sick of it."

This is no glib justification. This is deeply felt feeling from a man who is dead serious and sincere when he says, "There's a lot of good that can be gained out of almost any film that deals with sensuality or sexuality. I think pictures like *Throat* that have treated sex openly and honestly can only help. I don't think they're gonna hurt anybody."

Why is it, Damiano asks, looking out of soulful, weepy eyes, that "you can go out and see a film today that deals with horror, that deals with murder and mayhem and chopping bodies up and throwing heads in the sewer, and absolutely no one has anything to say about it? They just go and they see it and enjoy it. But the minute you deal with sex, everybody seems to be so uptight about even discussing it, to the point where people live together, man and wife, and they spend their entire life living together in misery, just out of convenience. Because since their earliest meetings they had never been able to openly discuss anything sexual, about how they feel, what they think about.

"I think this is terrible, to have a society so guilt-ridden when it comes to something that is only natural and human. How else can two people declare their love and their warmth or their affection for each other but in an intimate situation like that? Why is it that this is the one thing that everybody is afraid about?"

There are no ready answers, but that doesn't mean Damiano, who is unabashed about calling himself a moralist, hasn't tried to fix things. More than all the huzzahs his work has received, he is proudest of a feeling that "I'm changing the moral fiber, or the moral thinking, of the American people. I think there's so many people going around with guilt complexes who, after they see sex openly portrayed on film, can better cope with their own problems. I think I have opened a lot of doors for a lot of people. That is today the most rewarding thing that I have felt."

So there is this twinge of emotionalism about Jerry Damiano, a man who says, "If I have a level-headed approach, then I'm happy." And all his years of working, starting with the time spent as a busboy in a Manhattan Automat and in Catskill hotspots like the Flagler and Kutcher's, have developed in him a cordon of cynicism. Suggest that his life is a variant of the American Dream, and he will smile his wicked smile and say, "It sounds nice, if to be able to work hard and succeed is what America's like. I think America would like to be like that. Unfortunately, working hard is not part of the American dream. I think getting everything for nothing is part of the American dream."

For Damiano, though, work has always worked. "I think if my films have had any success," he says, "it is because the one thing I haven't given up is the ability to sit down and do the work myself, not legislate it to someone else. With *Throat* I spent a lot of time and effort polishing the film to where it would look like somebody knew what they were doing when they made it. I mean the cuts match, the color was good, the photography was good, it had all those elements. It's 20 per cent artistic temperament, but it's 80 per cent hard work."

It started seven years ago with the coincidence that Damiano's beauty shop accountant also worked for an independent, low-budget filmmaker. "I expressed a desire to learn film," he remembers. "I'd always been impulsive about different things. I would see something and fall in love with it and pursue it and then sooner or later would fall out of love with it. But with film, I think the first day I ever went on a set, as far as my life was concerned, it was all over, there was nothing else for me to do. There

151

hasn't been a waking moment, a day, an hour since that hasn't been involved in some way in film. Always, from that moment on, it's been film."

It was a time, Damiano says with a wan smile, "when it was very easy, all you had to do was work for nothing, and you could do almost anything in film. It reminded me of the Catskills, where anybody that wanted to work at their craft—comedians, musicians, anybody—could go up in the mountains in the summertime and get a chance to do it. And low-budget sex-exploitation films to a filmmaker were basically the same thing—it gave you the opportunity. I started off as a grip, then worked my way up to assistant cameraman and production manager and then finally director. I spent three years paying my dues, working constantly on half a dozen features."

There was one slight problem. "I never made a dime," he says. "It was hard trying to sustain your life because there was absolutely no money in it—everybody worked for nothing. And in three years I managed to go through everything to the point where we were having trouble eating. Thank God, I had a wife good enough to put up with my nonsense."

In the beginning, though, "it was very hard for her to understand what I was doing, my motivations behind it. She was very curious about what was happening. Then one day I asked her to come on the set and see what was going on. She spent, I think, fourteen hours with us, and then she understood. She realized it was just a lot of hard work with people that were dedicated to making films. It wasn't one big orgy."

The films Damiano worked on in those scuffling days are so obscure he's surprised when anyone besides him remembers the names. Flesh epics like *Teenie Tulip, Sex USA,* and *Marriage Manual,* trashy items that nevertheless were "basically invaluable" learning experiences. Especially a little number called *Night of the Rain,* the very first film he produced.

"We started out to make a low-budget exploitation film, and somewhere in the middle it got out of hand, and we decided to make an art film out of it," Damiano says. "We spent about ten grand on it and it was the worst piece of garbage that was ever assembled. So I taught myself editing so I could re-edit, I taught myself writing so I could rewrite the scenes that were necessary, and then directing. I changed the name to *We All Go Down,* and a distribution company took the film, and they took me as a filmmaker, and I've been working ever since. Out of that catastrophe —taking that film and changing it—I evolved as a filmmaker."

In addition, that experience taught Damiano a couple of lessons he not only still remembers but reveres as truths that ought to be self-evident. "You have to gear your film for the budget;

you cannot do it in reverse" is tenet No. 1. "All low-budget film-makers have a formula within which they have to work. And the reason most people fail is that they try to break out of the particular formula when the budget won't allow that. Usually what happens, you're halfway through the film, and you run out of money. And then you're in a lot of trouble."

This fiscal consciousness extends even to the present, when Damiano could have as big a budget as he wanted. Only he doesn't want one. "I was out in California talking to MGM about making a film for them," he says. "But I don't think films should be made for over $250,000. I think anybody that spends over a million dollars to make a film today is either a thief or an idiot. And in most cases I would assume they're thieves. What we've done is prove that you can go out, and for $25,000 you can make $3 million, rather than the majors spending $3 million to make $25,000."

Tenet No. 2, as hard-nosed and practical and, yes, level-headed as No. 1, is not to forget that "we're making films for a market, a public that is out there paying money. Anybody that makes a film for himself alone should make it in 8mm and show it in his basement for his relatives. If you expect to throw something upon the public, then you better have your public, whoever they are, in mind and make it for them. Everything I do is basically geared towards an audience, and if they like it, this makes me very happy."

It may sound like a godawful cliché, but it is the heart of Jerry Damiano's success. For behind the curly silvery hair and goatee that give him a satanic, satyric look works the canny mind of a solid, intuitive burgher. He is a man who somehow knows what the public wants before they've even figured it out themselves, like the legendary Harry Cohn of Columbia Pictures, who said he could tell by a feeling in the seat of his pants whether a picture would make it or not.

He is a man who seems not as comfortable as he might be with things intellectual, a man who had never read any Sartre, even though *Miss Jones* is, in places, very similar to *No Exit*. A man who is unashamed to say, "I've never been able to understand Ingmar Bergman." A man who shies away from self-analysis, admitting that "there definitely has to be something behind everything I do," but adding with genuine modesty, "I think my critics can probably characterize what I do better than I can. I'm probably too close to my own work to understand it fully."

Yet beneath it all is someone who has always guessed right, a man who has made a success of "finding out what everybody else was doing and then doing the opposite." A person who first does something "and then I have to look back and see what I've done

153

and try and understand it. I didn't have a vision, you know, a bell going off. But I think if I have anything that makes me unique it's that a lot of times I will go on instinct or intuition to do one thing rather than another. Basically, I have an intuitive feel for things that are going to work."

Sometime in 1971, for instance, Damiano decided that "what the industry needed was the people to put humor in sex-exploitation films. Up until then it had been completely taboo, because you were dealing with a limited hard-core sex audience that took their voyeurism very seriously. They didn't want humor; they didn't even want development of story or production values. They wanted somebody to come in, take their clothes off, and leave, and then somebody else to come in and take their clothes off. But I realized the public was ready for something else. In fact, they'd been ready for years—it's just that nobody took the time and the effort to do it before." And the result was *Deep Throat.*

Sometimes, though, Damiano gets the feeling that "I created a monster, because all of a sudden there's a lot of people who were unaware that there was such a demand for sexual enlightenment in the country. And the financial success of *Throat* has caused these people to start cranking out sex pictures, making a lot of money with crap, with just garbage, making a lot of money without ever having paused to learn the craft, to learn what making a film is all about."

There is heavy irony here, because the word in the industry is that Damiano didn't see a penny of *Throat's* profits, that his erstwhile partners eased him out when things started to look good. Damiano refuses to comment at all, saying only that "most of the things involving *Throat,* the politics that went on, I don't want to get into for personal reasons." When the *New York Times's* Ralph Blumenthal asked the same question, Damiano silenced the reporter by saying, "Look, you want me to get both my legs broken?" End of dialogue.

Not one to brood, Damiano formed another company and was "anxious to get a film out as quickly and inexpensively as possible." So he produced something called *Meatball* which "by and large was just another film. It had no message, it had nothing to say; it was just a film to make enough money to go on and do things like *The Devil in Miss Jones.*"

That film, made in two three-day weekends and costing twice as much as *Deep Throat*, is indeed, as its ads claim, "the only film of its kind to receive National Critical Recognition." It actually took an entire half-page in the Sunday *New York Times* to list the raves calling it, among other things: "the most technically polished erotic movie," "a breathtaking erotic odyssey the likes of which has never been so strongly depicted on screen," "makes

Last Tango in Paris look like a minuet at a Boston Social Tea
Party!" And it all happened because Jerry Damiano had another
one of his feelings.

"*Miss Jones* came about for basically the same reason *Throat*
came about, but adversely," he says. "With the success of *Throat*,
everybody and his brother was running around to make a sexy,
funny, camp picture. And I felt that if this is what everyone else
was doing, it was time to do something different."

In addition, Damiano felt that "having viewed sex in a humorous way would give the American public the impetus that they
needed to be adult enough to take their sexuality seriously. So I
used my real name [*Throat* was made under the pseudonym Jerry
Gerard], and I treated *The Devil in Miss Jones* as though it was a
very serious film, and I felt that that's what it was."

To play the part of Miss Jones, a spinster who commits suicide
and then gets a temporary reprieve to live it up before having to
go to hell, Damiano hired a thirty-seven-year-old ex-dancer. He
ended up with a film he felt was "much better on every level than
Throat. There's no comparison. *Throat* is a joke, a well-put-
together joke, but still a joke. But *Miss Jones*, I think, is a film.
That's the difference."

The critics saw the difference too, which gratified Damiano
no end. In line with his belief that "the only people that're worth
knowing are people that take what they're doing seriously," he is
quite serious about his films, "more serious than the average person. Maybe it was my own defense of what I was doing. If I
didn't take myself seriously, why should anybody else? So it
became very important to me."

And that, coupled with his feeling, unusual for someone in the
pornography business, that character development is important—
"to get you to understand the people, so that what they do and
what happens to them becomes important"—gave him a bit of
a problem. "I always had a great deal of trouble finding actors
that would take themselves as seriously as I was prepared to take
them. Most people in the sex-exploitation business felt they were
just coming on to ball, and that's not what I was looking for."

Sometimes, to fill in the gaps, Damiano would play some roles
himself. In *Deep Throat*, in a party scene near the end, he asks
a man, "What's a nice joint like you doing in a girl like this?"
In *Miss Jones* the role is larger: He is the man—called Albert
Gork in the credits—trapped in hell for eternity. "There's not a
thousand actors that couldn't have done it as well or better than
I," he says, "but we're still dealing in sex films, and it's very hard
to mesh the two together, sex films and serious actors."

Surprisingly, considering the amount of publicity his films have
received, little if anything has been heard from the man who

made them. This is by design, for in addition to peripheral fears about "the crap going on with police, FBI, this and that," he has "basically, always been an introverted person. I don't extend myself outwardly too much. I'm just involved in my work and doing what I do. I haven't been on the cover of *Esquire*, but that's okay, that's not where I'm at." And something else, too, the feeling that "up until *Miss Jones* I never had anything I wanted to say to the public. If people wanted to interview me because I was a porno filmmaker, I just was not interested in talking on that level. If anybody wanted to speak to me because I made films, then I was happy to talk with anyone. I just didn't want to be bothered with speaking to a lot of superficial idiots."

For it rankles something fierce, this feeling most people have that filmmakers who traffic in pornography are lucky to be considered even second-class citizens. "People still don't know what's happening," he says, shaking his head, not quite resigned. "I consider myself a filmmaker. And the only reason that most of my films dealt with pornography is because this is the only thing that would sell, the only media that an independent could work in. I was gearing my films to a specific market because there was not enough money involved to gear it to any other market.

"Working within a limited budget, working under $25,000, you could not do the great American tragedy or great American love story, you just couldn't do it. For that kind of money you had to stick in the bedroom, you had to stay in bed, and then every once in a while you would get an opportunity to express an emotion other than sex."

Damiano admits working in porno is limiting—"This *Kama Sutra* stuff, this 101 positions of sex, that's a lot of bullshit; there's only like three or four things you can actually do"—but adds, "that's what makes it exciting. You can sort of examine something under a microscope and see a million things that you didn't even know were there."

But then there is the intense irritation when "a lot of people that don't know any better assume that anyone who's involved in sex-exploitation films basically has to be a pervert. This isn't true. A lot of people assume that an actress has to go to bed with the producer because he's making a sex film. Now this isn't true. The actors and actresses that hire themselves out for exploitation films, they do their balling on screen. That means they don't have to do it before. Sweet young things, in order to get soap commercials—there's a lot of money involved in these sweet, pretty 30-second commercials that cost $100,000—they're the ones that do all the balling."

Basically, then, Jerry Damiano's life has not been traumatized by his emergence into fame. In fact, it's barely changed at all.

Though he has made yet another highly successful hard-core film, *Memories Within Miss Aggie,* he still lives with his wife and two children in the downstairs level of the two-family house in Jackson Heights, Queens, he bought when he was a hairdresser, and his mother, a former dancer who knows "her son was doing sexy pictures that the average person couldn't go to see," still lives upstairs. He is still the type of guy who will tell someone who wakes him up with a telephone call, "Naw, you didn't get me up. I had to get up and answer the phone anyway." And he absolutely delights in being what he slyly calls "almost like a real person."

"You know," he will say, "the thing that relaxes me most would probably astound everybody in that it's so normal. I like to cook. I like to spend a quiet Sunday afternoon with my wife, my family. I enjoy my family immensely. To me, to go away and to lay in the sun by a beach with my family is the most exciting thing in my life."

The thought of what Mr. and Mrs. Front-Porch America would say if they knew what the man who discovered Linda Lovelace did in his spare time makes Damiano smile again. "A lot of people must feel that my life is one mad sex orgy after another. But if sex films have proven anything to me, it's that there is nothing like a one-on-one relationship with someone you really care for, someone you can talk to. I mean, to me that's where it's at.

"But until you see the other side of the coin, you don't realize this. There are a lot of people in this country always dreaming that the grass is greener and that all the excitement and the fun of life is somewhere else. And it's not until they get to see it and to know it and to understand it that they really find out that happiness is the warmth, the tenderness, the understanding that you can find in the quiet of your own home with your wife and your family. I feel lucky I've been able to see that."

13

COMING OF AGE

THE BEST AND THE BRIGHTEST

"The thing that shocked me most about *Deep Throat*," said Universal Studios vice-president Ned Tannen, "was that nobody in the audience was a dirty old man with a raincoat. They were all young couples." It was true. Respectable people had discovered a new way to spend five dollars on Saturday night. When *The Devil in Miss Jones* opened at New York's prestigious 57th Street Playhouse, for example, an appreciative, middle-class audience came in such numbers that the weekly house take topped $35,000. Such commercial success was a response to the increased sophistication with which erotic themes were handled. Quality hard-core films were paying more attention to the psychology of recognizable characters and the exploration of intense primal human relationships. More money was being spent on actors, quality equipment, laboratory work, and better scripts that dealt with serious subjects such as male dominance and sexual mastery, confusion between fantasy and reality, sexual adequacy and dysfunction, and the role of games and masks in sexual affairs. There were also comic films mocking human pretensions and failures in the game of love.

One of the best of these was *Dynamite*, a short film directed by the Amero Brothers, who had been in the exploitation business since the mid-'60s, when they began producing soft core. *Dynamite* is an episodic slapstick comedy that follows the adventures of a sweet young thing who sells sex aids door-to-door. This hard-core Avon lady sells a special cream to one fellow that is

158

guaranteed to keep him erect for an extended period of time. The product succeeds all too well; not only can the saleslady stand on his stiff organ during foreplay, but he still has an erection after intercourse, a fact that proves embarrassing to him on the way to work. The heroine also becomes involved with a versatile couple who want to experience the ultimate thrill while making love—something she supplies by blowing them up with a stick of dynamite just as they achieve orgasm. The girl eventually ends up at a movie theater, which by chance is playing the Amero Brothers production *Corporate Queen*. Here, in *Dynamite's* rousing finale, she makes love to a strange man in the spotlit middle of the theater stage, while two employees dressed in red, white, and blue costumes tap dance to a Sousa march. The Amero Brothers have a gift for wacky farce, and the wit in *Dynamite* surfaces as the directors take potshots at the various ways sex is merchandised and sold.

In a similar vein is Danny Stone's *High Rise,* a visually inventive look at the games married people sometimes play. A young woman (Tamie Trevor) is advised by her psychiatrist to "screw her way through a high rise" in order to lose her sexual inhibitions. After a series of erotic encounters, she returns to the psychiatrist, who is not a psychiatrist at all but rather her husband. The woman relates the experiences cf the day and, aroused by her descriptions, the couple make love. The following day the woman takes the role of the psychiatrist and advises her husband to work his way through a high rise.

This ironic story is counterpointed by the slapstick quality of several of the episodes in the film. The first encounter, for example, presents a mother-fixated model railroad buff (Harry Reems) who is innocent of everything except how to make trains run on time. The heroine seduces this bewildered innocent, only to have his mother break down the locked apartment door at the moment of climax.

Another of the vignettes, of a more serious nature, highlights Danny Stone's talent as a director and his interest in the problems of filmmaking. The heroine seeks refuge in the apartment of two lesbians, who seduce her in one of the most elegant love scenes in hard-core movies. The three women occupy a bed that is wedged between large sheets of glass set at right angles to one another, with the result that the women's passion is mirrored in an infinite number of ways. Part of the scene is shot in slow motion, and it ends with a backward zoom shot that, as the image gradually broadens, reveals the crew that has been filming the lovemaking. The crew finishes its work and kills the lights, plunging the three women into total darkness. This is filmmaking of a sophisticated and highly self-conscious kind, and it is to Stone's credit that the Brechtian shot succeeds in radically altering the viewer's perception of the relationship between reality and fantasy in the film.

Stone is also good with his actors. Harry Reems does a clever burlesque turn as the infantile railroad buff, Marc Stevens acts his standard egocentric young stud, and Tamie Trevor performs with the requisite bland innocence.

Another well-known comic feature, *It Happened in Hollywood*, is a frenetic farce produced by Jim Buckley of *Screw* magazine, in a reworking of the classic saga about the making of a star. A budding thespian leaves her mundane job as a telephone operator and, after landing on every casting couch in Hollywood, rises to stardom in a randy Academy Award–winning version of *Samson and Delilah*. Not just another "rise-to-Hollywood-fame-and-fortune" story, *It Happened in Hollywood* has the technical quality to highlight its raunchy sex and violent humor. The first half of the film contains all of the usual erotic elements; the last half is a long orgy on the set of *Samson and Delilah*. *Screw* magazine promoted the film with shameless audacity, giving it 101 on the Peter Meter (one more point than *Deep Throat*), and Al Goldstein nicely summed up the virtues of the film, writing, "In the course of her upward rise to fame, our heroine, Felicity Split, gets eaten, reamed, rolled and banged in every sexual perversion possible. In all, I counted eleven come shots, and this film is more come-filled than the sperm bank." *Screw* was not alone in its praise for the film. *Variety* called it a pornographic version of Laugh-In, and *Playboy* saw it as *The Sound of Music* of the sexual revolution.

It Happened in Hollywood was directed by Peter Locke, a young filmmaker whose first, nonpornographic feature, *You've Got To Walk It Like You Talk It or You'll Lose the Beat*, was a zany satire that starred Zalman King, filmmaker Robert Downey, Allan Garfield (from *Cry, Uncle*), and Richard Pryor. Locke is an accomplished director with a gift for getting the most out of sight gags and screwball dialogue. At one point, for example, a hard-boiled egg pops out of Felicity after she utters that hoary cliché about her "cunt being hot enough to boil an egg." *It Happened* also features one of the most extraordinary devices ever invented to extend the pleasures of man- or womankind—a sexcycle worthy of an erotic-minded Rube Goldberg, with two suction cups, one for each breast, and two dildos. Operated by an obviously pleased female cyclist, what sounds like a cruel, degrading machine becomes the surreal manifestation of man's infinite capacity to invent tools for his convenience. The rider of this remarkable contraption is one of the members of The Flying Fucks, an extraordinary team of sexual acrobats. In a demonstration of their erotic agility, the woman bends over a hobbyhorse while her male partner (fully clothed and wearing a dildo strapped to his loins) swings across the room on a trapeze and impales her. During this scene and their other acts in the movie, The Flying Fucks perform with all the deadpan grace of a straight act preparing for the Ed Sullivan Show.

Dynamite, High Rise, and *It Happened in Hollywood* represent the best of the well-made comic pornographic features. Of those with serious themes, one of the most outstanding is *Behind the Green Door,* a film made by the Mitchell Brothers film group in San Francisco. Based on a classic underground story that has been circulated in mimeographed form in college fraternities and army barracks since World War II, the idea was adapted for the screen by the Mitchell Brothers in collaboration with Ed Karsh. Jim and Art Mitchell directed, and the camera work and editing were done by Jon Fontana, a gifted technician who had worked for the Mitchell Brothers for several years. Shooting and editing took seven months, at a total cost of almost $45,000— $18,000 outright, and about $24,000 in deferred payments. The Mitchell Brothers initially opened the film at a single theater, the O'Farrell, where it made $20,000 the first week and grossed $200,000 during a twenty-week run. Only then was it widely released, with heavy advance advertising and press screenings in New York, where it eventually became a financial and critical success. Adding to the favorable audience reception, together with the good reviews, was the fact that the lead—a willowy, blonde, Cybill Shepherd look-alike by the name of Marilyn Chambers—was the girl on the Ivory Snow box.

The opening scene of *Behind the Green Door* is shot with deliberate confusion. Two truckdrivers (one played by George McDonald) pull into a diner, and one tells the counterman about a strange experience he and his companion had. The rest of the film is a flashback. On the terrace of a resort hotel, the truckdrivers helplessly watch as a beautiful blonde woman (Marilyn Chambers) is kidnapped by two thugs (Art and Jim Mitchell). The intrigue deepens when the truckdrivers later go to an exclusive nightclub and must argue with the bouncer (played by Ben Davidson, the massive defensive lineman of the Oakland Raiders) before they are seated for the floor show. Toad Artell, the celebrated San Francisco mime, performs briefly, and then the mysterious blonde woman appears again. This time she is led onstage, through a green door, by six young women in nuns' habits. Over the nightclub's public address system comes an announcement that what is about to be seen—ravishment and subjugation—will bring the woman great and unexpected plea-

161

sure and that she will subsequently remember none of her terror or outrage. It is a highly theatrical moment and prepares the audience for the ritualized sexual events that follow.

The six women undress the heroine and kiss and caress her to prepare her physically and spiritually for what is to come. A spotlight hits the green door, and a black man (Johnnie Keyes) slowly comes out on stage to the accompaniment of African music. He is dressed only in black leotards that have a hole cut in the front, his erect penis jutting straight out from his body. "I just regressed myself," Keyes, who has been a professional boxer and dancer, told William Rotsler, "like I had just come out of the jungle, my natural trip, and nature just took over. I became what you saw. When I walked through the green door, I had become just a magnificent animal." Keyes begins to make love slowly to the still passive and bewildered Chambers. The pace gradually picks up, and suddenly, in a quintessential erotic moment the hypnotized Chambers realizes that she is in the grip of an exhilarating sexual charge that is carrying her over, fully conscious and sentient, into orgasm.

The ravishment of Chambers by the black man inspires many members of the nightclub audience to initiate sex acts with others in the room, and a full-scale orgy takes place, contrasting strongly with the highly ritualized sex on stage. This is followed by an intricate, bizarre, and extremely erotic sequence involving Marilyn Chambers and a group of men on a fantastic trapeze. The skillfully shot episode ends with one of the most inventive, technically complex scenes in pornographic films—a 10-minute come shot. The image of one of the men ejaculating into the heroine's mouth is shot in extreme slow motion, and it is repeated and reworked by means of dissolves, overprinting, and reverse printing. The color is solarized, and the image becomes brilliant, abstract, changeable. Chambers's elegant characterization of a victimized woman is achieved without a single line of dialogue as she moves with absolute conviction from terrorized, passive virginity to willing sexual maturity.

The *Resurrection of Eve*, the second Mitchell Brothers production starring Marilyn Chambers, was another aesthetically interesting attempt to use an example of the hard-core genre as a vehicle for social criticism. The pretentious plot, mixing memory and desire in a complex time structure, is largely incomprehensible for the first twenty minutes, but once untangled, the basic story is simple soap opera stuff: A plain young woman, sexually molested as a child, falls in love with a promiscuous disc jockey (well played by Matthew Armon). After being seriously injured in an automobile accident, her face is rebuilt by plastic surgery, and she is resurrected from a cocoon of bandages as a beautiful young woman. Faced with this new Eve, the disc jockey marries her, tires of her, and leads her farther and farther into sexual experimentation. Though reluctant at first, the woman eventually finds a particular rapport with Johnnie Keyes, the boxer who also appeared in *Behind the Green Door*. The husband becomes jealous, but he has lost her in a swinger's paradise.

The highly stylized erotic elements of the film, alternating among irony, pretension, and hard-core sex, distances the graphic impact of much of the sex footage. The photography is adequate, demonstrating once again that Chambers is a woman of great beauty. Without the protection of her mysterious silence in *Green Door*, however, she proves to be an uninspired actress.

It is altogether fitting that one of the last important pornographic films to open before the stricter Supreme Court decisions of 1973, *The Devil in Miss Jones*, is the best erotic motion picture ever made, a film that is the equal of many turned out by the legitimate industry. Director Gerard Damiano, the film's sole creator (he was producer, director, cinematographer, editor, and distributor through his own company, MB Productions) is the first filmmaker to work within the hard-core industry whose talent is mature and fully realized. With absolute control and a compulsive drive for excellence strong enough to create visually elegant movies on a small budget, Damiano is able to elicit effective performances from actors of variable skills. Guided by his own disturbing vision, he has brought dark, libidinal fantasies into being before the glaring light of the projector's arc.

The Devil in Miss Jones opens with a scene that is reminiscent of Jean-Paul Sartre's *No Exit*. A woman (Georgina Spelvin) sits on a bench in a cinderblock basement. She is masturbating and endlessly reciting, "I'm so close, so close. I want to come." Her companion in this nightmare is a demented man (played by Damiano) who is waiting for God to manifest himself in the form of a fly. The woman turns to him for relief, promising any and all kinds of sex, but the man, self-absorbed and indifferent to her needs, refuses to help her in her painful quest for orgasm. This then is hell, not the place of fire (prefigured in the title shot of a cauldron of poured molten steel) but of endless sexual frustration, waiting, and despair. The scene sets the disturbed, frenzied tone of the rest of the film, which details why this woman will spend eternity here.

In her New York City apartment Justine Jones (her Christian name borrowed from De Sade's classic innocent), a thirtyish spinster, is tormented by a harsh, self-imposed celibacy. She wanders about disconsolately, examines her nude body in the mirror, starts to caress herself but dares not. Instead, she goes into the bathroom, runs a tub of scalding water, settles in, and opens her veins with a razor. "Oscars have been won", *Playboy* critic Bruce Williamson has written, "for scenes no better than the poignant, unnerving opening of *Miss Jones."* For her suicide, Justine Jones is sent straight to hell.

The staging area of the netherworld turns out to be a lovely farmhouse in the Pennsylvania countryside, where Justine Jones is interviewed by a kindly man who does the Devil's work. As she stares in sick fascination at a burning match which the man holds between his fingers, the heroine realizes that, although she has led a spotless life, she will be condemned to eternal damnation. In despair, she suggests that she be allowed to stay out of hell until she has sinned enough to warrant confinement there. "If I have my life to live over," she says, "I would live a life engulfed . . . consumed . . . by lust." And it is the pursuit of lust that forms the rest of the movie. The virgin, whom life has passed by, sets out to sin and to learn all the varieties of love.

Harry Reems plays the character who initiates her sexual life. He teaches her the intricacies of oral intercourse, painfully deflowers her, and roughly takes her anal maidenhead, driving her to climax. Justine Jones is then introduced to lesbian love during a tender erotic encounter in which her partner rubs her all over with silver lotion and then makes love to her on a waterbed, the photography emphasizing the glistening textures of bodies and the swelling patterns of movement. She also plays lustfully with a snake.

Other traditional hard-core activities are not lacking in *The Devil in Miss Jones,* and Damiano has directed them with as much prurient interests as could be mustered by the most depraved stag film director. There is a masturbation scene in a bathtub during which the actress directs a stream of water from a rubber hose into her mouth, onto a nipple, and into her body orifices. In another scene two men make love to her simultaneously, one in vaginal intercourse, the other anally. In a third episode she and another woman take turns fellating a man, and, after he ejaculates, the women pass the semen from mouth to mouth. All of this action is shot in explicit detail, with the added erotic dimension of Justine's direct, seemingly spontaneous dialogue, her constant verbalization of her needs and feelings.

The Devil in Miss Jones made Georgina Spelvin, whose performance was almost universally praised, into a celebrity almost overnight, and she has made a number of films since, including *Well of Frenzy, Memoirs of a Male Chauvinist Pig,* and *High Priestess of Sexual Witchcraft.* The thirty-seven-year-old Spelvin—the name is a pseudonym—is not strikingly attractive: She has somewhat imperfect features and a sharp speaking tone.

Her acting talent, however, is substantial, and as she performs, she projects a beauty of spirit and character that makes her fascinating to watch. In *The Devil in Miss Jones,* she makes the audience believe in the lonely, frustrated spinster. One can accept her descent into lust and the obscene monologue she recites with conviction and genuine feeling, and she has a way of making sex seem intellectual as well as animal.

Little in Georgina Spelvin's background would lead one to expect this excellence. She has been around the edges of show business all her adult life but without a sustained career or great success. She has sung in USO shows, spent some time in the ballet corps at Radio City Music Hall, danced at the Latin Quarter, worked in the chorus of Broadway musicals, and performed with three small ballet companies. She has also been around the motion-picture business, doing some Nudie inserts for Radley Metzger in the mid-'60s and for several years producing and editing television commercials for a large Manhattan advertising agency, where she first met Damiano. During 1972 Spelvin returned to work in sex films because she was flat broke, and it seemed like an easy way to pay the rent. She performed in a couple of routine hard-core films and then went to Damiano looking for behind-the-camera work on *The Devil in Miss Jones.* "She came up to do commissary," said Damiano. "She was going to cook, and then we got to talking, and I realized that she was the person for the film."

Damiano discovered something special in Georgina Spelvin that he felt was right for the main character, but the actress herself makes it quite clear that she is *not* Justine Jones and that the film is not a spiritual autobiography. "Miss Jones has a whole set of mores and hang-ups that we talk about all the time," Spelvin said in a candid interview with Al Goldstein. "She finds herself in her mid-thirties never having had been able to love anything or anyone. This includes herself. She feels that she has been a very virtuous person, that she's done everything she's been taught, and therefore doesn't understand why her life is so barren." Georgina Spelvin does not believe that of her own life. She speaks of past husbands and lovers and now lives openly with Claire Lumiere, the woman who is her partner in the lesbian sequence of *The Devil in Miss Jones.* Spelvin does, however, have a real sympathy for the character of Justine Jones. Describing her cinematic transformation from spinster to sensual woman, she says Justine "experiences a complete reversal in which she makes everything around her an object of her own sexual gratification, of her own need for warmth, but she's not loving. She's not giving anything of herself. She's demanding; she's taking."

The character's final lonely, fruitless pursuit of orgasm is the

165

logical extension of sex without personal commitment. The only quality that Justine Jones values in any man is the stiffness of his erection, and thus the men in *Miss Jones* are without personalities and sometimes without faces, mere sex objects. *Miss Jones* neatly reverses the traditional male and female polarities in hard-core films by presenting a situation in which a woman uses men solely as a means of sexual gratification. Only in one scene is there some sense of genuine communication and feeling between the performers. Some of this material, involving Spelvin and two men, was shot by Damiano while they were rehearsing (Georgina is arousing the men and assisting them in achieving penetration), and they did not know that they were being filmed. It is the immediate, spontaneous, sympathetic quality of the sexual activity that makes the episode among the most powerful in the film.

As a whole, *The Devil in Miss Jones* is a sexual fantasy that uses the direct presentation of the sex act to create a portrait of depravity and damnation. Damiano beautifully weds the hard-core action to plot and character, and his interest in the consequences of sexuality—seen through the erotic life of one particular woman—leads to what everyone has always called for—a sex film that is both good and dirty. The pansexualism in *Miss Jones* expresses a fear of sentimental attachments, demanding personal relationships, and lasting commitments. Those who were upset by the film, who found it disturbing and depressing, were really complaining that it was in a sense too good, too close to the harsh, unpleasant realities of the dark side of the erotic imagination.

14

THE ELVES IN SANTA'S PORNO WORKSHOP

AN INTERVIEW WITH THE MITCHELL BROTHERS

"We're giving one of those 4-hour interviews that last only thirty-five minutes."

—Jim Mitchell

The Mitchell Brothers are not crazy about chitchat. "I'm not interested in sitting back and acting like we've done something, because we haven't. We made a few fuck movies," says brother Art. Not in the habit of being reflective, if they had their druthers they'd be out somewhere shooting film or dubbing sound or checking the grosses. The joy is in the action, not the reaction. "It's worthless to talk about doing a thing," Art continues. "You gotta go do it."

The talk this day is in the office of their movie theater, the O'Farrell in San Francisco, a square, garage-like building painted a delightful shade of baby blue and punctuated by huge multi-colored floating flowers that probably embarrasses the stolid washing-machine showplace across the street. But don't be fooled. The atmosphere inside is business, strictly business.

And the Mitchells, twenty-eight-year-old Art and thirty-year-old Jim, are tough cookies. Intense, somewhat cynical, whimsical when it suits them, and very hardworking, they are serious about what they do and perhaps just a bit tired of constantly having to explain, justify, and defend. Almost identical, with their receding blond hair, mustaches, tinted sunglasses, and hip-casual clothes, they are the makers, the doers, the tireless elves in Santa's porno workshop.

Together they form what might be called a hard-core conglomerate. They have made *Behind the Green Door* a million-dollar-plus-grossing feature, showing it in their own theater and distributing it themselves to nearly two dozen other theaters around the country, and followed it with another successful big-budget feature, *The Resurrection of Eve*. And that was not beginner's luck either, for the Mitchell Brothers have been in the industry as long as anyone, long enough for the wonder and strangeness to have gone out, long enough to make it a job of work, nothing more or less.

Almost alone of the people who started the pornography wave, they have made the jump from quick cheapies to classy features that get reviewed in the right places and exude the desired élan. They are the first to admit that "the old fuck-movie days are over," proud of the hard-won expertise they have brought to hard core's *nouvelle vague,* as well as the hard-nosed and, yes, businesslike way they run their end of it.

"It's a real business," emphasizes Art, "and we've really learned it by ourselves. We haven't brought in a bunch of outsiders. We've never believed in the idea that if you want to do something go ask someone else to do it for you. I mean you gotta do it, you gotta be in on the doing of it. If you don't, you miss all the fun, the experience, the money."

And so the Mitchells set up their own distributing company, and now, boasts Jim, "We're booking our fucking movies on a percentage basis. We're making more money per ratio per capita than a lot of people in the movie business." And that money has allowed them to take care of their own people, like actress Marilyn Chambers, who, they estimate, will make a minimum of $25,000 for her share of *Green Door* because she is getting a percentage of the profits. "No one's made that kind of money in hard core before," Jim says. "We were the ones who started paying actors residuals. We know we're the first, no one has even come close to us."

It all started modestly enough back in 1969 when the boys were at San Francisco State working out of the film department. "Yeah, we wanted to make movies," says Art, "but, shit, who doesn't? That's like saying, 'I want to be a rock star.' " Or, as Jim says, "We figured, 'Let's make movies, why be a lawyer, why be a dipshit?' I was a college punk, you know, you didn't know shit when you were in school."

They had grown up in the East Bay area, some fifty miles from San Francisco. "We both came from like a rootless middle-class kind of thing, transient, almost like up from the dust bowl," says

Jim. "My father was like a con, an ex-con, kind of a highwayman of sorts in his earlier days, settled down a bit you know, married when he was thirty-five. I got out of it when I was seventeen, shit, you know, I ran away from home kinda like everyone else to get the fuck out of the house and to get out of a small town." After two years in the army he tried college, but it didn't last. "The same semester I was gonna graduate, S. I. Hayakawa came in, there were riots, strikes. I was on strike, and I never went back."

Instead, he and his brother went to the corner of Polk and O'Farrell and in January of 1969 bought a building more than thirty years old that had done time as a garage, a Buick salesroom, even a gay after-hours pub. Six months later they opened it as the O'Farrell Theater, and the fun began.

"It was beaver in those days," says Jim, laughing slightly at how little it took to please the folks. "Bill Osco'd come up from L.A. with loops in a suitcase, $50 each. We'd take 'em in the back and hold 'em up to the light. It was always the girl on the bedspread. We're saying, 'Hey, honey, get your finger in there.' At the time that was hot stuff. It was really hot sticking a camera up some girl's box, run it on the screen, and everybody'd file in. You know that was really hot shit."

Things got hotter soon enough, and the Mitchells claim they just might be the first people to ever show real live hard core in a theater. And the police came soon after and handed the Mitchells the first of some thirty-odd busts. "The next morning it's in the fucking paper with a front-page picture—you know, 'Horny Theater Raided,' or something like that," says Jim. "I mean like that was like unbelievable. Theoretically, this is San Francisco." Endless trials followed, which mostly came to nothing, and, says Jim, they "got really good at going to court, being loose and laughing and joking, giving tickets out to all the judiciary and all the fucking jailers."

More important, in the same relatively short period of time they also became proficient at filmmaking. They poured out, by their own count, 236 films with titles, albeit titles like *Wild Campus, Rampaging Nurses,* and *Runaway Hormones,* to show at their theater and any others that were interested. In a dazzling tribute to the Protestant Ethic, they would grind them out every week, sometimes two or three a week, feeding an insatiable public. These films weren't great, the Mitchells realize, but on the other hand, they were made, which is something.

"I think they're pretty good for what they are," Art allows about the old days. "We were under the limitations of time and money. Now for that kind of film, for that time, I think they're great. 'Cause I'll challenge anyone to get together and do a movie like that and turn out anything better. We couldn't even do it anymore; we couldn't do it now, no way. We could only do it then because we were much stronger and hungrier."

Without money, unable to "learn from making the kind of movies we wanted to make," the Mitchells learned from shooting hard core. "We learned about fucking and about people and about bodies and we made a lot of money because the turnover was easy and we had low costs," Art continues. "We learned the business, we learned how to, what it's kind of all about. You can't step into something, you know. You need a lot of hard work, millions of hours, that's all."

The culmination of that was *Behind the Green Door,* which pulled in, says *Variety,* $100,000 a day since its star was discovered to be the lady in the picture on endless boxes of Ivory Snow. Pegged for an eventual $10-$20 million gross by the ever-optimistic Mitchells, it is also the only film of its type to feature an honest-to-gosh National Football League star, albeit not in a porno role. "We asked ourselves, 'Who's the baddest ass in the Bay Area,' and came up with Ben Davidson," says Jim. "He said he'd talk to his wife. He played a bouncer for $500, but Pete Rozelle (NFL commissioner) was pissed off when he found out."

Despite the acclaim that greeted *Green Door*—"sex as ritual, sex as fantasy, sex as it could only be in the movies," celebrated Arthur Knight; "a kind of sexual *Space Odyssey*" added *Playboy*'s Bruce Williamson—the Mitchells' heads have not been turned. Although their success has increased their self-confidence and resulted in a couple of invitations to address, no kidding, the local Lions Club, Art still says, "I don't really feel famous, I really don't. It's not something you really think about a lot; it doesn't really affect you." And they realize that pornography, as Jim says, "is still out on the edge" of accepted culture. Even a favorable Supreme Court decision wouldn't have mattered, he says, because "it's not gonna affect Nixon's head, nothing a court could say would change his mind on how he feels. And as long as there's that kind of official sentiment there's not gonna be any radical embracing of hard-core pornography. Nixon's got to go. When he's out, and you have a different administration, and all of a sudden, say, a guy's invited to the fucking White House or something to show his flick, hey, everything then becomes big business. Until then, it'll be like little minnows swimming through the pond."

Little minnows, though, can do big business, something that the Mitchells have never forgotten. "Our early motivation was almost a hundred per cent, you know, in it for the money," says Art, and Jim adds, "There was never any other motivation, it's always a hustle, this was a hustle, a way to make some bucks. It was an opportunity to make money and we latched onto it, you know. I mean, I wouldn't want to take it so seriously and think it was anything else than that. It's like, if it all fucking folded up tomorrow, then I'd have to get by somehow. I'd have to get into something."

Still, despite all this hard talk, the Mitchells have a soft spot for their films, a tendency to try for quality when faced with the dilemma of whether "to do a great film or just to stop trying to be so pretentious and fucking knock 'em out, man, people like to see a new one every week."

"We've been trying to make the best movies we could all along, but we've been trying to look at the problem realistically," says Art. "Our movies," adds Jim, "have always been dirty, hard core; that was the idea. And at the same time we tried to put a title on them when no one else did. We tried to put a music score behind it when nobody else did. It was always, you know, 'Make a better fuck movie.'"

And if there is a path to better pornography, what could it be except, you guessed it, the sweat of the old brow? "Yeah, a lot of hard work, that's all I can say, a lot of hard work," says Art. "A lot of hours solving our own problems and trying to struggle forward, trying not to be too naïve was the only way we were gonna get something out of it. We have a real ethic; there's no reason to sit around and bullshit each other all day long, you know. Like I'm trying to tell you, it's what we can actually produce that actually means something." Even Richard M. Nixon should be able to understand that.

15

HARD-CORE STARS

TWO INTERVIEWS

"It's like learning the Ivory Snow girl made blue movies."
—Summit County Prosecutor Stephen M. Gabalac discussing the possibility that the 1973 All-American Soapbox Derby was rigged

•

"If the International Olympic Committee authorizes copulation as an athletic activity in the 1976 Montreal meeting, Harry Reems has to be the winter-book favorite."
—Andrew Sarris, *The Village Voice*

"I think he could ball at high noon in Macy's window, or center stage on the Johnny Carson show. . . . When I say it's a pleasure to work with him, I think you know what I mean."
—Linda Lovelace, *Inside Linda Lovelace*

"It's a beautiful marble tower, so smooth, so hard, so warm. You throb in my hands, I can feel the strength, the life, the power."
—Georgina Spelvin in *The Devil in Miss Jones*

MARILYN CHAMBERS, 99 44/100 PER CENT PURE

Marilyn Chambers is an angelic child, a WASP princess, a vision of the Fantastic. Long, soft, cornsilk blonde hair, blue eyes, a jailbait smile. A stunningly vulnerable waif, the secret center of every dirty daydream, clean and wholesome enough to be sitting pretty on the front of millions of boxes of Ivory Snow. But for how long?

Procter & Gamble awoke one morning to find that their baby-cuddling cover girl was also doing time as the hard-core star of the highly erotic *Behind the Green Door*. "Mrs. Clean Is Porno Cutie," headlined the irrepressible *New York Daily News*, while the *New York Post* called her "A Girl Who Gets Back to Basics" and *Variety* labeled the whole brouhaha "the biggest non-criminally angled publicity break for a porno feature in New York." And Marilyn Chambers, just turned twenty-one, thought the whole thing was, well, kind of goofy. "If they were smart, they'd play it up in a good way. They'd sell more Ivory Snow boxes," she says, grinning. "People who like the film can just buy Ivory Snow and wash with it, wash their souls clean."

Perhaps the most beautiful woman in hard core, ethereal enough to make it seem she might just float away, she delights in the fact that "a lot of people are surprised when I tell them, 'Yeah, that's me.' 'What, are you kidding?' they say. 'I expected to meet some chick with VD or extremely dirty hair and zits and stuff and fat.'

"See, my image is clean, wholesome, all-American, Ivory Snow. That's what people want to see; that's their vision of a person maybe they'd like to go to bed with, a sexy person, right? So give it to 'em, that's what I figure. I'm a very simple person, you know. That's fine with me. I'm kind of straight to a certain extent. I believe in love. I don't think there's too many people that could say I'm disgusting and crude."

What she is is disarmingly candid, especially where sex is concerned. "It's outta sight, just outstanding," she says. "I find that one of my biggest releases is sex. It gets rid of so much tension. It's so healthy. You have a good lay, and you know how good it feels. You can just go out and face the day and you feel great." All said with the sweet voice and smile of a giggling ingenue talking about her first big date. The contrast can be disconcerting.

Marilyn's background corresponds pretty much to the way she looks: Connecticut-born, upper middle class, working in commercials in New York since she was fifteen, "a lot of television, a lot of bullshit, Clairol, Pepsodent—just the regular run-of-the-mill stuff." By the time she was eighteen she was working full time in the Big Apple and soon had a small part in a big movie, *The Owl and the Pussycat*, starring Barbra Streisand and George Segal. In less hectic, more conventional times, that might have been the beginning of an upwardly mobile Lana Turneresque career, but for Marilyn Chambers it was the start of a disenchantment with what passes for conventional cinematic sexual morality, a disenchantment that led her to the world of hard core.

In her *Pussycat* part she was in bed, presumably quite naked, when Barbra and George bring a television over to a friend's apartment. "For Christ's sake, I'm sleeping in bed, and they made me wear underpants, a bra, and a body stocking underneath that bed, that's how uptight they were," she says, still annoyed, talking with the righteous anger and wrinkle-faced intensity that seem unfortunately to belong exclusively to the young. "And all these union guys are just standing around, standing up on the rafters, and they're whistling and going, 'Hey honey, want to meet me after?' It's just so obnoxious and sleazy." And, she adds, dishonest as well.

"This fake simulation stuff, that's a bunch of crap," she says, as upset as any bluenose. "Faking it is horseshit. I don't want any part of that; I don't agree with that at all. If there is a sex scene, *fuck it, do it, don't be so uptight!* I think the thing that bugs me the most is going out and seeing a film that's really far out and then it turns out to be a lie as far as sex goes." Like *The Virgin and the Gypsy*, f'rinstance.

"Oh, Franco Nero, he is *really* sexy," she says, becoming a fetching, coy Lolita, her voice going all gooey. "There's a scene where he starts to take this girl's clothes off, and I said, 'Fantastic, oh wow, I've gotta see this.' But"—and her voice edges quickly into outrage—"*you don't even get to see her boob!* And then that's it, the scene goes blank, and you just go, 'What?' I think that's so damned dishonest. Why do people do this? Why don't they just show it? Not for a long time—don't flaunt it—just do it when it's called for. Because it's a part of your everyday fucking life. Because too many people fake it, and that's our problem."

And so, when the people shooting Clint Eastwood's *Magnum Force* in San Francisco became intrigued enough with all the Ivory Snow publicity to ask her to do a small part, she turned it down very, very cold.

"I'd get killed, fall out of seventeen stories, you know, it's just this blood-and-guts, cops-and-robbers stuff. That really turns me off," she says, making a face. "Plus my part was supposed to be some chick that didn't have any clothes on, pretending to go down on this guy. That's a lot of shit. I don't want a part of that. I don't agree with that at all. I just said, 'Bleah.' "

But all this was still in the future when Marilyn first came to California as part of an *Owl and the Pussycat* publicity tour and very definitely liked what she saw.

"I'd never been here before, and I just freaked out. I said, 'Aachh, what am I doing in New York? I'm crazy.' I went back to New York, I packed all my stuff, and I just came to California. I didn't know what I was gonna do—I didn't care."

For what Marilyn had been running into in New York was "a lot of producers and all this crap that all they want to do is sleep with you if you want to get a part. Yeah, that thing still exists. That really kind of got me down. It's a really sleazy, sleazy, under-the-table deal, all these guys in pin-striped suits and ties saying, 'Hey, well honey, want to do a fuck film?' " done with just the right degree of mimicked leer.

"New York was just the most unprotected place in the world. There are a lot of freaks in that town, and as far as sex films go that's where you're gonna get in trouble, because those guys just want to get into your pants. It was really a hard-core trip, it made me so nervous, so uptight. It made me afraid of getting back into dramatics again, because of all the nasty people I met in the past."

So Marilyn Chambers was out in San Francisco, fully prepared to be "just another old hippie chick, probably living with my old man and living off welfare or something, working as a waitress." However, two gentlemen named Mitchell happened to see a film called *Together*, and none of that was necessary. Marilyn had more or less starred in that benighted cheapie about a sensory perception school—"you know, couples go, touching and feeling and all this crap." The *New York Times* called it "a load of drivel slapped together as a movie," and Marilyn agrees, calling it "a rip-off that made about 6 million bucks," while she herself got only $250 for acting plus "doing voice-overs for the whole movie in a closet." But the Mitchell Brothers liked her in it and inquired about a role in what was to be their first full-length feature, the soon to be infamous *Behind the Green Door*.

By this time the Mitchells' quickie movies were getting a lot of competition. "Sex was being crammed down everybody's throat in this country," and since they weren't about to desert their audience, they decided, says Marilyn, "if it's gonna be crammed down their throats, let's do it right." So they got a sizable amount of money together and began what was to be more than "just a regular old fuck film." It was to be, if such a thing could be possible, a genuine pornographic epic.

At first, Marilyn wasn't quite sure where she wanted to fit into this sexploitation extravaganza. "They asked me if I wanted a balling or a nonballing role, and I said, 'Nonballing. Jesus, I don't want to get too dirty, you know.' " But the Mitchells talked her into it. "They made me see it was cool even though I did go through the 'Oh, God, I feel guilty' and 'Oh, what am I going to tell my this and that?' I liked their approach; they didn't say, 'Well, honey, you gotta screw me first.' It was, 'Here, smoke a joint,' you know, far out."

There were, of course, other considerations. First was money.

Marilyn was offered a terrific deal in comparison to the rest of the industry—$2,500 up front plus a percentage of the profits equal to about a penny for every dollar the film makes, which has been working out to between $2,000 and $2,500 per month. So much that Marilyn has turned herself into a corporation, "putting her in a better position," *Variety* says, "to capitalize on her gross national product." They also gave her—another rarity —some choice as to who she'd be working with. "I don't have to put up with these weirdos, ugly, yech! If I say, 'Oh, God,' then they say, 'Okay.' " Moreover, she had faith in the Mitchells' general aura of being straightshooting good guys—"They're honest, and they pay you, and they don't try to fuck around with your head"—and their willingness to treat her the way she wanted to be treated: as an actress, buddy, and don't you forget it.

"I'm a serious actress, you know," she says in a serious way. "I've been to acting school and all that shit. Balling on the screen is not embarrassing at all; it's just another phase of acting. It's just a very little part that a lot of people are afraid to express that is being brought into the open. I have faith in myself personally that I can be a good actress, and that's my main goal."

The acting experience she got via *Green Door,* while unconventional, has been tremendous, she feels, even though she doesn't get to speak a single line in the whole movie. "In the beginning I said, 'You mean I don't get to say anything? What is this?' But I found out in the end that if I had said anything, it would have blown it. It would've been just like everything else. People would've said, 'For Christ's sake, why doesn't she keep her mouth shut?' " So she did, and found herself in the difficult position of trying to convey everything with her actions. Things like orgasms, which, she feels, "people are getting tired of. So you have to make it different every time, which gets harder and harder. But it's definitely a challenge."

She is serious enough about her acting to be thinking about advanced age—"I'll play the older woman; I won't take my clothes off any more"—and to fantasize about really hitting the big time. "Jeez," she says, "someday I'd love to meet Ingmar Bergman and do something with him. He sounds like a great kind of person to work with, that relaxed scene he has. That's my dream."

But for now she has other plans. She has made a second Mitchell Brothers' film called *The Resurrection of Eve,* announced by a very tasteful full-page ad in *Variety.* She has also become a nightclub performer under the tutelage of Chuck Traynor, Linda Lovelace's former husband. And now more than ever she is trying to avoid the tawdry boring productions that characterize most of the industry, looking for that evanescent "good part" that will convince the doubters that, yes, there is some real acting going on here. "I'm in a position now to be able to choose what I want to do," she says. "And if I make the mistake of going and doing something stupid, then I'll blow it. Maybe I'm being naïve, I don't know, but I think if I stay away from things like that and only settle for something really good, then they'll accept me for the things I do on screen, may it be sex or whatever."

Sex films, it must be said, have had an advantage for Marilyn that more conventional fare may lack. "You know," she says, obviously pleased, "it satisfied a lot of my innermost desires. It was definitely a fantasy trip. I still have some little fantasies—like a guy screwing a guy from the back and then a girl sucking the guy off, that'd be freaky—but I don't have as many as I did before.

"You know, every woman has a fantasy of wanting to be raped and done in by six chicks and everything else. It's been a pretty prevalent one with me, I know. There's nothing you can do, like you're strapped down, and, you know, that kind of turns me on a little bit. And I say, 'I can't get out of here anyway so I might as well enjoy it while I'm here. Why fight it?' "

Some parts of the ravishment were less pleasant than others—having someone ejaculate in her face was "very humiliating at first" and "the trapeze things, I mean that's not a fantasy, that was just exhausting"—but the lesbian scenes, those were something else again. "I'll tell you something," she says, her face lighting up. "Those chicks really fucking turned me on. I mean they really know what they're doing; they really impressed me. I really got off behind that because it was a fantasy. I didn't want to do it, really. I wouldn't do it in private with another woman at all. Because as far as lesbian scenes go, I'm really not into it. I mean, when I was younger, a lot younger, when I lived in New York, I had a couple of experiences with women that were great. I mean to me it wasn't a guilt-ridden experience. It was by a much older woman who really turned me on to something that was far out. Of course, I worried, 'Oh, Jeez, am I a lesbian?' But I found out that I really enjoy men a lot more. In the *Green Door* scene with the six women I was lucky. I was the submissive one. I was the one that everything was being done to. So I didn't have to initiate, see? That's what I've been afraid of. So I could fantasize even more on what was happening."

As far as other folks' sexual fantasies go, Marilyn says, "I'm sure a lot of people think that people in erotic films are dirty, have clap, syphilis, everything. It's surprising, but nobody I know had it, nobody in the last two films. We have tests before we do anything; we make sure everybody's got the test. And everybody has been fine, because they know it's their business, so they're interested in being clean. I mean, who wants to get the clap? Nobody."

And what about all those wonderful on-screen orgasms, the ones you write home to the boys about? "Those are secrets of the trade," Marilyn says, smiling that teen temptress smile again. "I can't say I don't enjoy it, 'cause if I didn't I wouldn't be doing it, but, you know, you can't come every time. A woman can fake an orgasm; at any time, any place in her life, a chick can usually fake it.

"I find it thoroughly enjoyable, but I just kind of let my feelings stop at a certain point, you know, just physical pleasure. In sex you can't be concentrating on what you're doing, where in a film I would say that you are concentrating on what you're doing, making sure you're doing everything right. And, well, when you're really doing it, you just . . ." Even for Marilyn Chambers, some things can't be put into words.

Yet like any true believer, she is something of an evangelist. "Our movies," she says with as much hope as pride, "are changing the American people. Sometimes they say, 'What is this *Deep Throat*? What are they doing? My God, I can't handle it.' But actually I think it really helps couples free themselves. Your mother always told you that masturbation was bad, sex was nasty, 'Now don't do it,' and that's a bunch of shit. 'Cause it's one of the healthiest things you could ever do for yourself.

"Our goal is, I don't know what to call it, to un-hang-up people. They wouldn't be so uptight about sex, I think, if they see the people on the screen not being uptight about it."

Besides, the Mitchell Brothers' O'Farrell Theater in San Francisco, where *Behind the Green Door* played for more than a year, is "a nice place to go," Marilyn feels. "You're not embarrassed to walk in there; you don't have to hide under your raincoat. It's not like that any more.

"We went on a radio talk show once, and this woman called and said they were having a bridge party—there were eight women there—and they were so turned on by hearing about *Green Door* that they were going to drag their husbands to it that night. I just said, 'Oh far out.' You know, that's where I'm satisfied, where people like that, people who are really hung up about sex, can get off on it and be curious."

Marilyn estimates that the reaction to the film has been 90 per cent favorable, but there is always that other 10 per cent, who say, " 'This is fucked up. My wife and I have never had oral intercourse for our whole lives and we're not gonna start now, and how come our kids are listening to this?' " and so on. There have also been some obscene phone calls, which soon ceased being a goof, and are in fact one of the reasons why Marilyn prefers to go by a stage name. She doesn't use her parents' name, either, and that's another story.

"Have they seen my films? Not on your life. They know what I do, but we don't really talk about it too much. I can dig it. I don't want to push my trip on them; they haven't been pushing theirs on me either. I hope someday they'll come to realize it's not as bad as they think. It's something that I do want to do; I'm not being forced into it 'cause of the money or whatever. I feel it is an important subject to get out into the open for everybody's benefit, and if I can be one of those people to help, I will."

And so we take our leave of Marilyn Chambers, a typical California girl who can't quite understand why "sex is such a touchy subject. It shouldn't be, you know. It's everyday life. But so many people want to hide it; they want to cover it up and make believe it doesn't exist."

For someone whose earliest memories, "ever since I can remember being a little girl" were being told "sex, sex, terrible, bad, awful thing," Marilyn Chambers has come a long way. She can't quite empathize with people who "turn bright red to the point of dying when they think about or speak about masturbation." She reads "a lot of dirty books, as many as I can get my hands on," and recommends smoking a joint before going to bed in order to open up sensual awareness. She feels "our world will be a hell of a lot better when people have healthier attitudes about sex" and wonders angrily why "they can put a man on the moon and they can't find some birth-control technique that's not going to hurt you to take or do."

Yet underneath this flash Marilyn Chambers is the woman who says, "People who take themselves too seriously get boring after a while," the radiant, spunky, sexual child who turned down a Hollywood producer's offer of a house in Los Angeles, a car, acting school, plus a sizable monetary stipend in exchange for one conjugal visit a month. "I had the choice of being in a plastic world or being in my own world," she says. "I didn't want to be what somebody's else's computer wanted me to be. I wanted to be me."

HARRY REEMS, THE GP
BODY IN X-RATED FILMS

Up a little earlier than usual, Harry Reems stumbles a bit in the kitchen of his Manhattan apartment, trying to get his bearings. Suddenly he sees the jar he wants, takes out a pill, and holds it up for inspection, his naturally bright eyes positively twinkling.

"He takes his Vitamin E every morning," he announces sturdily. Then, his voice deepening, he adds, "He doesn't let his public d-own-n-n-n." He swallows, chuckles, and, dressed in faded cut-off jeans and a patchwork flannel shirt he made himself, ambles off into the next room.

Suntanned, well-built, and handsome, with curly black hair and a triumphant mustache, Harry Reems is one of the biggest male stars ever to hit hard core. "In New York, out of, I'd say, eleven or twelve films that have made over a million dollars, I'm the lead in about nine of them," he says, citing a list that includes *The Devil in Miss Jones, It Happened in Hollywood,* and, as the doctor who discovers what ails Linda Lovelace, *Deep Throat.* He is one of the few porno stars to command a guaranteed minimum salary and was the first totally nude male to grace the pages of *Playboy.* And what does he say about it all? "You could call me the Shirley Temple of fuck films, take an X film, and make it an R because I have a GP body."

For though he looks like pornography's Burt Reynolds, he is more like one of the Marx Brothers, mugging, joking, laughing—a genuine, lovable zany. He has endless accents and intonations, switching easily from Scottish burr—"So ye want to be interviewing me, lad?"—to crusty old farmer—"Woo, some whiskers you got." When he tells you he was "an avid track fan, a long-distance runner" in his youth, he just can't resist adding, his voice rising, his grin expanding, "He still is, he's a great endurance man!" He surrounds himself with people he calls characters because "I like happiness, I love to smile. It's sunshine. It's pink balloons and bubbles. It's tripping in the park on a Sunday afternoon. We've only got one life to live, and people that hang themselves up with 'I've got to do this so my future is this'—it's wrong, it's wrong, man. It's day-by-day living. It's a real day-by-day life."

His name isn't really Harry Reems, a tag thought up by Gerard Damiano. "It's such a stupid name. It's really awful you know; you wonder what kind of a guy has the name Harry Reems, but suddenly I'm stuck with it," he says. Stuck with it because he gained his popularity under it and because he can't afford to use his real one. For Harry Reems is a rarity in the hard-core field, a genuine legitimate actor. "I came into the market when there weren't any real actors; they were kind of dying for people. Not that I'm any kind of great actor, but I can take written words and not make them sound like I'm reading them. I can make them sound half-assed as though they're coming out of some kind of character. And I got an awful lot of notoriety in the business because I could handle lines, and I did understand cameras, and I knew what film was all about. I was not there phoning in blow jobs."

But being an actor means membership in both the Screen Actors Guild and Actors Equity, organizations that sometimes have maximum fines of $5,000 per picture for the things that Harry does. So the plays and films and theater companies he's been in have to be off the record, though he likes to talk about his commercials—"a lot of water sports as well as the usual young husband stuff and a lot of athlete stuff before I let the hair go and the moustache and dissipated and debauched myself into some kind of scarecrow here. Marilyn Chambers is the Ivory Snow baby—okay, I did three Wheaties commercials. Breakfast of Champions!"

Twenty-seven years old, the product of a "quite normal" Westchester County family, Harry dropped out of the University of Pittsburgh—"you can quote me, Pittsburgh is the armpit of the earth"—after his first year and "went into the Marine Corps, like a crazy man. It was kind of a childhood thing, like being a cowboy." When he got out, having narrowly missed Vietnam because of illness in the family—"my original outfit really got slaughtered, 87 per cent casualties"—he bummed around for a couple of months and then gravitated toward acting. "I was legitimate and struggling and pushing and doing the dance classes and the voice classes and acting classes," he says. "And one Christmas, I needed money. And somebody said, 'Well, gee, I know where you can go.'" And so it began.

The man told him where he could make $75 an hour "doing this little 'oink-oink' number—of course you can't read what an 'oink' is; you can say, 'He motioned obscenely with his fist.' So I called this guy up, a very seedy-sounding character. He said, 'You got a good hanging thing? You know, it looks good? I mean, you got a nice body?' And he just hired me right off the telephone. And I went over there and the whole time I'm walking I'm looking behind me thinking the cops are following me, really superduper paranoid."

But as soon as he went in the door "and saw these beautiful young ladies, I immediately got hard, pulled my pants down, and came instantly, totally oblivious to all those people behind the camera, just totally into those two ladies. I was just so excited about the whole situation—there was something dirty and yet exciting about it. And, well, actually, I was nervous. I was afraid. I didn't want people to watch—nobody's ever watched me before —I mean, it was a private, you know, dark-room number for me in the past."

The filmmakers were as excited as Harry, but for a different reason. "I came instantly, inside the girl, and that was not kosher. Not only did they not get enough film, they didn't see the come shot," he explains. "I'd blown the whole scene; they went flipping-out crazy. By the time they settled down from being crazy I was ready to go again. It took no more than ten minutes for me to be ready again. 'Hey guys, look, try it again, you know, I'm sorry.' "

Messing up that first scene was an ironic prelude to his porno career, because Harry Reems made a reputation as one of those rare people with "the ability to always get it off. I've never had a problem getting it off. And usually I can regulate it, it seems that when they've got enough in the can in the way of film, I'll say, 'Okay, I'll give you twenty seconds' warning.' I usually can put my head into getting off or not getting off, you know, start concentrating on basketball, 'What'd the Knicks do this week?' and hold myself back."

And to people who say, "Gee, I could get up there and fuck that girl" and "Let me up there," Harry Reems says they just don't understand. "They can't understand why three guys are waiting around and not getting hard-ons, or why a producer's standing there yelling, 'What the hell's the matter with you guys? I hired you to fuck.' It's not an easy number. It has a lot to do with the vibes on the set; it's got a lot to do with the physical condition of the person, what he did the night before, the looks of the girl, the looks of the guy. Yeah, it's not easy, you know; a lot of people fail miserably at it."

Harry Reems did not fail; in fact, he prospered. After that first $75 "I said, 'My God, I have other gifts I have to buy, too,' and the very next day went to work with some other people on some more loops," as well as one-day features, and inserts, too, for the distributors who "would buy European soft core and spice them up with hard core." Cashing in on the rising popularity of so-called educational films, he did "an awful lot of these documentary doctor-type things, where they'd have a doctor talking and then six different things, and I was one of those couples all the time." Admittedly hung-up on making money, though still ambivalent about what he was doing, during his first year in the business Reems worked about three hundred days, the same the second, making so many pictures "I don't even know the titles of half of them," so much in demand because of his acting ability that there was "one weekend when I made myself $700 from a Friday night to a Sunday evening." Titles like *Post Graduate, Heart of Marriage, Dark Dreams, The Making of the the Blue Movie,* somewhere between two and three hundred features all told, enough so that he can say, "I was used in most every major film that was made, every feature that came out of New York or the East Coast."

It was a time of "a lot of legal hassles. People were always afraid of busts and locking doors and had guards posted and all that kind of stuff. It was a very seedy, raunchy kind of business. The guys were all fucked up; the girls were all fucked up. There were a lot of dope addicts. I'm not the criminal type, but I was in a criminal form, and I was kind of anxious to either get out of it or see it go legitimate." But there was the tremendous sexual kick, being in kind of a real-life wet dream. "You'd hear about the scene, and it's where these two girls are the aggressors and they take your clothes off and they go down and they blow you until you come, right. Wow, great! You know, outrageous! I love it. That was a great number."

Harry Reems, though, was not just another pretty face, not just a well-oiled body; he was something more. Along with his legitimate acting experience he brought a professional attitude to the set, an attitude that seemed to make people, especially new people, less uneasy about what they were about. "People, especially when they've never made one before, they don't know how to handle the situation: they're uncomfortable," he explains. "I had an ability to relax people, especially new girls coming into the business. We'd sit and talk; it made people feel comfortable, you know. I brought hundreds of people into the business. I was like A-number one in New York as far as the amount of work that was coming to me."

As an offshoot of this, Harry often found himself behind the camera, directing, lighting, doing whatever was necessary. The pictures he made were not exactly blockbusters, but they gave him experience he feels he couldn't have gotten elsewhere. "You go to a union situation, and you are a sound man or you are an assistant cameraman and for the rest of your life that's what you are, and you never get to handle the other equipment," he says. "But working on hard-core crews, you're taking sound one minute, loading magazines the next, shooting the next, and lighting the next. I mean, I've done it all. It's a toy, you know. One day I can act, one day I can shoot, one day I can direct. And I'm getting a tremendous amount of knowledge out of it."

If this sounds quite like the way director Gerard Damiano thinks, it's because Damiano and Harry Reems have done a lot of work together, much of it behind the camera, with Harry doing a lot of Damiano's production work. In fact, for *Deep Throat* Harry went down to the shooting in Florida "as key grip and organizer, trying to slap the whole thing together for them. I'd worked with Jerry in front of the cameras a hundred times, and I said, 'If we get in trouble I'll go in front of the camera for you.' And we couldn't cast that part of the doctor. So we stopped at a barber supply place to get the white coats, and I was learning lines with Linda in the back seat, improvising, and by the time we got to the place I had the lines memorized. A lot of it was

183

improv; it was a very skeleton kind of script. We did what you call a wing. We winged it."

A very successful wing it turned out to be, but, Reems feels, a total fluke in terms of the money it made. He himself made very little, and that does irk him, but he made up for it in the shooting of *Deep Throat II*, where he again has the leading role. As for his famous co-star, Harry, ever the gentleman, says, "She's a sweet, sweet, sweet girl, she really is. She's a beautiful person, a very together person. She's not super bright; she's not an actress —she's the first one to admit it—but she's totally open and free sexually. She's got this thing where sex is to be enjoyed and not slandered, and she follows it. She really believes it." And as for that highly touted technique, though Linda "loves it so much, it really is a turn-on for her, that's where she is at," Harry feels "there's not a lot of contact and warmth and lubrication in that kind of getting technical and giving head. It's almost 'Look what I can do.' It's nothing superduper special."

This nonchalance aside, Harry is aware that *Deep Throat* has made him what he calls "some kind of a half-assed star." His family and neighbors take pride in what he does, talk shows and magazines request interviews—everyone from David Susskind to Gloria Steinem—and, after seeing a "Linda Lovelace Blows My Mind" T-shirt, he thought of getting one up saying "Harry Reems Sucks My Soul." And his recognition apparently knows no social strata, either. On the one hand, "I get picked up by the international jet set as kind of a conversation piece, a toy"; on the other, the doormen at porno theaters recognize him and yell out, "Doc, hey doc! Come on over." And then there are the women.

"Star fuckers all over the city, phone calls, absolutely," Harry says. "That's why I use Harry Reems. Very few people know my real name, but still they somehow filter down to me. They got my number from somewhere and 'Oh, please, blah, blah, blah.' I just got a letter yesterday from some girl who's seen all my films and thinks I have a sexy smile and will that get her anywhere and all this ridiculousness."

Yet to all the people who figure "I've probably got the greatest sex life in the world," Harry says, "Well, I probably do. I mean, let's face it, I don't have any problems anymore. Especially, I don't have to look anymore. I don't have to play the games, you know? 'Do you want to go home and fuck?' they say. 'Hey, you want to fuck me?' They say it to me."

Many males in the hard-core business have found to their horror that their sex lives have turned into kind of a perverse reversal of what they'd dreamed about. "It just fucks them up," explains Harry. "They have no social life left anymore, or they're afraid people are recognizing them and they're embarrassed they just sexually won't be able to get it off anymore." Yet that hasn't happened to Harry, who doesn't believe man is naturally monogamous and who "kind of feels as though I'm missing something in life by not being bisexual. I still love sex. It's a great number, you know; it's a beautiful number. And I've gotten quite good at it, too. I've got all the little tricks."

In fact, working in sex films has been a liberating, loosening-up experience for Harry. "It was real therapy for me. I really enjoyed it. It suddenly opened me wide open; I grew philosophically. My God, my whole life changed altogether," he reports, sounding like some kind of off-base Jesus freak. For one thing, he's worked out just about all his sexual fantasies. "God knows I've done everything that could possibly be done. I've been licked from head to toe by six girls at once, poured honey all over me, foods, poured foods on other people, and gone through every kind of fetish you can imagine." Having gone through all this, his views on sex changed from "the dark-lit room to having a lot of fun in my sex. I really enjoy laughing and joking and carrying on and having sex. Because it's fun. It's not only a great sensation and that kind of thing, but it also should be fun. It shouldn't be heavy and serious and bogged down in love. People should share themselves with each other."

Ironically, what all this sex has also done is lead Harry to feel that in and of themselves "the physical pleasures are limited. You like to get into people's heads. I am so jaded sexually from going through all these numbers that I enjoy people's company now more than I do in bed." Even though he knows people must figure that "I'm into all kinds of whacked-out numbers, they figure you're freaky sexually," and though he can't resist saying, "I'm not, you can ask the three girls in the bedroom," he really isn't. "I'm not into swings and orgies and any of that kind of stuff," he says. "I'm very promiscuous now. I love to ball and generally fuck anything in skirts, but if I'm like this ten years from now I'll become a sad person, because it's not life, it's not where it's at. You see these guys running around and leching and drinking themselves to death and trying to screw everybody and play the roles and do the games, and it's sad to watch them. A guy I hadn't seen in probably ten years—goes back to high school days —called me up the other day. And he goes, 'Hey, I've seen you in the movies. Man, you're out of sight. I'm into that whole scene, man. I love to fuck; I love orgies. Gee, I did a number on a girl, I stuffed a pickle up her ass, and I cut her pubic hairs off, man. Now that is out of sight. Did you ever do that?' I said, 'Gee, no, I haven't. Listen, I've got to go to Nebraska now. Why don't you give me a call in a couple of weeks?' I'm really a normal person, really straight and all. I'm not all fucked up, and I'm not all into this, you know, fuck on, fuck on, fuck on."

It got so bad that Harry stopped working for a while. "I did too much balling. There were situations where I've come eighteen, twenty times a week because there was a lot of work." And, naturally, this got in the way of the type of off-screen relationship Harry wanted to have with women. "I wanted to share my life with somebody, you know? It's nice to have somebody to share life with, man. I miss it. I need it," he says. "And there were people I would have liked to do it with, but it was an unfair situation. How could I go out and say, 'Well, I gotta go to work, can't ball tonight'? Because if you've got three come shots to do in a day, you don't want to come home and ball for a day or two."

So, slowly, Harry began to change his life-style. "I went through the years when I just didn't do anything but dissipate, and I went through my excess smoking and my excess dope and now I'm kind of reverting back to the health number," he says. He has bought a farm in Pennsylvania—the setting for *The Devil in Miss Jones*—and spends as much time as he can up there. "It's another therapy, crawling up barns, and tearing down lumber, driving pick-ups, and singing country songs," he says, wistful as a small boy. "I love the solitude. I love the country."

This same ambivalence, the attempt to reconcile things that won't quite mix, comes out a bit in Harry's attitudes toward the work he does. "I love it, man, I truly love it. To me it's not work, it's play." And it has, he says, helped his acting, too. Because of the amount of relating and concentration it involves, he thinks "fucking on film is one of the finest acting exercises anybody could go through." It has helped in small ways, too, like giving him a better sense of improvisation and showing him he has a knack for comedy where before "I was always the serious actor, bogged down in Ionesco and Sartre and all the heavies." And more than anything else, the range of acting experience has been staggering. "How many actors in this world get a chance to work in front of a camera as often as I do, to work with as many different directors and different crews as I do?" he asks rhetorically. "Where else can a guy like me get a chance to play all these different kinds of characters and then see it back on films on a thousands-of-dollars kind of playback system? I know actors that are doing very well. They get their occasional shows, they'll go out for stock, and they'll do maybe one commercial a year or a bit part in a movie, and they really don't know what they're like acting. But I can sit back and study myself in 60-minute films nonstop from now till next year. You just don't see yourself on film that often."

Then there are the other times, times when he's felt exploited by what he calls "the grindo-type guys who make ten bad films just to get the market going." Times when he's felt what he does is "a cheap form of prostitution," that "I did sell myself out, I did not wait for the good scripts and things in the theater and so on and so forth." He gets insulted when he's thought of as nothing more than a copulation mechanism, like the time Queens College wanted him to make an appearance, but he said no because "just to stand up there and say, 'Here I am, you know . . .' " The thought was too distasteful to finish. "I'd say every week in New York a magazine or newspaper article comes out dealing with hard core," he says, "and very few times do people pick up on the person—they're always talking about the sex machine." To Harry Reems, who takes his acting as seriously as anyone, and with as much reason, that hurts, that hurts a lot.

The calls still come in, "people that don't pay more than $75 to anyone else saying, 'Please, I'll give you $200,' because there's nobody else that can act." But Harry Reems isn't answering them much anymore. Though he knows that "if I do make it as an actor it's not going to be because of my legitimate work, it's gonna be because of this," he has decided that it's time to try to get out of the business. "It's not that I don't really want to do it; it's just that I've done it all," he explains. "I can't go out and make loops anymore, I can't go out and do these one-day features anymore, because there's nothing to them. I just got tired of doing the same thing over and over and not growing at all. It was all the plumber-comes-into-the-house kind of situation, or instead of the plumber maybe it would be the milkman, so eventually you get to the point where you want to do decent scripts. Once you learn the nuts and bolts, it's time to move on to working with people that are better than you. I'm not down on hard-core films, it's just that I'm ready for a professional field."

Harry Reems, like everyone else, has his "ambitions, things that I want in life that I hope to get someday. But if they don't happen, well, they don't happen, you know?" And whatever happens, there will be absolutely no regrets about the past. "It's been a good period in my life, and I wouldn't change it, would not change it," he repeats for emphasis. "If somebody said, 'Go back five years, and I'll put you in a major motion picture, and your career will flow, will blossom out of that,' I would be a different kind of person than I am now. A sadder person, not as wise, not as open, not as knowledgeable as I am now. I wouldn't want to change it. I really dig what I've done."

16

ALL MALE

THE HOMOSEXUAL BLUE MOVIE

Male homosexuality as the subject of Hollywood films and of sex-exploitation films made for a largely male audience has had a short, swift history that compresses as it mirrors the development of the heterosexual erotic film. During the first years of the '60s, for example, there was no theatrical exhibition of all-male films, and—with the exception of "posing-strap" films made for the home market—depiction of explicit homosexual activity and male nudity was confined to serious artistic motion pictures produced by filmmakers of the new American cinema and shown in cinematheques, film festivals, and art galleries. Among the most widely seen of these early titles were Kenneth Anger's *Scorpio Rising* and *Fireworks*, Jack Smith's *Flaming Creatures*, and several early Andy Warhol films, including *I, a Man* and *Blow Job*.

The first significant theatrically released gay exploitation films were the work of Pat Rocco, a Los Angeles filmmaker whose shorts and features were designed to show off the beauty of the male body. *Marco of Rio, A Night at Joanni's, Mondo Rocco*, and *Sex and the Single Gay*, to name just a few, were gentle, romantic, soft-core paeans to male form, feeling, and friendship. Gone were the over-age queen and the mincing sissy (played to perfection in Hollywood films by Franklin Pangborn and Grady Sutton). Instead, Rocco's young, handsome, and virile stars played characters who openly advocated male love and asked for respect instead of expressing self-hatred. In general, Rocco's films celebrated the "coming out" of the homosexual and his acceptance

188

of his own nature, and their release proved instrumental in opening a market for gay films. It is a market that has never become very large. About fifty theaters in the United States currently exhibit gay films, but because they do not generally play alternate dates with heterosexual sex-exploitation films, their profitability is limited.

The soft-core films of Pat Rocco were followed in 1969 by hard-core male loops and features. Such quickly and cheaply made 16mm films as *Sticks and Stones, Trick and Trade, Friday on My Mind, The Collection, Stud Farm, Earth Child,* and J. Brian's *Five in Hand* were, in the words of director Gorton Hall, "more or less fantasy for the lonely man, to get the blood going again, fantasy for the guy to extend into his own personal dream, either in the theater or at home. It used to be a supplement, like a vitamin. Pick the most beautiful boys and have them do the most beautiful things, and you can sit there and relate and think, 'Wow, that's me.' Ammunition to build a dream on, that's what it used to be." These movies, which featured endless pairs and groups of young men making love with one another, worked within many of the same conventions and liabilities as 16mm heterosexual hard-core films. The requirements for sex scenes—*x* number of acts in *x* number of minutes—were as rigid as those for sainthood, and the advertising for these beefcake or meat-rack productions, as they were called in the trade, simply played up the presence of the male bodies. "Cassidy vs. Dakota," boasted an ad in the *Los Angeles Times*. "Maledom's greatest action star vs. Gaydom's number one model, together 'n' terrific in *Manpower*," a movie that claims "from any angle it's the double-barreled, triple-powered, forty-five calibre, rocker-socker of the year."

A few filmmakers did try to break out of that pattern, and in 1970 two soft-core movies dealing rather more thoughtfully with homosexuality were released. The first, *Song of the Loon*, was based on Richard Amory's 1966 paperback classic, of which more than 2 million copies were sold. Set in the North Woods, this tale of a love affair between an experienced trapper and a young man troubled by the thought that he might be promiscuous was the first production of Sawyer Productions and was seriously and ambitiously directed and edited by Andrew Herbert. Robert Maxwell photographed the beautiful outdoor scenes, which were shot on location in the Trinity Alps and the Big Pines National Reserve. (In the credits, the U.S. Forestry Service is thanked for its "cooperation and understanding during production.") Perhaps the most distinguishing aspects of the film are its lyrical and sentimental qualities. As Vincent Canby wrote in the *New York Times*:

189

The film is quite different from most exploitation films, not because it is homosexual, but because it is so unabashedly romantic. ...There are lots of nude shots and several graphically photographed lovemaking episodes that are technically good and numbingly lyric.

Parker Tyler was less charitable; he singled out for criticism the actors (one is "flabby and dissipated"; the other "looks at times about to burst into tears because the pebbles hurt his feet") and the generally arty and pretentious quality of the photography. He also complained that the sexual activity was discreet and that the whole film was a perversion of the direct, masculine attributes of the original novel.

The second important film produced around this time was *Meat Rack,* a first effort rather crudely directed, photographed, and edited by Michael Thomas, a twenty-one-year-old theater manager, that was released by Sherpix in a grainy 35mm print enlarged from a 16mm negative. *Meat Rack* strung together a series of sexual encounters between a bisexual San Francisco hustler called J.C. and a number of his clients (mostly male) and lovers (mostly female), including an aging queen, a bored housewife, a couple of violent, knife-carrying young men in drag, a masochist, and a virgin runaway from New Jersey. The cast was strictly amateur, but despite the clumsy and dramatically trivial soft-core erotic scenes, the street scenes have a gritty authenticity, and on the whole the movie offers an unflinchingly honest portrayal of life in the gay bars and bedrooms of San Francisco.

One of the more unusual gay films is *Pink Narcissus,* which was directed, produced, written, photographed, and designed anonymously and released by Sherpix in 1971. Originally made in 8mm and definitely outside the mainstream of all-male films— it more resembles an experimental film than an exploitation film —*Pink Narcissus* focused on a brooding, introverted street hustler who retreats into a fantasy world in order to avoid the sordid realities of his chosen way of life—pick-ups in public lavatories, endless street cruising, sexual humiliation. The young homosexual's largely narcissistic fantasies, setting him in scenes of bullfighting, Roman slavery, Middle Eastern harem life, and a romp through the woods, showed no explicit sexual activity but contained a great deal of posing, dressing up, preening, parading, dressing down, and undressing by the star of the film, Bobby Kendall. The most noteworthy aspect of the peculiar production was its total artifice: All the sets, indoors and out, were handpainted, drapery was skillfully used, and much of the photography was decadent and arty. Its extraordinary qualities were summed up by Vincent Canby:

Pink Narcissus is a fragile antique, a passive, tackily decorated surreal fantasy out of that pre-gay activist era when homosexuals hid out in closets and read novels about sensitive young men who committed suicide because they could not go on. . . . It is sad and very vulnerable and as serious as it is sappy.

In the early '70s, although such run-of-the-mill gay films as *Confessions of a Male Groupie, All About Alice, Bob and Daryll and Ted and Alex, Pleasure Cruise, The Boys and the Bandit, Fire Island, First Time Round, Gay Guide to Hawaii, Twilight Cowboy,* and *Midnight Geisha Boy,* continued to be made, the audience seemed ready for something else. As Gorton Hall noticed, the viewers "want their mind to be jarred as well as their innards. They want to see acting; they want to see drama, situations they can relate to. They want to see a story, a point made." Buoyed by this belief, he and a number of other directors—Wakefield Poole, Fred Halsted, J. Brian—invested a substantial amount of time and money in their films, and the care and artistry with which they made them paid off with notoriety, critical praise, and financial success.

Wakefield Poole's *Boys in the Sand,* which opened December 29, 1971, at the 55th Street Playhouse, was, despite some artistic flaws, one of the more remunerative of the quality hard-core films—it grossed almost $400,000 on its $8,000 cost. Each of *Boys'* three fantasy episodes features Casey Donovan (the pseudonym of actor Cal Culver), and the success of the movie cannot be considered apart from Donovan's presence, for his legitimate acting experience and his model's good looks lend the film a certain credibility as a sexual document.

One of the hero's encounters begins with the unlikely appearance of a bearded man walking up out of the ocean. Another lover materializes in the swimming pool after Casey drops in a small pill, and the third episode begins with Donovan, quite naked, wandering around in his house, "cruising" a black telephone lineman. *"Boys in the Sand,"* said Wakefield Poole,

basically deals with a progression. It starts out with innocence in the first segment, "Bayside," which is very romantic. The second segment is a little more realistic, as far as looking for a mate and the dream of finding Prince Charming on his horse. The third one is the acceptance of the fact that there is no such thing as Prince Charming on his horse. The third segment is the most sophisticated sexually. [Casey] cruises a black lineman and loses him, and he can't stand it. So he keeps imagining the guy all around the house in different areas. So finally he goes and he takes out a dildo, and it happens to be a black dildo. It's a private moment. It's not someone else shoving a dildo up his ass, it's him doing it to himself and freaking out on losing that guy and saying, Well, if I lost him there, I'm gonna get him in my head anyway.

The final scenes of passionate lovemaking between Donovan and the black man, well shot and well edited, are among the best in gay movies.

The financial success of *Boys in the Sand* enabled the director to devote more time and money ($22,000) to his second feature, *Bijou,* an eerie, artfully lit and composed, but strangely affecting work that Poole calls "a statement about sexual freedom—just to take it as it comes, and whatever happens happens, and don't have any guilt about it." A rugged, well-hung construction worker (Bill Harrison, who also plays in heterosexual films) sees a woman run down by a car and steals her purse from the scene of the accident. He returns to his narrow apartment with its Playmate foldouts tacked on the wall, goes through the contents of the purse, and finds an invitation to a place called Bijou. Once he is there, reality disappears. The blackness is broken by a sign telling him to remove his clothes. It is a whole new world in which the construction worker finds an orange foam rubber sculpture by John Chamberlain, an infinity of mirrors, and a room where movies are projected—films of the woman he saw run over, of masturbating men who will soon initiate him into homosexual love. He wanders farther and discovers a young man with long blond hair lying on his stomach. The construction worker makes love to this man, who remains a passive, androgenous figure of indeterminate response and motivation, and others join them, in what grows into a six-sided homosexual encounter. The sex is explicit but curiously distant; Poole is more interested in the formal and hierarchical aspects of the scene than in the sexual activity, which is treated as a ritual initiation. The hero dresses and goes out the door into the cool night air. Then, in a freeze frame, he smiles. This timeless smile, enigmatic and effective, seems to signal his acceptance of, and pleasure in, homosexual activity, something beyond his sterile fantasies about *Playboy* Playmates, but the ending is open to interpretation. Poole himself has said, "That grin at the end is ambiguous. You could think, 'Well, it was a hoot,' or you could say, 'Sonofabitch, did I get myself into a situation.' Now that's what I mean by ambiguity; you can interpret that smile fifteen thousand different ways."

Another filmmaker who became famous at this time was Fred Halsted, a Los Angeles director-star whose films are among the most notorious to come out of the gay film movement, both attacked and championed by proponents of gay lib. *L.A. Plays Itself*, shot in 16mm, begins with tedious, aimless scenes of a man driving around the streets of Los Angeles, accompanied by a long, poorly recorded and almost totally incomprehensible soundtrack. The words that can be understood are spoken by a young man who has come to Los Angeles and has been warned to beware of the unkindness of strangers. A man cruising in the car (played by Halsted himself) picks the boy up and takes him home, where he physically beats him and subjects him to protracted sexual abuse. After this vision of sex as cruel abasement, however, the tone of the movie changes; the second half is shot in the woods and features two handsome young men who engage in several homosexual acts in a forest and under a waterfall.

Despite its lyrical, idyllic ending, L.A. Plays Itself attracted a good deal of adverse attention. It seems clear that Halsted's violation of the taboos on showing sadomasochism accounted for its being raided by the New York City police. An earlier film, The Pledgemaster, which had played Manhattan in late 1971, had a similar theme but had placed its violence in a socially redeeming context. Billing the action as an exposé of college hazing, The Pledgemaster followed four pledges through a rough fraternity ritual that featured beatings, humiliation, and forced feedings, and the ties between homosexuality and ritual violence were brutally drawn.

The police moved against Halsted's film on the basis of complaints by homosexuals in one of the first instances in which gay films were raided in Manhattan; previous crackdowns on straight porno houses in 1970 and 1971 had ignored the all-male theaters. The police shutdown of L.A. Plays Itself had an amusing aspect. The undercover police who made the arrest went into the theater, saw a few minutes of hard-core sex, and lodged a complaint against the film. What they saw, however, was another film by Halsted, a short called Sex Garage, which depicted a variety of unusual sexual activities, including a man making love to his motorcycle.

Halsted's other movie work included a short called Truck It and an appearance in a tedious, badly edited, feature-length history of the gay movie entitled Erotikus. In the latter, excerpts from Boys in the Sand, L.A. Plays Itself, and a number of the 8mm posing-strap films from the '50s are intercut with Halsted's narration, which he delivers while masturbating before the camera.

Up until 1972 filmmakers sporadically produced films that were then distributed—in a limited and uncertain fashion—to gay theaters. With the establishment of Jaguar Productions, a production company that made films and distributed them to a fixed circuit of twenty-two theaters, all that was to change. Since February 1972 Jaguar has released its motion pictures, many of which were produced by Gorton Hall or J. Brian, regularly and reliably, accompanied by press kits, audience questionnaires, and trade paper reviews. In general, the movies boast coherent plots and character development in addition to sexual activity, and the leads are chosen for acting skills as well as for looks. As one director boasts, things have gotten to the point where "a guy can be, quote, gorgeous, and if he can't act worth a nickel, he will be rejected for that role." In the world of hard-core gay films, where stars can sometimes be seen cruising on Hollywood Boulevard, that is saying quite a lot.

The advantages of Jaguar Productions have spilled over into the technical side of filmmaking as well, as Barry Knight, a twenty-seven-year-old photographer-editor who got into hard-core films after making hundreds of TV commercials, including some of the staggeringly idyllic Salem cigarette extravaganzas, testifies:

"We have an art director. I'm so proud we have a full-time art director. And a still photographer who's a real pro. We're doing the best to get the best photographic image possible. We fight all the time with the labs. In fact, we were the first outfit to use a camera crane in a male film.

"When I talked budget with the executive producers, they said, 'You know, this won't net a nickel at the box office; it costs money to rent a crane.' And I said, 'I know, it's just my personal pride and satisfaction of trying to upgrade the quality level of the pictures.' We didn't overdo it. It doesn't look like 'Hey, look, I've got a camera crane.' We used it discreetly, and it shows.

"All the male porno pictures that were made before ours, they shot them in a day. They just quickly set up, shoot the picture, and get it done, the cheapest way they can. I fought so that now we have five and six production days to do a picture in. Gorton [Hall] has fought to have two weeks ahead of time for the actors to rehearse lines, two hours a night, three or four nights a week. No porno people have ever done that before to get a better quality."

Hall, a chunky, cherubic Peter Lorre type, talks just as seriously about that artistic quality. "We were the first ones," he says with honest pride, "who ever attacked one of these with a script, dialogue, rehearsals, and made the actors learn lines and learn interpretation. When I approached the distributor on my first film, he said, 'Oh no, you can't get these kids to learn lines.' And I said, 'Let's try it, why not?'" And, just like in some classic Busby Berkeley movie about callow youths stepping into the spotlight, "the actors were delighted, absolutely delighted. They couldn't wait. They'd start on their own rehearsing. Honest to God, they found talent they didn't know they had. They were marvelous, and I was amazed."

Of course, Hall makes a point of giving his performers a story line and motivation to go along with the sexual action. What he looks for is "good stories and good drama. It's the *only* reason I got into this field. If it was just strictly porno . . . anyone can shoot two people having sex. I'm interested in drama. We're not ashamed of sex, I don't apologize for sex scenes, our sex scenes are erotic as hell! I just make damn sure it's a good sex scene and that the characters are properly motivated—that they're not doing anything they wouldn't do in that situation."

The contrast between Hall's work—a cinematic illustration of his belief in "blowing the mind, so to speak, instead of the body" —and some of the more mundane gay films in circulation is remarkable. And even against more sensational competition, such as *Lodestar*, which its producers claim is the "most controversial film ever made" and features Jesus Christ himself coming off the cross to perform a homosexual act, Hall's concern for his audience's intelligence has paid off. His best-known film, *The Experiment* (made with Barry Knight in 1973), brought to life the story of two young boys who discover their homosexuality, and how the father of one—played by Hall—reacts to the revelation. It was called "the most brilliantly executed gay film of our time" by the *Gay Film Review*, and *The Advocate* noted that Hall and company "are to be applauded for their daring, for affirming their belief that audiences do not park their mentality at the door of a porno theater." The reaction from the audience was no less favorable. "There were people with tears in their eyes at the end of *The Experiment*, absolutely crying," the director remembers. "One guy told me, 'Damn, I wish now I'd told my father when I was that kid's age.'"

Some other Gorton Hall films run along rather different lines. *A Ghost of a Chance* is a porno comedy with more than a passing resemblance to *Blithe Spirit*—doors mysteriously open, and the protagonists fight invisible men—but the comedy gets bogged down by the obligatory sex scenes. *Devil in the Flesh*, with polished black-and-white photography by Barry Knight and story and direction by Hall, features a murder mystery plot involving a rich, callous young man, his male lover, and a homosexual hustler. The movie is quickly paced, with sex scenes that contribute to the story line, and the performances by Mark Taylor, Brian Reynolds, and Van Stewart are more than adequate. Gorton Hall once again makes a personal appearance, this time as a police detective. As Harold Fairbanks, film critic for *The Advocate*, wrote, "The actors pay as much attention to their lines as their loins, and the original screenplay by Gorton Hall has provided them with dialogue they feel comfortable speaking."

Another mainstay of Jaguar Productions is filmmaker J. Brian, whose early works—*Five in Hand, Seven in a Barn*, and *First Time Around*—were straightforward, well-photographed action pictures, short on plot and character but featuring good-looking, athletic young men. His film *Four More Than Money*, released through Jaguar, was somewhat stronger artistically. Based on a

195

collection of first-person short stories, the film starred San Francisco model Joe Markhum; the various episodes paired Markhum with a thick-headed weightlifter in a Chicago gym, with a black hustler in Dallas, and with a country innocent whom Markhum turns into a hustler.

A more recent Jaguar product directed by Ignatio Rutkowski, *Nights in Black Leather*, is a strange mixture of brutal and idyllic lovemaking in the mold of Fred Halsted's *L.A. Plays Itself*. Peter Burian plays a young German visitor to San Francisco who keeps a diary about his homosexual experiences. After a masturbation sequence, the hero picks up a fellow homosexual in a suggestively choreographed encounter, and their lovemaking in the woods is shot in lyrical and almost endless slow motion through vaseline and cobwebs. A second episode in which the protagonist discovers a "victim" in a lavatory, depicts pain and sodomy in equal proportions. The film ends with a final pickup as the sun sets over a tranquil sea.

From their beginning as all-male Nudies to thoughtfully plotted features boasting creditable acting performances and sensitive direction, from uncertain distribution in sleazy theaters to reliable showings at respectable movie houses, homosexual films have come to show their heroes as men of physical and spiritual pride. The genre has to a great extent mirrored the emergence of a more liberated attitude toward the gay experience itself, and the making of gay films has, in turn, changed the attitudes of the people involved.

Gorton Hall, for example, says, "I profit the most from these pictures, more than anybody, from Jaguar down to the last customer. It's an education, an absolute gold mine of philosophy for living. I really have learned a lot." Perhaps the catalysts have been the actors he occasionally casts by picking up hitchhikers along Sunset Strip—tawny young men in denims and tanktops, whose open, wholesome smiles symbolize the sexual accessibility, the you-name-it-you-got-it erotic openness that fills the atmosphere in Los Angeles like a perfume whose number Chanel hasn't quite gotten yet. "I learned a lot of values from these kids," Hall points out. "They have no qualms about taking off their clothes, about me saying, 'We're on schedule now, let's get something going,' that sort of thing. They just say, 'Well, give us a couple of minutes alone because, you know, we have to groove on each other.' I learned how absolutely normal this whole business is, that sex taboos are such a farce; they're so prehistoric."

Hall's summing up could apply to all gay films, perhaps to the entire sex-exploitation industry: "Nothing human is dirty. Tennessee Williams said that, and I believe it."

17

"I MAKE 'EM ALL FOR ME"

AN INTERVIEW WITH WAKEFIELD POOLE

Wakefield Poole would like to take this opportunity to thank the person or persons responsible for a hard-core homosexual film called *Highway Hustler*. "Whoever made that movie's gonna kill me," he says, laughing, "but I have nothing but gratitude to whoever it was."

It was on one of those Friday nights in New York City, where seeing anything decent demands standing on lines that refuse to end, so Poole suggested to a quartet of friends, " 'Why don't we just go see a porno movie.' And we went to the Park-Miller, and we sat down, and halfway through the film one friend was asleep, two were nodding. And they kept playing 'June Is Busting Out All Over' on the soundtrack. They were doing all these horrendous things, and I said, 'This is ludicrous.' Now that was $25 sitting there, and it was a piece of shit we were looking at—it was so terrible. So I just said, you know, let's try and make one just for the hell of it, just for fun."

Wakefield Poole's idea of fun turned out to be an item called *Boys in the Sand*. Made on less than a five-day shooting schedule on Fire Island—such a short time Poole says he's ashamed to admit it—and costing $8,000 "at the most," it really is, as its ads insist, "the most acclaimed male movie in the history of the cinema." Besides its phenomenal financial success, it almost single-handedly legitimized the gay hard-core film—"moved it uptown," says one critic—as well as, its maker says, everything that has happened since. "I think without tooting our own horn that we're responsible for half of the revolution that's going on now," Poole says. "I think everything is a progression, and I think we were just that little tiny cornerstone. *Deep Throat* couldn't have happened without us; I firmly believe that."

With a thin, monkish face set off by elliptical, metal-rimmed glasses, a single tiny round gold earring, and close-cropped hair and beard, Wakefield Poole manages to look like an animated, energetic, aesthetic pixie. He speaks rapidly and forcefully with a remnant of a Southern accent that comes of being born in Jacksonville, Florida, at some indeterminate time in the 1930s. "I really don't even know; I don't think about that anymore," he says, explaining, "I just had a birthday and I thought I was a year older than I was. And when I realized how old I was, I went, 'Oh boy, I got one, that gives me an extra one, a free one,' because for a year I'd been telling people I was a year older than I was."

Though his interest in film barely predates that peek at *Highway Hustler,* he has a background in the performing arts that is thoroughgoing and surprisingly extensive. "I've really dabbled in just about everything," he says. "I was a performer since I was like four years old, singing, dancing, acting, all that stuff." By the time he graduated from high school, Poole had decided he wanted to be a ballet dancer, and after nine months of study in New York joined the Ballet Russe de Monte Carlo. Two years later he joined another company, touring the Orient for ten months under State Department auspices. "Sometimes we performed for 150,000 people in outdoor theaters—incredible." When he came back to New York, he began dancing in Broadway shows, including *The Unsinkable Molly Brown, Tenderloin,* and *West Side Story.* He moved on to being an assistant director-choreographer to Joe Layton on shows like *No Strings, George M,* and *Do I Hear a Waltz.* He directed *No Strings* in London, staged TV's Phyllis Diller show for twenty-six weeks, did some off-Broadway shows, and some summer stock, choreographed some ballets—the list is almost endless.

"I had in my head that I was going to be a Broadway director-choreographer and that's what I was striving for and striving for and striving for," he says. "I knocked around the theater for a long time, trying to get a break or trying to get a good property. Unless you're somebody or unless you're very lucky, you don't do it right away. And I was really at the end of my career as far as I was concerned. I'd been successful and down, successful and down, you know, and suddenly I did something that I really wanted to do. This other thing was there all the time boiling, but I had those blinders on—I had that image in my head. And suddenly all this came to the surface, and now I can relax, you know. I can just make movies."

Of course, when Poole made the first of *Boys in the Sand*'s three segments, it was not with anything nearly so lofty in mind. "It was really just done out of fun, you know." But that first part looked pretty good, and so he joined with Marvin Shulman, a shaved-headed Fu-Manchu-mustached theatrical accountant, to form Poolemar Productions, shoot two other segments, and then possibly release all three as a film.

However, when one of the actors in the first section heard that, "he pulled a whole switch, he wanted a lot of money and blah, blah, blah, which we didn't have. He'd get paid for his work, but he suddenly saw a chance to say, 'I want 20 per cent.' He's doing a 15-minute segment and he wants 20 per cent of whatever we're gonna make on the movie. So I said, you know, 'Fuck you. I'll do it over, you know, double fuck you.' So we got Casey Donovan through a friend of mine. He'd seen this segment and said, 'I'll make anything for you because it's fantastic.' So I reshot that segment with him and then decided to use him for the other two to make a connecting line, and it worked. So I believe in playing with accidents. If something happens, don't make it negative and defeat yourself; turn it right around and make it positive. And that's what we did."

Someone whose only previous experience with film was working on multimedia shows and taking 8mm stuff as a hobby, Poole admits that *Boys* was not as polished as it might be. "I did everything wrong, you know. I mean, you name it, I did it wrong," he says. "I went into this lab and said, 'Look, I've got a movie here, and I don't know what to do with it.' I told them it was already cut, and they blanched. They turned white. They said, 'You mean you cut your original footage?' and I said, 'Yeah,' and they said, 'You've got some balls.' But they took me under their arm; they put it together for me. I think they were so refreshed that a filmmaker came in and said, 'I don't know what the fuck I'm doing,' that they were very nice to me."

Despite inexperience, Poole did have very definite ideas about what the film was to be like. First of all, it was to be silent, because, like *Sunset Boulevard*'s Norma Desmond, Poole says, "I don't like talking. As long as the situation can be explained with cinematic terms, you don't need the words." Remembering again *Highway Hustler,* where the character's exaggerated swishy accent "blew the whole movie," he felt that if *Boys* was silent, "there was a little ambiguity to it, so that the person watching it could freak out. Sex is all involved with fantasy anyway, and the person watching it could see Casey's face and look at the glint in his eye and could imagine him saying whatever he wanted."

199

Secondly, Poole was adamant that there would be nothing remotely degrading about the picture, "nothing that anyone would wince at when they saw it on the screen." And when it came to distributing the film, Poole followed the same dictates. "We were offered $12,000 for it, and I said, 'You're full of shit, you know, sell it,'" Poole recalls. "I decided we'd distribute it ourselves, and we'd do it first class." And this, everyone feels, was the key to all that followed.

The 55th Street Playhouse, a stranger to gay films, was hired, and an ad campaign was mounted, the likes of which no hard-core film—gay or otherwise—had ever seen. "We got an artist to do a sketch for us, and we did a lot of breakthroughs as far as advertising," Poole says. "We advertised in big magazines, you know. *After Dark* took their first ad for a movie like that. We were in the Sunday *New York Times,* big ads in the *Times,* on the same page with *Minnie and Moskowitz* and *X, Y, and Zee* with Elizabeth Taylor. We were reviewed in *Variety.* They said, 'We never saw any film with credits before.'" And to give it just that much more legitimacy, Poole put his name on it. "He's the original flasher on the subway," Marvin Shulman puts in archly, but Poole says seriously, "I think that gave it validity, the fact that I put my name on it. I'd done a few things in the theater, and even though I wasn't well known, people in the industry knew me, and they all freaked that suddenly I came out with a homosexual porno film with my name on it, you know? And more than anything else, the fact that we did it right and we did it first class and we didn't sneak it in," that made the difference.

And although Shulman dryly asks, "I wish you'd leave the humor to me," Poole can't resist telling the story of how *Boys* met its public. "We'd done maybe four private screenings, and everybody said, 'Oh, it's wonderful.' But you can do a piece of shit, and people pat you on the back and say it's wonderful and then they go back and say, 'Oh did you see that piece of shit?' But anyway, we went over right at twelve o'clock when the doors were to open, and Marvin was hanging a sign up on the door: 'This product is for mature adults over twenty-one who are not easily offended.' And he's trying to glue it on because the doors are metal.

"They open the box office and suddenly people start pouring into the theater. Well, the Jew here was going crazy, seeing the thing come through like this. He couldn't get the sign up, and the sign was crooked, and we both nearly fainted. Because if we had had fifty people there the whole day we would have been delighted. But, I mean, it was just zoom, zoom, zoom, coming in there, and those five dollar bills going down, and Marvin was going crazy. He had a hammer in his hand that didn't work on the metal door and glue, and the thing was cockamamy, and we just didn't believe it. We were like nervous wrecks. The people in the box office didn't believe it either; they even called the night manager on the phone and said, 'Get here and take this money to the bank.' They were petrified, the business was so good."

It was very good—$5,300 the first day, to be exact, better than that Liz Taylor movie, and close to $25,000 the first week. It made *Variety*'s top box-office fifty, and the paper ran a major story on the two men, headlined " 'Amateurs' Bring in Bonanza" and saying its makers "seem to have managed the impossible." The first week's grosses paid for all expenses, Shulman went out and bought a Mercedes after the second, and Poole began getting calls on the order of "I'd like to book Casey Donovan for a gang-bang I'm having tonight." *Boys* ended up running nineteen weeks. Designer Yves St. Laurent said it was the thing he'd enjoyed most in New York; *Variety* noted, "There are no more closets"; and Poole himself heard "two queens in the booth next door" at a Manhattan baths "talking about the movie, critiquing it, and getting it all wrong. I thought, 'This has got to stop.' "

Now withdrawn from theatrical distribution, an 8mm version of *Boys* is for sale by mail for $99, with an average of fifty requests coming in per day. "Suddenly it became big business, it was no longer sleazy and underhanded," Poole says about that initial 55th Street spurt. "We were the first one to go legit. We started the revolution, especially the fact that we were homosexual and got the recognition that we got. Then I think the straight filmmakers got more courageous because they thought, 'If a homosexual film can do that and run and not get busted, I mean, fuck it. Why are we sitting here making these sleazers?' And they got better and better. I think really we're responsible for the quality getting better and better and better."

After all that success, Poole is well aware that he could have made *"Boys in the Sand II,* we could have done another $8,000 movie, we could have gotten into the grind of turning them out every three weeks, we could've just kept going and going and going. But Marvin didn't need that in his life. I didn't need that in my life. I said to Marvin, 'I don't want $400,000 a year. What am I going to do with $400,000 a year?' I want to be able to make movies, keep making movies, and making them better and learning and growing."

Wakefield Poole feels an instinctive commitment to the cinema of titillation, and he believes that "if erotic films are gonna continue, they have to develop. Somebody's got to do it; you just can't keep making *Deep Throat* and making passels of money, right?" Not that he has anything against money, mind you, but his basic philosophy, based on the unexpected off-the-wall success of *Boys* is "Never say, 'Hey let's do this 'cause we'll make a pile

201

of money on it.' We make what we want to make and if it works, fine, if it doesn't work we're prepared to take that loss. Because I think if you make a movie saying, 'Everyone's gonna love this movie; boy, are we gonna make money on it,' you're gonna turn out a piece of cliché shit. I'm much more into making films I want to see and keeping my fingers crossed that they work."

So Poole tries to ignore people who ask him, "When are you going to make a real movie?" and turns down the type of legitimate offers many porno veterans fantasize about. For instance, "I was offered a black film, like a James Bond–type film. The budget was about $800,000 or something like that; I mean, it was outrageous. But then, you see, I'm just taking someone else's ideas and translating them to film, and that's not my bag. I'm at the state where D. W. Griffith hasn't made *Birth of a Nation* yet. I really don't think at this point in my life I could handle a crew of five hundred people. I'm still playing around, and I'm learning. My aim is to just keep going."

After *Boys in the Sand*, then, Wakefield Poole did the very different *Bijou*. Shot in the 18 × 24-foot living room that now belongs to Cal Culver, it was originally going to be a boy-girl porno vehicle, but "we thought, no, we'd made one gay movie and it'd been successful, why should we cut off and go into another market that we knew very little about?"

Variety, which had called *Boys* "so cinema verité that at times the viewer feels the camera itself is going to get into the action," had quite a different reaction to *Bijou*, calling it "a head picture, part ersatz Kubrick, part raunchy Disney," with the result aimed straight at "the boys on the grass." It captivated, of all people, *Screw* Magazine's Al Goldstein, who said he got "culture shock" when he saw this "gay masterpiece of masterpieces . . . the most ambitious and successful hard-core film to emerge from the depths of the porno underground." But other, more devoted fans of the gay cinema claimed that *Bijou* was too esoteric and intellectual, arty fantasy masquerading as raunchy pornography and, worst of all, it simply did not deliver on the sex. Wakefield Poole, though, has no regrets, because he did it the way he wanted to, and for him that's all that matters.

"With *Bijou*, we put our nose on the line," he admits. "We'd made a hot movie, the hottest movie supposedly ever made as far as the gay porno world is concerned, and now we tried to get a little arty with it. We tried to get a little more cerebral and heady with it, make sort of a head trip out of it, rather than just the nitty gritty. The reaction was either very good or very bad; there's no middle of the line. No one said, 'Oh, it's okay.' "

And the people who say it doesn't deliver—the ones who "want to see more cocks in mouth and fucking"—Poole feels those people are simply "crazy. There's a lot of action in that movie, you know. I mean, it's not a soft-core film; there's a lot of hot stuff in there. There are orgasms, but, except for the first one, I don't pull out and show the come, and that's why they say it doesn't deliver. You don't see the come, so people say it doesn't deliver. That irritates me because that means people are not looking. They're looking at this"—he points to his crotch—"they're not looking up here"—he points to his head. "They're not looking at the emotion; they're not looking at the way the body reacts, that's what irritates me. I want to go into the human side of it, not just the cock in the hole. I mean, once you do that, what do you do?"

Poole's latest film puts even greater strains on his normal constituency. First of all, it is not specifically gay-oriented, though the director feels, "If a gay person is human and has his head in the right place, it's gonna affect them." Secondly, its subject matter is, well, a little strange. Variously titled *Wakefield Poole's Bible*, *B. C. Scandals*, and *Wakefield Poole's Scandals*, the film had a brief, unsuccessful run in New York, but Poole, unconcerned, released it again in 1974. The stories used are Adam and Eve, filmed (where else) in the Virgin Islands; Samson and Delilah, with midgets in the supporting cast; and David and Bathsheba, with Georgina Spelvin of *The Devil in Miss Jones* as Bathsheba. He, is not, he claims, "trying to compete with Cecil B. De Mille," nor, except for one actress who said, "My head is just not together, I've just stopped going to Mass, I just can't do it," has anyone thought his idea particularly outré. "Everyone I've talked to about it, their mouths have all dropped open, and they say, 'What a fabulous idea,'" Poole says. "My family knows; they know I'm making the Bible. They think it's a goof."

It is the third difference, however, that may be most crucial, for, in line with a decision made well before the Supreme Court's, *Wakefield Poole's Scandals* will not in any sense be hard core. On the other hand, Poole says, "It's not gonna even be soft core; it's gonna be something that's never been done before. It's gonna be an erotic film, an erotic film with no penetration, but it will go right to the line. I'm trying to make a film that will go as far as we can possibly go, I mean, to the very edge, without showing penetration—I mean, right to the razor's edge. If they say *Bijou* didn't deliver, they're probably gonna say this movie doesn't deliver, but they're crazy. It's one of the hottest things."

Take for example, the Samson and Delilah scene, where, in Poole's version, the latter is about to perform oral intercourse on the former. "That girl, her face will knock you on your ass," he says, fired by the stream-of-consciousness spirit of the true believer. "When she looks into that camera, and she's blowing him, and you don't even see his cock, and suddenly she just goes out of the frame and she opens her mouth—for the first time in the film she opens her mouth when she goes to blow him—and she opens her mouth and you see her head disappear out of the camera. If that doesn't get you hot, kid, there's something wrong, you better go to a doctor. I mean, if people don't have their hands under their raincoats, something's wrong."

Really, though, Wakefield Poole is not all that concerned with what the public thinks or where its hands are. Though he is grateful that film "opened up a whole new can of peas," enabling him to "take everything I learned as a choreographer, everything I learned as a director, everything I learned as an actor and a dancer and put it all together," he doesn't really see himself as "you know, the up-and-coming filmmaker." And as far as his connection to the gay film scene in general, "I don't really see myself in relation to them, and I don't care, I really don't." For to Wakefield Poole the ultimate kick of it all is that he can do just what he pleases and have people line up at the box office to see the result. "That people would pay money to see my fantasies, I mean, that was the gratification," he says. Or, to use the phrase he favors, "I'm jerking off and making money."

By way of further explanation, Poole talks of seeing artist Jim Rosenquist one day. "I didn't know who he was, and I saw his face, and I thought, 'Holy Jesus, that man looks so fantastic; he looks so together and so at peace with the world.' Because an artist doesn't have to answer to anyone, you know? And I think I'm getting there, because I'm able to do what I want to do without someone saying, 'You can't do it' and 'Don't do this' and 'Don't do that.' "

Ultimately, Poole's films have only one audience in mind. "I make 'em all for me. Yeah, I make 'em all for me," he says with satisfaction. "If the people buy it and happen to like it, that's what makes it a jerk-off. I'm doing my own trip, and the fact that people come and pay to see my trip is what makes me feel good. That's why I equated myself with an artist, you see, without being pretentious and saying, 'I'm an artist.' But I've got the same feeling inside me that an artist has, with no one telling him what to do and no compromises. He's not making that for you to buy, he just does it."

So Poole, who can sit on the subway and visualize scenes from *Wakefield Poole's Scandals* and then have them turn out in the camera "exactly like I did it in my head," is pleased to say, "I never had so much fun in my life doing things as I do now. Marvin (Shulman) can tell you I've totally changed in the last two years, and it has nothing to do with the success. It has to do with the fact that I'm doing something that's pleasing me and also pleasing the people, you see. I'm really having the time of my life."

18

EVERY GAY'S DREAM

AN INTERVIEW WITH CAL CULVER

"Cal, to me, is beautiful. Just the way he looks. There aren't too many Casey Donovans around. There just aren't people put together like him. Casey's number one. He's just a turn-on, period. I can't put it in any other words. He's beautiful. Everyone else in the picture was very nice, but like I said, Casey—there's no comparison."
—George Payne, co-star of
The Back Row, quoted in
The Advocate

Welcome to Cal's world, and to its main attraction, Cal Culver, a.k.a. Casey Donovan. It is a world that could only exist in New York, a world that radiates out from Cal's $450 a month Upper West Side duplex apartment with the 24-foot ceilings and the huge climbing plants. It is a world where the good things are a hoot, the bad ones tacky. It is a world of flash and filigree; a world of seeing and, more important, being seen; a world that is filled to the top with people who are inordinately pleased to have the pleasure of Cal Culver's company.

And Cal Culver is a stunning guy to have around, possessed, he has been told by admirers, of "a charisma that Robert Redford had when he first started." Twenty-nine, closing in on thirty, he is devastatingiy handsome, with a smile that rolls over you with an almost physical warmth. He is a person very much pleased with himself, but in such an easygoing, guileless way you end up being just as pleased for him yourself. Because he so wants to be liked, you like him, and when he says, "I would like to be a star, I mean, I really would, and I don't think there's anything wrong with wanting to be that," you feel like pitching in and helping any way you can.

Not that he appears to need much help. A successful New York model, he pulls in $60 an hour and was on the cover of *Newsweek's* "The New Sex Therapy" issue, its second biggest seller of 1972, he likes to point out. He has been in legitimate films, including *Ginger* starring Cheri Caffaro, something called *Fun and Games,* as well as Radley Metzger's *Score,* and though he doesn't believe in acting lessons, has both Broadway and off-Broadway credits, having appeared in the Repertory Theater of Lincoln Center's *Merchant of Venice* and toured with Ingrid Bergman in *Captain Brassbound's Conversion.* Accomplished under the name Cal Culver, all this is overshadowed in many people's minds by what he's done as Casey Donovan.

For as Casey he has been the main attraction in three hard-core homosexual films—*Casey, The Back Row,* and the classic *Boys in the Sand*—and become the undisputed A-No. 1 gay heartthrob, the man you'd love to love. "Everyone will fall in love with this philandering fellator," deadpanned *The Advocate,* adding "Casey Donovan wins them all and is every gay's dream." *The Gay Insider* gushed, "It is impossible to ignore Casey's magnificence or to minimize his impact . . . I adore him." All of which has caused such a stir that the man himself can talk with some justification of "a Casey Donovan cult. I mean, to some extent I am sort of a legendary character."

Considered individually, neither the fact that Casey has a tidy legitimate acting-modeling career nor his hard-core homosexual exploits would cause an undue amount of stir among interested parties. But his being able to combine the two, his adroitness in high-stepping his way from one to another makes him just about unique in the pornography field, a uniqueness that has not sat easily with his peers.

There was, for instance, the young model a friend of Cal's met at a party. "This kid started rapping about me," Cal began with relish. "'Well,' he said, 'anybody who's done modeling in New York just doesn't go around, just doesn't go out and make a *fuck movie!* I mean how can anyone dare do that?' The guy started carrying on, and he's doing this whole number saying, you know, 'You just don't do that,' and finally he says, 'Well, you know what, that son of a bitch did it and got away with it.' And that's sort of the attitude a lot of people have had. They think it's sort of fascinating that I've been able to make it work."

And making it work have been a whole row of factors, prime

among them being what Cal, who instinctively knows the risks of saying it with a totally straight face, refers to archly as "my charisma." And really, there is very much the air of the golden boy about him, the feeling that things will always go right for him, the implicit knowledge that things always have.

Like many another product of upstate New York—in this case Canandaigua, near Rochester—Cal had wanted to live in Manhattan for just about as long as he can remember. He went to college upstate with a career as a teacher in mind and took his first job in Peekskill just so he could be near the city. Next he got a job as a permanent substitute at Ethical Culture, a private school that features a lot of celebrity children—"Harry Belafonte's kids, Steve Lawrence and Edie Gorme's kids, Eli Wallach and Anne Jackson's kids. My favorite student was Roberta Wallach. I saw where she was just in the film *The Effect of Gamma Rays on Man-in-the-Moon Marigolds.* Isn't that neat? Roberta and I becoming stars at the same time, who woulda thought six years ago?"

Next came summer stock in New Hampshire—"bitten by show biz"—and then back to New York and an appearance in *Pins and Needles* off-off Broadway, to be followed in the next couple of years by similar slots in similar productions: an understudy in *And Puppy Dogs Tails,* a role in *Circle in the Water,* another one in something called *Brave* that was closed by a newspaper strike. And in between there were a boggling collection of odd jobs. Like selling at Saks Fifth Avenue, working as a waiter at Serendipity, being a doorman for four weeks during the Christmas season at Cartier's—"they bought me a fabulous Pierre Cardin suit, the whole bit"—even a stint teaching at a public school in the Bronx. "I went one day and I felt like Sandy Dennis in *Up the Down Staircase.* It's being a zookeeper; it's horrible. There was no way. I called up the next morning, I never went back. I love teaching, but that was ridiculous."

Cal had better luck with his modeling, to the point where he has done everything from ads that have appeared in *Reader's Digest* to flying to Rome to do Valentino's fall collection. He has been in catalogues, on record and book covers, in filmed spots for the Bahamas, on underwear boxes, in a six-page, full-color, totally nude spread in *Viva,* and, most of all, in *After Dark,* an entertainment magazine with a strong emphasis on beautiful people. "They've been really good to me," says Cal, talking about his two covers, one of which came out the same week as the *Newsweek* one—"Me and Liza Minnelli, two covers" —plus the seven-page spread featuring two full-page nude shots of him on a trapeze, the ones "my former lover said would make Burt Reynolds pee with envy." It's gotten so that "another old friend of mine said the other day, 'Well, I guess they'll have to recall this month's issues, you're not in it!'"

None of this had happened in February of 1970 when Cal answered an ad in a trade paper that got him the part of Rodney David Allworth II, "a rich kid involved in this gang of sex and drugs and blackmail" in *Ginger,* a sexy-violent, female James Bond–type picture. "And I must say, in the *Variety* review for the movie, I was the only one of the entire cast who was singled out. They said, 'Only Calvin Culver as the thrill-seeking jetset blackmailer shows any indication of better things to come.' That was kind of nice, but nothing ever happened to me after that. I mean, I couldn't get anybody to go see it; no one would go 'cause it was so bad."

Well almost no one. Cal's mother, "who just wants me to make a G picture so she can take the grandchildren," came down to see her son's unclothed debut. The producer told her, " 'I hope you're ready for this; I hope that you won't be shocked.' And my mother said, 'Oh I don't think I'll be shocked . . . maybe bored.' So when I came on the screen nude, she laughed a lot. And when I got my balls cut off, she thought that was very funny."

But even kind words from *Variety* aren't enough to sustain life, and about a year after *Ginger* Cal appeared in a very different kind of film, a hard-core gay number called *Casey.* "I originally did it for the money," he says simply. "I was desperate, and I needed bread, and it was a lot of money at the time—$125 a day. That's a lot of bread. A lot of people are lucky to make that in two weeks."

It all started with a girl Cal knew. "She'd do anything for money, and she and her boyfriend were very into fuck movies. And she called one day and said she knew a guy who was making a porno film, and the guy who was supposed to have the lead backed out at the last minute, and she thought I'd be perfect for the movie. I had no money, no money at that time. So I went to see this guy on a Wednesday, and on Saturday we started filming."

A fun experience it was not. In fact, it was "kind of a very uptight situation. One kid turned out to be married and was very straight. I don't think he'd ever been involved with a guy before and was obviously doing it for the money. And I thought, 'Wow, you know, come on, if you're gonna do it, be into doing it, because if you're not, you're gonna look terrible.' But he was cast, so what could I do. And there was another guy who was very uptight, and the problem was my having to make them look good.

"I mean the film was fun, and I played my alter ego; I played my fairy godmother in drag. I looked just like Doris Day shot through linoleum, it was just incredible. I really thought it was going to be a piece of real shit, and I thought, 'Take the money and *run.*' But when I saw it all put together, I was absolutely amazed what happened to it. It was really pretty good."

In addition, the film provided Cal with his *nom de guerre.* "I didn't want to use my real name, with my family and with my modeling career and the whole bit; I didn't want to blow anything at that point. So I decided since the film is called *Casey* I'll use Casey, right? So one day when we were filming, the radio was on and this Donovan song came on the radio. I thought, 'Donovan, that's a neat name. Casey Donovan, hum, that's got a nice ring to it.' " And so it does.

All was now ready for the big moment—Cal's meeting with Wakefield Poole, the man who made him a star by putting him in *Boys in the Sand*, the *crème de la crème* of gay erotica, a work so artful in its own way that the conventional British film journal *Films and Filming* said it might even be "a great leap forward in high quality dirty movies." At any rate it was good enough to make Cal Culver, a sort of male Linda Lovelace, or, in his own words, "the East Coast fucked-up star."

In fact, it all started in the very apartment Cal lives in now, which used to belong to Poole and where the latter showed the former a couple of experimental movies he'd made for his own amusement. "They were just fabulous," says Cal, "incredible, brilliantly done, so lush and so tasteful, the most different things I'd ever seen. I was impressed," so impressed in fact, "I said, 'I'll do it, I'll do it, I want to do it. You don't even have to pay me.' That was a mistake, I shouldn't have said that."

Paid or not—and he was, including a $500 bonus, a porno first —shooting took just three successive Mondays on Fire Island, and featured performers virile enough for *Variety* to write that the casting "appears to have been done by Dial-A-Hustler." And Cal was as relaxed as could be, blessed with "a marvelous working relationship with Wake. I knew where his head was at. I knew what he was trying to do. I really owe it all to Wakefield. I simply trusted him. And I think that's why it worked, because I did have this great trust in him."

It worked so well that the film turned out to be "just a cut above everything else that had ever come out. I love *Boys in the Sand* and I'm very proud of the film. I checked out the competition, and they were so dreadful, they were terrible. And I thought, 'Jesus, I'm sure doing a hell of a lot better than this number.' And the word of mouth on it was just wonderful. I mean, my God, everywhere you went people were talking about 'Did you see *Boys in the Sand*? Did you see *Boys in the Sand*?' I mean it was really incredible."

So a star was born, or at least "a minor celebrity," a status

Cal finds much to his taste. "There was even a blurb on me in the *Johannesburg Star*. It said 'Calvin Culver, who was seen in *Boys in the Band*.' Obviously somebody thought it was a typographical error and changed it. But as the guy said, it doesn't matter what you're seen in as long as you're seen."

Not that it's been all fun and games, mind you, for gradually Cal has "really realized the responsibility of my being a star. I mean, I can see why people start to drink and why they start to take pills and why they've got to have ups and downs. The pressures are just incredible."

Take, for instance, his first time back at Fire Island after spending a summer in Europe during which that "quite spectacular" *After Dark* spread came out. "It was the talk of New York," Cal says. "In a way it was like being a new face but not exactly a new face. But it was really incredible that first weekend back—everybody knew who I was. It was really frightening. I went through the whole recognition trip, people doing numbers and people sort of stopping and doing double takes. And I thought, 'Wow, now I really realize why people in Hollywood want their privacy, and why they don't go out in public, and why they don't like to sign autographs, and why they don't like to be recognized, and why they want to be left alone.'

"And the intimidation of people was incredible, like how afraid people are to come up and talk to me. I mean they'll see me in a bar or restaurant or on the street or in the subway. And you see them, but sometimes I play it very cool, and I pretend I don't see it. But I'm taking it all in, 'cause it's really a hoot.

"Sometimes it's a great deal of fun, and sometimes it can be a bummer. Sometimes it's annoying, you don't want to be bothered. And I really realized what a price you have to pay to your public. And I thought, 'Jesus, if this is happening to me, think what Bette Davis has gone through all these years, or Robert Redford or Paul Newman, the letters and the phone calls and the kooks that must come by.' "

The kooks haven't exactly overwhelmed Cal, but they've been there. Like the annoyance phone call who dialed up between 3 and 6 A.M. almost every day for a year only to hang up as soon as Cal picked up the phone. Or "these strange ugly people," New York's collection of professional autograph freaks who follow actors like second skins. More of a problem has been keeping a vigilant eye out for things that would cast him in a bad light, that might prove impediments on his path to stardom, things like an article someone wanted to write on him that was "so bad and so tacky and so tasteless it would have absolutely ruined my career.

"I can't go to bars that much, and I have to play it cool when

I do go," Cal continues. "I mean, I'm certainly not going to walk in and be outrageous, 'cause the talk would be all over New York the next day. I'm afraid tongues would be ˏwagging. Friends of mine are always telling me stories of conversations that they hear. And my name comes up all the time, and that's kind of frightening. Because I don't want any bad rumors to start going around, you know, anything tacky, because the word spreads fast. You really have to play it cool."

Cal seems to be bearing up pretty well under the strain, "try-ing to not let it fuck me up," because, after all, "it's kind of fun to be up there on the screen. You can kind of become a fantasy figure for a lot of people. I sort of get off on that. Look at how many people fantasize on Clark Gable or fantasize on Marilyn Monroe. I mean, I think if people don't fantasize on you as a movie star, you're not gonna be a star. And a lot, a lot of people have gotten off on Casey Donovan."

And Cal Culver has gotten off on what being Casey Donovan has done for him. "Everything that's happened to me in the last year and a half has really been an indirect result of that movie. You know, it got me a lot of attention. I mean, I met John Schlesinger and Raymond St. Jacques; I met a lot of people in films who were curious to meet me and find out what I was like. We'd talk for a while, and they'd say, 'You know, you're very nice, I didn't think you'd be this nice. I thought you'd be sort of, I don't know, a creep or whatever.' People had some conception that I would be sort of a cunt or something, that I would be very offensive, a hustler type. And I thought, 'Well, why shouldn't I be nice. I'm a nice guy.'"

So nice in fact that there is this whole list of people who have been nice in return. For instance:

• TV gossip Rona Barrett, who "did a whole-minute number on me in November, and it was really nice. Her opening line was 'Calvin Culver, of X-rated film fame,' and then her last line was something like 'It looks like we'll be seeing a lot more of Calvin Culver—of his talent that is.' So I'm really in on her side, I hope. And evidently she knows the two sides of my life, and I wouldn't put it past her that she hadn't seen *Boys in the Sand*. So when she's done those couple of bits on the show, it's been with this marvelous little glint in her eye, tongue-in-cheek, like 'I know something you people in Kansas don't know.' She's really heaven. What a lady to watch. She really just clawed her way to the top. I think it's fabulous, I mean, I think it's terrific. How to build a name."

• an unnamed filmmaker who has "exquisite taste and great ideas. And he's got a lot of money behind him; everything he

211

touches turns to gold. He's coming out with a feature, and my friend thinks it's gonna be dynamite, and he really wants me to do it."

- actor-director Raymond St. Jacques, who wanted to use Cal in his *Book of Numbers*, which Cal had to pass up. "I haven't signed a contract yet, but Raymond has asked me to do his new film," Cal relates with pleasure. "He said, 'I think you're gonna make it big in the film industry, and I would like to help you in any way I can.'"

- a Greek gentleman who owns the rights to Mary Renault's *The King Must Die* and "approached me to do a part in the movie. He was very impressed with me and really wanted to help my career and put me in this film. I mean, the part is not set, what I'm going to be doing, but I have been promised a part in that film. It's in the works."

- a director-choreographer "whose name I really don't want to mention at this point" who is working with Cal on a nightclub act, hopefully to open at the Continental Baths and to be called, what else, *Casey at the Baths*.

- another director, also unnamed, who "came up with a fantastic idea for a musical that he's writing for me—it's incredible, just brilliant, completely original. He had become very kind of infatuated with me. He just felt that something was going to happen to me, and he wanted to help me make it work. So I have been sort of collaborating with him, giving him a lot of ideas for it, but my job is to really get my voice together and learn to tap dance. And it's my own undoing 'cause I created this incredible tap number for the show, so I've got to get it together."

- photographer Roy Blakely, the man who does Cal's annual nude New Year's Eve card, who is collaborating with him on a book of fan letters. "I've gotten a reasonable amount of fan mail," Cal says. "I mean, it doesn't come flooding in by the hundreds every week, but every once in a while I get a letter. After *Boys in the Sand* a friend wrote and said, 'My dear, I always knew you could do those other things, but I never knew you could swim. I'm throwing away all my Esther Williams pictures and concentrating on you.' I've saved all of them, and doing a book of fan letters is an idea I've had for a long time. And then someone recently said, 'Well, why don't you use photos in the book as divider pages?' So I said, 'Mmm, fabulous idea.' Again, it's that sort of cult thing, of buying a book with pictures of Casey Donovan. But a lot of people have made money on me, and I'm going to start making money on what's happened."

Somehow, in the midst of all this good feeling, which may or may not materialize into the real thing, Cal has managed to keep his career plugging along. There was, for instance, the twelve weeks, including two on Broadway, he did with Ingrid Bergman —"the greatest lady in the world"—in *Captain Brassbound's Conversion.*

And he appeared in *The Merchant of Venice* at Lincoln Center, where he had "about five different shticks," the main one in "this incredible masque, with huge heads and headdresses and costumes and a boy on stilts wearing a dress. It was just incredible, really a nightmare, and I played Jesus Christ. I had my crown of thorns and my G-string and my 8-foot cross and that was it. So it was quite a moment."

There was to be another play, a production of *The Children's Mass*, which would have been a major coup except "I was released from the show 'cause I was just not right for the part. A lot of people are going to be very disappointed, because of course I was in the big ad in *After Dark*. They realized when they let me go that they were losing a great box-office potential, because you know my name has a certain draw and was going to sell tickets.

"Anyway, it's very chic this season to have your contract terminated. Everyone I talked to, agents and people who read the play and whatever, they all said they were very glad I wasn't doing it after all, it's probably the best thing that happened to me, 'cause evidently it's just not working. If it wasn't meant to be, it wasn't meant to be."

Cal has done something else since *Boys in the Sand* that he has not been too happy about. It's yet another hard-core film, *The Back Row*, made at nights while Cal was rehearsing *Captain Brassbound* during the day. And though he has a percentage of the take, Cal just has to say "a lot of it is really, really bad. And that's very disappointing. The film is better than a lot of other films that've been done, but people really, really hate it. It's a very trashy movie. It's like really dirty sex, a whole different trip.

"Because a lot of people expect to go see Casey Donovan in another *Boys in the Sand*, they want to see me in glossy sunshine and on the beach and whatever. And it's Casey Donovan in the johns, and it's very grubby. A lot of people are offended by it, they don't want to see that sort of aspect. Still, I mean, it's in its twelfth week. I thought it closed last week. I couldn't believe it; I thought that turkey closed."

What is closing instead is Cal's hard-won hard-core career. Though he still feels that "sex is not dirty, it's a function, and it's terrific," and still believes in giving hard-core patrons "a fabulous thing to watch, do a number on it, and don't fake it," he himself has gotten out of the business all it has to give. "To me, the three porno films have been a fabulous chance to experiment in front of a camera. One of the directors said, 'Cal, you're incredible.

213

You're the only person I know who looks very at ease but you know exactly where the camera is every minute.' And I'll push hands or legs out of the way so that things can be seen. Other people don't think of that, but I'm thinking camera every minute I'm doing a number.

"And I've learned how to relax in front of the camera. When I met Raymond St. Jacques, he said, 'When I saw *Boys in the Sand* I thought to myself, "If that kid can be that relaxed doing sex in front of a camera, there's gotta be something there in being able to act." ' I mean, that was very sweet."

And just because Cal has always been very honest in admitting what it is he has done, that doesn't mean he hasn't been worried about what effect it might have on his future. On the one hand, he says, "I don't have any regrets. I've done it, I have to live with it and cope with it. I can't turn back and say I wasn't in it. There it is, for all the world to see. I'd never deny that I've done it. I mean I can't, why should I?"

On the other hand, though, Cal has always been conscious of taking a risk, and at some times the risk has seemed greater than others. "I really thought I was gonna get the ax from my agency [Wilhelmina] last year," he says. "I've had a couple of instances where I've lost modeling jobs because people know who I am, and they're uptight about using me because they're afraid that somebody in East Podunk is gonna know who I am."

So having served its purpose, having advanced Cal Culver down the yellow brick road to the success he so dearly wants, pornography must be left by the wayside. "Did you see Addison Verrill's article in *Variety*?" he asks. "I mean that was incredible. He singled me out; he said I was the first one to come along and bridge the gap from hard core to straight. I mean Addison really made me a star in that article. He absolutely legitimized my career." Free at last, God almighty, free at last.

"Well," Cal continues, "If someone comes along and legitimizes my career, there's no use going backwards. And I just feel that porno's going backwards, it's not going to advance me. I mean my agent just came back from California, and evidently I have a big, big fan following in California, and people do talk about me. I'm sort of an interesting commodity, but a lot of people are afraid to take a chance with me because I've done the porno films. You see, that's why I don't want to do any more. Because I'm really afraid now of jeopardizing, now that I do have a legitimate film career going, and I don't want to jeopardize any good modeling jobs."

And getting out of the porno biz will have another advantage for Cal Culver: No longer will he have to take a back seat to that fellow Donovan. "It's a very funny thing being recognized and being known by some people as Calvin Culver and being known by other people as Casey Donovan," he admits. "A friend of mine said the other day, 'Jesus Christ, you talk about Casey Donovan like he's a third person.' And I really do, because I just have to separate him. I feel he's an entirely different person, someone else.

"Now I'm at the point of my career where that's really difficult, because I'm absolutely schizophrenic, I have to play one against the other. I haven't exactly killed Casey Donovan. I thought at one time I was going to take out an obit in *Variety* and I was going to put 'In Memoriam Casey Donovan,' and I was going to officially kill Casey Donovan. Then I decided I better not because I might need him one day when I need some bread, so"—and that great smile flashes one last time—"I decided he's just away."

PART 3

WHO ARE ALL

THESE PEOPLE?

19

WATCHING IT

FANS AND FANTASIES

The owners of theaters that show sex-exploitation and hard-core films have trouble with the police, the courts, the Catholic Church, local newspapers, building inspectors, fire inspectors, dishonest distributors, picket lines, and arsonists. The people who give them very little trouble are the patrons of the theater, who form one of the most polite, discreet, and passive audiences in the world. People sit as far apart as possible, unmoving, seldom laughing even when the film being shown is a comedy. The explanations for such good behavior vary: the fear of being arrested, or even noticed, in a sex theater; a disinterest in any kind of physical relationship, violent or loving, with another human being in the auditorium; or a total absorption in some inner fantasy life. And although there is evidently a certain amount of covert onanism (leading to jokes about unusual uses for hats, raincoats, briefcases, folded newspapers, and popcorn boxes), there is very little overt mess. Even the prostitutes who reportedly work the theaters are generally unable to compete with the hard-core fantasies on the screen. On Eighth Avenue in New York, where masseuses walk through grind houses (connected to massage parlors by a common entrance) late at night calling out, "Last chance for a massage," there are few takers. Given the choice between local and media massage, the rapt audience chooses fantasy over reality.

There has been endless speculation about the dirty old men in semen-spotted black raincoats who frequent sex theaters, but until recently no one bothered to find out who all these people really are. It was the researchers for the Commission on Obscenity and Pornography who did the obvious, going into the streets and interviewing the patrons of adult film theaters, with a mixture of predictable and startling results.

Harold Nawy and his researchers made detailed observations of adults in the San Francisco adult theaters and determined that there were

> ... a preponderance of male (96 per cent), white (69 per cent) customers, the model age group of which was thirty-five to forty-six years. The average customers observed were dressed casually but neatly (49 per cent) (the second most popular attire was coat-and-tie—38 per cent), were of average physical appearance (91 per cent) and entered the theater unaccompanied (85 per cent).... Our data also indicated that over 50 per cent of the adult movie theater business is conducted during the 9 A.M. to 5 P.M. working day. This is in sharp contrast to general motion-picture theaters.

These patrons were asked to fill out a detailed questionnaire, the results of which, when compiled, showed them to be predominantly married, college-educated, upwardly mobile white-collar workers with an average income of $12,000 a year—not exactly the traditional picture of lonely men troubled by the symptoms of advancing age and missing something in their lives. In fact, these men, according to the Nawy study, were in the prime of their sexual life. Nawy states:

> Frequency of intercourse was also high for the majority of the respondents. Most stated that they had intercourse twice a week or more. In addition, we noted that a significant degree of promiscuity was evident in our respondent population. Most had had intercourse with two or more different persons during the last year. More than half of the married men responding were included in this category, and more than half of the respondents state that viewing sex movies has improved their sex lives.

The erotic film thus seems to be not a replacement for sex but rather a sexual stimulus, helping to maintain a high level of sexual awareness and even arousal by repeated exposure to nudity and explicit sex.

Harold Nawy's findings in San Francisco were expanded by those of Charles Winnick, a sociologist at the City College of New York, who conducted a survey of the consumers of adult films in Manhattan, interviewing a hundred white, middle-class patrons as they were leaving dirty-movie houses. More than half of those interviewed attended regularly—a few of them with compulsive regularity—always seeing a new film on the first day in order to view it before the hot parts were cut out. The patrons chose their movies in two ways. The casual, spontaneous moviegoer went to the theater that was the handiest, but the hard-core buffs chose theaters on the basis of movie quality. Few of the patrons read reviews. Most came because word-of-mouth was good or because they had seen a trailer and remembered the elaborate come-on as promising. (The role of trailers in the sex-film business is a crucial one. They are usually longer than the average Hollywood trailer, and they sometimes show the most explicit part of the film, not until recently being subject to prior censorship in many localities.) The fans interviewed by Winnick displayed a high degree of consumerism. They discussed innovations and variations of conventions, noted mistakes in production, and even speculated about the circumstances surrounding the making of the films from internal evidence. This is not as strange as it might sound, for hard-core films are often patched together from bits and pieces, with old come shots edited into new films. The men also complained about the retitling of old films and poor sound quality.

Many of the men who responded to the Winnick interviews stressed the importance of the didactic aspects of the movies they saw. "It really is educational," commented one viewer.

> I saw one film, about fifteen minutes long, where you could actually see a vagina, covering the whole screen, and throbbing, with the fluid running. You know for sure that she is coming, the same way you know a man is coming when you see the sperm moving out. Where else could you see a vagina twenty feet high, and learn how it works and looks. They look so real.

The men prided themselves on the ability to judge the beauty of the performers and complained that some of them were unattractive, evidencing every affliction from hemorrhoids to heroin addiction. One man accused an actress of being unfair because "I could tell that she was wearing a toupee over her pussy." And another viewer said, "I watch the girl to see if there is something special in her eyes, something human and personal. I can respond to that, but just seeing the body of a girl doesn't grab me any more the way it did. I'm sorry about that. I miss it." This comment, and others like it, corroborate Joseph Slade's hypothesis in his *Transaction* (November-December 1971) article, "Pornographic Theaters off Times Square":

> The reality on screen is simply physical presence wrapped in artifice, and the audience, fighting the threatening impersonality,

turns in desperation to the little individuality that physicality can reveal. Thrown back on apprehension of one dimension, the patrons plumb it for a source of fantasy. Physical idiosyncrasies are savored: moles, caesarian and appendectomy scars, a tattooed "Property of Hell's Angels" on a buttock, even hair styles, dangling earrings, a crucifix bumping between breasts. Fantasy requires fairly specific stimulus, and wherever fantasy is thwarted, the mind searches for some individuality to offset the impersonality. For this reason, a good stag film will concentrate on the faces of the participants, especially the females, for faces indicate dimly what the actors think and feel. . . . When a novice cameraman focuses on what he thinks should be the center of interest in a sex film, holding close-ups of churning genitals, the audience goes to sleep. When an ingenue accidentally glances straight into the camera and smiles shyly before averting her face, the ripple of attention from the silent rows is perceptible.

In general, qualifications for stardom in sex-exploitation films are minimal. The veteran performers usually have in common average good looks, the ability to do what little acting is required of them, and the willingness to work in a profession that does not pay well and does not, with certain extremely rare exceptions, lead to a Hollywood career. But the best-known actors also have something about their personalities or their pasts—something of that individuality the audience so values—that can be exploited successfully both on the set and in subsequent advertising campaigns. The first name performers were already famous strippers like Tempest Storm, Blaze Starr, and Candy Barr who only worked in specialty scenes in the early soft-core movies. Other soft-core actresses stepped from the folds of *Playboy* into sex-film stardom, including Lorna Maitland (*Lorna*), Sarah Kennedy (*The Telephone Book*), and Connie Mason (*Blood Feast*). A third route to fame was some unusual physical gift. Marsha Jordan, Ann Myers, and Uschi Digart became stars because they are possessed of larger-than-life breasts, and while exposing themselves before a camera, developed the ability to perform capably in a demanding industry. The first two women have each made extensive personal appearance tours, keeping in touch with their fans and building up audience loyalty.

Uschi Digart has been featured in innumerable magazine spreads and posters, in addition to sex-exploitation films like *The Politicians*, *The Godson*, and *Getting into Heaven*. Swedish by birth, Digart's first important role in the United States was a part in Russ Meyer's soft-core fantasy, *Harry, Cherry and Raquel*. She has nothing but respect for Meyer. "He is a beautiful person, and he knows what he is doing," she told an interviewer for *Adam Film World*. "I can't think of anyone in the industry being better at photographing big-busted girls—he's fantastic . . . he knows how to do it so the breasts look beautiful and not distorted."

The men who appear in soft-core sex exploitation films are generally overshadowed by the nude women, and therefore fewer have become famous. One who has succeeded is John Alderman. The darkly handsome Alderman, in particular, has had a long career and is a reliable actor, delivering his lines well and working in sex scenes without the suggestion of embarrassment or prurience. His acting career began in the late '50s with a part in Saroyan's *The Cavedwellers* on Broadway and continued on the West Coast, where the MCA talent agency sent him, along with George Peppard and Rip Torn, to play a foot soldier in Gregory Peck's war film, *Porkchop Hill*. During the next few years Alderman made an unsold television pilot and appeared in several more Broadway plays, but he was broke in 1967 and under a pseudonym took advantage of a part in a sex-exploitation film called *The Animal* to earn some money. He has made several soft-core films since that time—for example, *The Fabulous Bastard from Chicago, Starlet*, and *The Erotic Adventures of Zorro*— and is generally typecast as a villain. It is a long way from drama school at Syracuse University (where Alderman's fellow students included Jim Hutton and Suzanne Pleshette) to the sound stages of one of Bob Cresse's S-M psychodramas, but that has not made Alderman bitter. He now uses his rightful name, does the best job he can, takes the money, and works toward the chance to do something that will justify his years of waiting naked in the wings.

As for performers in hard core, the story has been somewhat different. Acting talent was not the first prerequisite, and in the old stag films coarsened prostitutes tended to have the leading roles. In the more recent hard-core features, however, the actresses are generally very young and often disturbingly pretty. Women now perform not only out of a need for money, but also out of the conviction that what they are doing is an act with liberating political and social consequences. Says Mary Rexroth:

> Sex in public has always been taboo, which is what makes pornographic films so strange to people, because they think you're breaking something very basic to the structure of society. Sex films are a way of saying to society, "Well, somebody cut off your balls and you didn't even notice."

It is an act of defiance against institutionalized decorum and propriety, like the shouted epithet at a student demonstration— an open revolt against parental authority and guidance. As one San Francisco theater owner said, "Most of the girls come from

223

well-off, middle-class families. They have gone to college, if not graduated. Their appearance in sex films is a way to show off their new-found sexual freedom. Dad is probably the real target if you want to get Freudian about it."

The new sex performers do not generally stay in the sex-film business for very long, only an estimated three months on the average. Financial need is usually the impetus, and most of the women get their first role by answering advertisements in underground papers. When the need—financial or psychological—that got them started disappears, they move on to something else.

The financial rewards, though, are substantial. The average fee for a female sex-film performer ranges betwen $75 and $125 a day for a full day's work, and most performers neglect to pay taxes on that sum. Moreover, there is generally plenty of work to be had, so that it is possible to earn $500 during the normal white-collar work week, money that is sometimes supplemented by unemployment checks or money from home. There are, to be sure, occupational hazards—disease, rough action, the occasional police bust, pressure from parents, boredom, and fatigue—but there is always the lure of becoming a star.

That is certainly an incentive for Rene Bond, a *zaftig* West Coast actress who, although not as notorious as Linda Lovelace or Georgina Spelvin, has made approximately a hundred features, both simulated and hard-core. Her most celebrated film is *Teenage Fantasies*, where she appears between each of the several segments of the movie and fellates a different man to climax, talking meanwhile about what she is doing and how much she is turned on by oral sex. Bond recites her lines with carnal conviction and an undercurrent of erotic feeling, and she has capitalized on that ability to build one of the most prolific, professional careers in the business. Though she seems to lack the talent for self-promotion that is necessary to manipulate the media, she is surprisingly articulate about the work of making sex films. "You're saying things that aren't normal for two people making love," she has commented in an *Adam Film World* interview. "There's fifteen people around, and there's five hundred degrees of lights burning down on you for two hours." Thus, she does not become erotically involved even when she works with her steady boyfriend. Instead, she considers filmmaking a career, a lucrative source of present income (she makes $100 a day) and future employment.

The requirements for male hard-core stardom, unlike those for women are quite definite: the possession of a large sexual organ and the ability to use it on cue and thereby safeguard the producer's substantial investment. One who fits the bill is George McDonald, onetime president of his senior class in high school at

Merced, California, and eventually an actor for the Mitchell Brothers. McDonald worked his way up from loops to features and by 1970 was making $150 a day, with *Schoolteachers on Stage*, *Behind the Green Door*, *School Girl*, *Reckless Claudia*, *Flesh Factory*, *Easy Woman*, and *Family Affair* among his better-known efforts.

Mary Rexroth has said of McDonald:

> He could turn himself on just like a technician. It's like a technical skill and a kind of pride in that would be the turn-on ... doing a good job and doing it well. For a while in San Francisco, every film in this city had George in it, so if you went to pornographic movies once, his image could be indelibly placed on your mind. He got recognized all the time. Guys would walk up, shake his hand. I think the men basically relate to the guy in the film.

Whoever it is that they relate to, there is a seemingly insatiable desire on the part of the public to learn about the lives of the new porno stars. Hence, interviews with Linda Lovelace on local television talk shows; the columns by Joyce Haber, Herb Caen, and Kevin Thomas on the antics of the new stars; and the revealing autobiographies by the performers themselves. Tina Russell's *Porno Star*, for example, is a fascinating cultural document, partly reliable fact and (evidently) partly erotic fantasy designed to verify what is commonly believed about women who perform in sex films: that sex performers are turned on by what they are doing, that they will do "anything," that they get off on every kind and variety of sex, and that they are insatiable and shameless. These "confessions" are structured like hard-core pornography, and they feature all of the intimate details of the uncommon sex lives of those who live on the outposts of sexuality—biographical minutia, childhood experiences, deflowerment, recent indiscretions, favorite ways to achieve orgasm, love affairs of the flesh, and affairs of the heart. Such composite pictures portray the hard-core actress, the Sex Goddess, as a woman who has an intimate knowledge and experience of love and who represents the life-style of a new generation—shameless, uncommitted, permissive. She is wise in the ways of the body, instinctive and sensual, consuming her life in lust and caprice. Whether married or living with a man, she and her partner share their love lives with others, both together and apart. Most important, erotic films and the acts she performs in them have changed her life. And through fantasy, she will now be able to change the lives of those in the audience.

The men who sit in the comforting darkness of grind houses

and minitheaters become involved in fantasies that are without consequences, that exist outside of the frustrations and unrealized expectations of real sexual life. There is ultimately only the dreamer and his dream, and quite often the formless and disoriented movies being shown on the screen are not what is being experienced by the viewer. The realization of erotic fantasy is ultimately what sex films are all about. They offer the chance to see the things that one has always wanted to see and the chance to have things be, at least for a short while, as one has always wanted them to be. In fact, the unreality of the situation is crucial. As Washington, D.C., psychiatrist Irving Schneider has pointed out:

> Obscenity may be defined as a border phenomenon. That sexual material which lies just on the other side of the currently accepted boundary line, regardless of the specific content, has by virtue of its location the power to excite. What now appears to be a tame romantic passage in a novel by Ben Ames Williams in the early Forties had as much power then to stimulate the reader sexually as does an explicitly sexual scene in a current Harold Robbins book. It is that one step further that is arousing. . . .

The great majority of hard-core sex films are heterosexual in orientation, with content generally limited to intercourse, oral sex, and group sex, the three forms of sexual activity that are most favored by and acceptable to the white, middle-class audience that attends sex films. Harold Nawy discovered, for example, that the respondents to his questionnaire had a positive reaction to those practices and a negative preference for social and political comment, long hair, sadomasochism, homosexuality, bestiality, and pedophilia. These attractions and aversions, according to Nawy, are

> . . . reflected by the content of the movies, the majority of which contain admittedly explicit depictions of sexual activities between members of the opposite sex. . . . We can conclude that even by the professional professed standards of the San Francisco Police Department the usual content of erotic movies does not deal with deviant sex; it merely renders more graphically behavior which in other media remains subliminal.

And more recently, *Screw* magazine took a poll of its readers and asked each of them to rate several standard sex activities on the basis of the desire of the respondent to see the act performed on film. The results correspond with the finding of the Commission on Obscenity and Pornography: Rape and homosexuality scored lowest on the rating scale of one to four, female masturbation and cunnilingus fell into the middle ranges, and most popular were normal heterosexual and anal intercourse and fellatio.

There is, however, a small audience for films that present all the kinds of sex behavior not precluded by bodily limitations or insurmountable human reluctance. Actor John Holmes, for example, who refuses to do genuine sadistic routines in his films, has spoken of a friend of his who made a Roughie that was for real: "I know a girl who's really a sadomasochist. I mean, pain, blood, anything. And a guy offered her $500 to do a film. He hired two motorcycle dudes. I mean, ugly-looking dudes, and they beat the fuck out of her. But she dug it. I mean, the chick was getting off on this." Another of the forbidden themes is bestiality, and although there have been relatively few films that have included anything more than the suggestion of human-animal contact, the few that have, such as the Danish *Animal Lovers*, have been successful in finding at least limited audiences.

Erotic films are designed for male audiences and are therefore almost exclusively about the sexual experiences of women. Yet the erotic cinema hardly offers profound explorations of the needs and nature of women; it offers, instead, the product of directorial fantasy, based on the familiar stereotypes of the virgin and the carnal woman, variously portrayed as housewife, career woman, prostitute, innocent, servant, and pretty girl.

The virgin is the passive, innocent victim, the one who is brutalized, violated, and despoiled. Innocent of sex and sin at the beginning, she is slapped and beaten by a man, cries bitter tears, and is deflowered. But this physical violation does not render her frigid; indeed, it turns her into a real woman. She becomes aggressive, carnal, pleasure-seeking. The other stereotype casts the women as experienced, vital, sensual, demanding, and fiercely passionate—a creature of impulse and instinct, quickly and easily aroused, taking her vital pleasures when and how she can, enjoying her own sexuality. She is the one who will moan and call for love, mouthing obscene and outrageous things.

The role of the man in hard-core pornography is a simple one: He is potent, dominating, seeming inexhaustible—the oppressor and the outlaw. Ironically, however, the male is often reduced to a trivial tumescence. As Dr. Schneider has noted,

> . . . the more explicit the pornography, the less competent and powerful the man appears. Women can much more easily simulate sexual arousal and capability; while the man in a stag film is desperately struggling to get and maintain an erection and to achieve orgasm within the time and angle demands of the cameraman, the woman is confidently bouncing around meeting all the challenges

227

and demands. The fantasy may be male chauvinist, but the performance clearly establishes the female superiority.

Thus, the hard-core film has a built-in level of erotic realism, unlike written pornography, which can be full of unreal, outrageous sexual incidents and accidents and irresponsible affirmations of sexuality. The cruel and complicated fantasies of the Marquis de Sade are generally beyond the means and purposes of the camera.

A 16mm film called *Two on Two* provides a good illustration. The plot is typical: Two men break into the apartment of two women, raping them and forcing them to submit to sexual indignities. The recorded image, however, bears another message. One of the men cannot sustain an erection during fellatio or intercourse; the other is clumsy and unimaginative in his lovemaking. The women, nominally the victims, are eager, inexhaustible, and understandably contemptuous. They are beings of infinite and expansive sexuality, far deadlier than the male.

Ultimately, the erotic cinema is a source of knowledge about human sexuality, both a rehearsal and a compensation in the lives of those who see the films. As Morse Peckham has written in *Art and Pornography*:

> Pornography . . . provides a functional corrective to the folklore notion that a good sexual performance is a simple matter of letting yourself go and doing what comes naturally. The themes of instruction and initiation into each more complex and publicly unacceptable mode of sexual and genital activity are central.

But the films have a wider importance as well. In realizing communal sexual fantasies—views of sex—pornographic films have, in turn, helped to shape and change those views. In terms of sheer numbers they cannot help but have some effect. The Report of the Commission on Obscenity and Pornography found that in 1969–70 alone there were between 50 and 100 or more individuals and companies—traditionally working without a studio system and with budgets ranging from $2,500 to $25,000 per film—producing about 150 sex-exploitation films. William Rotsler estimates that there were around 5,000 films produced between 1959 and 1973 (approximately 2,000 of the soft-core variety and, between 1970 and 1973, 3,000 hard-core examples). If these figures seem staggering, it should be remembered that in 1971 there were a hundred minicinemas in Los Angeles alone, and all of them changed their features once a week. With many of the theaters showing double bills, the demand on the part of each theater could be as high as 104 films each year, a demand that kept a lot of 16mm hard-core producers in business.

Sex films, by accurately reporting what Henry James once called "the great relation," have become the largely unacknowledged artifacts of our times. How long they will be produced and what they will, in the end, tell about the quality of our lives remains to be seen, but it is certain that these films have created a new image of the erotic that, liberated from localized phallic sexuality, transcends the limits of the copulative act and becomes symbolic of larger human consciousness and feeling. The final question is whether pornographic films indicate that we are a sick society, enjoying a Roman decadence that presages the barbarian at the gates and the plunge of Western civilization into the abyss of blood and darkness, or whether they prove that we are becoming a more tolerant, permissive society, one in which the expression and enjoyment of sexuality is an accepted fact of life.

20

MAKING IT

FILMING A DIRTY MOVIE

On a grubby, overcast, typical New York morning, at a small apartment within hailing distance of the Plaza, Tiffany's, and the Museum of Modern Art, a group of people were working on that wonder of the modern age, a dirty movie.

Though it featured industry stalwart Harry Reems as the male lead, this was not one of those heavy productions that dare you to draw the line between social importance and smut and that cause the critics to stand up and cheer like small children at a birthday party. It was pretty much small beer, a film like many many others to be shot in as brief a period as possible by a director used to shooting quickies and who says right off the bat, "It's a cheap film; we admit it's a cheap film." Yet in its utilitarianism and lack of pretension it is typical of an industry that only recently has ventured above ground, an industry where the financial risk is very little because the demand for new bodies to fuel erotic fantasies is never-ending, a commodity far sounder than the dollar, an industry where speed is the essence.

The writer, director, and producer of this film is Bob Mansfield, a forty-five-year-old native of Boston who started out in show biz as a seven-year-old actor. A former writer for Screen Gems, once a producer for ABC-Television, he has let his graying hair grow long and wears crisp dark blue pants, a red-striped turtleneck, and a range finder around his neck, all combining to give him a distinguished look, a Ralph Richardson air of being somehow too good for it all. And though his wife is disappointed by what he does—"She feels that I'm not living up to my potential as an artist; she would like to see me make a great film"—he entered the exploitation industry because making low-budget movies was the only way to get started on his own. Between what he has done on his own and in collaboration with others, he has made an estimated forty films, features like *Eyeball, Knock 'Em Over, The Relatives Are Coming, Stroke of Nine,* and *Tales of a High Class Hooker.* Number forty-one, about to begin shooting, has been given the tentative title of *Doctor on Call.*

"I happen to dig old-fashioned burlesque-type humor, and I wanted to see if I could put it on film and make it work," Mansfield explains as he munches on a Danish. The story, such as it is, concerns a young doctor who unknowingly goes to work in a sex clinic, tries desperately to maintain some medical decorum, and finally runs off and joins the Foreign Legion when things get too much for him. "Essentially, there is very little story thread because what the film is is essentially a series of comedy blackouts all related to the doctor's office or the doctor," he says. "In a sense what it is is another *Oh! Calcutta!* That's in a sense what I'm trying to do."

The shooting is scheduled to take four days and cost $40,000, a high figure for this type of business. The director is "pushing for a classy film," which is one of the reasons he hired Harry Reems to play the old doctor who runs the sex clinic. And since "everybody in this industry knows one another," hiring the rest of the cast was mainly a "word-of-mouth kind of thing." If that fails, ads are placed in the *Village Voice* and show-business papers on the order of " 'Girls wanted, exploitation films, nudity required.' We make sure all our people are of legal age and there's no problem." Scheduled to run seventy-five to ninety minutes, *Doctor* will be shot both hard- and soft-core, Mansfield says, with the distributor making the final decision as to which way it will go. "You know people can't fuck all day long," the director explains patiently. "I mean, they shoot soft, and then when they want the hard-core footage they just have the guy get it up and give it the business." So much for that.

Mansfield has been chatting in what is the apartment's *de facto* cafeteria, a back room where a table of assorted Danish and a pot of coffee have been provided for one and all. Next door is the bedroom, where most of the film's ten actors and actresses are sitting on portions of a sloppy double bed, littered with day-old newspapers and even older tennis shoes. One of the women is leafing through a girlie magazine, and Harry Reems is standing before a corner mirror, slapping his suspenders, joking with the girls, and gradually transforming his dark hair and mustache to a shade of salt-and-pepper most befitting an elderly doctor.

231

The apartment's main room has been made up to look like a doctor's office, with certificates lining the walls from institutions as diverse as St. James High School, Haverhill, Mass., and the Yehuda Horowitz Benevolent Society. Wandering around the room, fiddling with lights, dragging huge coils of wire, looking for sockets, and so on, is the film's 12-man crew, including cameramen, light men, sound men, gaffers, production assistants, and just all-around handymen and go-fors.

No one looks over thirty, except possibly the cameraman, who presides over an awesome piece of machinery known as a Mitchell 35mm BNC reflex, a $30,000 camera identical to the ones used to film 90 per cent of Hollywood's epics. "What you see is what you get," he says proudly, as he offers a peek through the lens, noting that the beast rents for $150 a day, almost a quarter more than the type of camera usually used in exploitation work. It looks slightly out of place here, sitting in a dark lobby littered with ominous black boxes, lonely tripods, and blankets to be used for soundproofing. There is a decal pasted onto the film magazine: "Serving the World's Finest Filmmakers." It gives one pause.

Before shooting starts for the day, Mansfield calls everybody into the bedroom and announces that a writer will be present for that day and the next. No need to panic—no one's name will be used, no reputations will be ruined. In fact, no one seems to be at all interested, except for a heartthrob-type blonde in a nurse's uniform who says she is Andrea True and wants to make sure her name *is* used. After the meeting ends, the film's sound man, his hair long and his expression peevish, sidles up. "Don't mention the sound man's name," he just about whispers. What name? "Just don't mention the sound man's name," he repeats and sidles off.

Harry and Andrea, doctor and nurse, engage in some repartee as they wait for shooting to begin. "The only cleavage rated GP, and you can quote me," Harry says as she buttons up her uniform. "The dirty old nurse," one of the crew yells, smiling, and Andrea agrees, "Yeah, the dirtiest nurse in Manhattan." After a moment she adds, seriously, "You know, sometimes I feel bad doing a put-down on people who are doing such good work, a profession I really respect." Harry allows as how he understands.

The first scene of the day, Mansfield explains, is one of the oldest of burlesque sketches, the medical transference bit. The doctor invents a machine where a patient's disease is transferred to a dummy. Some unlucky fellow substitutes for the dummy by

232

accident and has disease upon disease transferred to him, "building the comic value," as it were. Playing the dummy is a genuine
old burlesque comedian, an Abbott-and-Costello type complete
with baggy pants, string tie, and funny hat. He sits in a chair, is
connected to the machine—in reality something called a Jacob's
Ladder, a miniature version of the crackling electricity-producing
gizmo that livened up the lab in *The Bride of Frankenstein*—and
waits while the patients file in.

First comes a woman with an itch, then a woman with a lisp,
then a homosexual, and finally a pregnant woman, at which point
the dummy rebels and the skit ends. It is rehearsed twice and
then filmed right straight through. The sexiest thing about it is a
couple of bumps and grinds by Andrea and *double entendre* dialogue on the order of "A guy had ptomaine poisoning and they
cut off his toe? I'm getting out of here, 'cause I've got prickly
heat!"

Pretty dull stuff, but Harry Reems comes over to sympathize
during a break. "Ah, the hard core, that's the meat and potatoes,
that's when the paper really flies," he says grinning, then changing
voices to chant, "He fucked her to the left, he fucked her to the
right," finally grabbing his own stethoscope and announcing,
"This is Howard Cosell at the Screwing Olympics." General
laughter.

A visitor on the set is Cindy West, voted the best actress in
the New York Erotic Film Festival. Modish, even collegiate-
looking, in a red leotard top and brown superwide bellbottoms,
she talks shop with Harry, comparing notes on who's been working where. Around her neck she wears a huge metal Jewish star,
which, she informs one of the technicians, is a *yarmulka* (skull
cap) emanating from Turkey. "In Turkey," she says with mock
gravity, "Jews have to be strong."

Harry Reems heads for the kitchen to get a Coke. He offers to
share it with a crew member who drinks it down and then says,
kidding but wistful, "Maybe I'll inherit some of your prowess."

After the transference skit a lunch break is called, and the
apartment becomes a mass of unclothed and half-clothed people
wandering around, showering, changing clothes, eating the cold
cuts that have replaced the tray of Danish. The nudity is so unselfconscious and functional, it loses all excitement value. It is so
deglamorized you forget to look twice.

In the main room, Bob Mansfield sits behind a big desk, takes
out an oversize checkbook, and pays the people whose work on
the film is finished, while they sign releases for their services.

"Are there going to be credits?" one girl asks. "I don't want any, I'm union."

Last to leave is Andrea True, who hands over a business card so her name won't be forgotten. "I didn't even get a chance to take my clothes off," she complains slyly to Mansfield. "It'll ruin my reputation."

The afternoon shooting will involve the attempted seduction of the clinic's naïve young doctor by two sex-mad nurses. The first of the nurses, a redheaded Judy Holliday type, arrives with a plastic shopping bag from a health food store, out of which she pulls her uniform of the day: black, see-through shorty nightgown, see-through panties, and black shoes with white pompoms the size of tennis balls. She glances through a copy of *Backstage* and takes out some macrame embroidery to work on until the shooting begins. "Is that a noose for me to hang myself?" Mansfield wants to know and ambles off into the bedroom to take a quick nap while the crew laboriously pushes the quarter-ton camera across the floor to its position for the afternoon.

In the back room the young doctor, played by a tall, lean, blond actor who has a marked resemblance to Richard Chamberlain, is sitting on the windowsill rehearsing the upcoming scene with the other nurse, a short-haired blonde who has just returned from Florida with one terrific tan.

"Come on, doc, slip it right in there; it feels so good," she reads from a typed script in a twangy monotone, and they both giggle at the inanity of it all. "Squeak, squeak," they read together, imitating the script's notation for bed noises, and Mansfield's assistant, who has been overseeing the reading, notes dryly, "I think Bob wants you to ad-lib around this part of the script."

With one final grunting heave, the camera is pushed into final position. "Are we lit? Is this a big sex scene?" the cameraman wants to know. "What's a big sex scene? Do you consider this big?" one wit asks, picking up an eight-inch length of pipe. Everyone laughs except the cameraman who patiently asks again, "Is it more than tits and face?" "Well," Mansfield's assistant answers dubiously, "there's a hard-on," and the cameraman says that's all he needs to know.

Mansfield has roused himself by now and joins the group kibbitzing about what type of panties the topless blonde nurse should wear. A white pair is rejected, despite choruses of "aren't those cute?" and "wedding-night panties." No one seems to mind that the black ones selected look incongruous against the pattern the Florida sun has left on her body.

Final preshooting precautions begin now, including shutting off the phone and taping sound blankets to the windows to cut off sunlight and try and hold out the noises of the city, like those of the garbage truck that held up shooting a couple of times during the morning.

The young doctor has meanwhile removed all his clothes and jumped into the freshly made double bed that served as the general dressing room only hours before. He thumbs through a large book that is supposed to give him a scholarly look and goes over his lines while a small army of technicians wanders back and forth, measuring the distance of various objects to the camera. The two nurses, one in the black panties, the other in the shorty outfit, stand to the left of the bed. With the shooting about to start, there are a total of ten sweaty people in a small, overheated room. "Okay," Mansfield says, "This is a take."

"I need a treatment, doc; I need some lovin'," the blonde says. "That's unethical. What's wrong with everybody?" the doctor counters, and the blonde tells him, "It may be unethical, but it's a lot of fun." She points to the redhead, who looks like she'd rather be back in the other room doing her macrame, and says "Pretty, aren't we? And hot and willing, too. Let's give him the business," at which point they both jump on the bed, and the scene is over. Well, almost over, because the sound man, huddled in his earphones over a little table where a tape recorder sits, announces that her voice didn't carry, that he needs some filters, that the whole thing will have to be done again. They start from where the doctor says, "This nonsense has got to stop," at which point Mansfield can't stop himself from chuckling. "How many times," he asks no one in particular as he shakes his head, "have I written that line?"

The next scene has the blonde alone in bed with the young doctor. They lie nude in each other's arms waiting for the technicians to finish, she rubbing his chest and he looking pleased but a little too embarrassed to appear too pleased. It is getting warmer than ever in the room, and Mansfield takes off his turtleneck, revealing the tops of white boxer shorts. "Okay, take her and bring her over the top to the other side," he says, but just as they begin the cameraman announces that the scene is not light enough. The embrace does not break, but the doctor can't help grinning self-consciously at the absurdity of being in a torrid embrace while a crew member sings, "Shine a little light on me" as he moves over a new spot.

Finally, all is in readiness for a run-through, and the girl is instructed to pull the covers off the bed, hopefully revealing the doctor with an erection. "Whip it down," Mansfield barks. The covers fly, and the girl says, "You're human after all." "Now

235

turn him on," orders Mansfield, and the girl locks him in her arms, rubbing her breasts against his chest. At the same time, she's supposed to be turning off the light on the night table, but the tightness of the embrace won't allow it, and she starts to giggle. Finally, a crew member is designated to watch the action closely and pull out the plug at the appropriate moment.

It is now time for an actual take. "Quiet down—we have a mood scene to do," Mansfield says, grimacing and hiding his head in his hand. But there is one final problem. The doctor doesn't have the required erection. "Think sexy," Mansfield orders, and the young man laughs and says, "Give me a few minutes" and begins working on it with his hand. Suddenly, with perfect though totally unexpected naturalness, the blonde girl bends over and begins to help with her mouth. "That'll destroy everything," the doctor says, managing a weak laugh, but everyone is suddenly very quiet, as if a secret ritual were being unexpectedly revealed. Mansfield lets it go on for a minute or so and then says, "All right, that's good enough, it doesn't have to be perfect." Slightly flushed, the couple parts, and the scene is filmed straight through, ending with an embrace characterized by much rolling around, groaning, and grunting, all obviously simulated. "Oh my God," the doctor says, the technician pulls the plug, and Mansfield, pleased, announces, "Okay gang, that's a wrap for the day."

And so what seemed racy and risqué in expectation has been in reality very matter-of-fact and businesslike, even commonplace, a job of work as John Ford would say. One quickly becomes inured to the sight of naked flesh interacting, for without an emotional context it seems totally divorced from and unrelated to anything people might do in real life. Everyone treats it so very casually and unselfconsciously, from the actors down to the go-fors now busy cleaning up the litter of cigarette butts and half-finished Cokes, that you are forced to think of it the same way, as no big deal at all.

"Is this your first shoot?" asks the burly, bearded electrician, a pleasant fellow in a plaid flannel shirt. "It's appallingly wholesome, isn't it, and boring as hell."

The weather the next day is as awful as the day before, and the doorman of the apartment house where the filming is being done looks churlish at best. "He is Hungarian and he disapproves," says a woman who is taking the elevator up to her apartment. "He says, 'Every actor, every singer, every bum in New York is here today.' What kind of film are they making, anyway?"

The scene for this morning will be hard core and will involve the old doctor, the young doctor, and a plain-looking girl with brown bangs and bright red fingernails. The older doc is interviewing the younger one about a position on his sex-clinic staff, Mansfield explains, but unbeknownst to the youngster, "there's a nurse under the desk, blowing the old doctor, and at the end of the interview he appears to have a heart attack and the young doctor walks around and sees it." Is his face red!

While preparations for that scene are under way, the sound man sidles up again and begins to unburden his mind. "Never have I been on a skin flick before where there were less than 10- or 12-hour days," he says. "This is a joke. The director goes to sleep, comes in half an hour late; he doesn't give a shit. Getting out at three or four o'clock in the afternoon is a first. Usually you bust your balls to get good production values. I've been on shoots where we worked twenty hours a day for lack of a big budget. This is very lax. Is it going to affect quality? You can answer that yourself." And off he goes.

The run-through starts with Harry Reems behind a desk and the young doctor in a chair in front of him. "Am I anticipating the blow-job?" Harry asks Mansfield, who says yes, causing Harry to go through a series of outrageous rasps and pants that has the crew in hysterics. When he finally keels over and the young doctor comes over to see what's happened, the brown-haired girl gets up from under the desk and Harry manages to introduce her as "our head nurse" before expiring with a huge sigh.

Mansfield decides to shoot the girl exiting from under the desk before the actual sex scene. She starts getting in position wearing only a pair of panties, but he reminds her, "Everything off honey, this is a take." She crouches nude under the desk, and Harry laughs and pats her head, saying, "No extracurricular activities down there, dear." Mansfield instructs her, "When you come out, whip the panties over your shoulder, saucy-like." The first take isn't right; the sound level is too low, due probably to the girl's nervousness. The second isn't that great either, and the sound man asks, "Do you want to take it from the top or live with it?" "I'll live with it," Mansfield says, and the sound man doesn't say anything.

In the break before the hard-core scene, Harry chats with the actor playing the young doctor, who says he isn't going to do summer stock this year, because "there's too much money in the city in work like this." "Finding a new field, eh?" Harry says with a leer, and the conversation turns to the city's current big porno shoot, allegedly a Black Mafia–run operation where the cast gets stoned on cocaine and alcohol every morning before getting down to work. Harry, for some reason, has not been asked

237

to participate, and he seems a little downcast at missing the fun.

With a few minutes remaining before their scene, Harry goes over and sits down on the floor next to the brown-haired girl. "What's your name?" he asks, and they chat for a bit and then Mansfield indicates he's ready to begin. "C'mon kid, we're up," Harry says, offering her his hand. As they walk over to the desk he makes a flourish with his hand and begins to sing, "I'm building a stairway to paradise, with a blow-job on every day."

The first order of business is raising the desk to give the cameraman, who will be using a hand-held 35mm Aeroflex, more room to operate. The girl takes her place, and Mansfield, despite Harry pleading, "No stand-ins for this scene, Bob," sits down in the doctor's chair and shows the cameraman how he wants the scene shot.

"This is your first angle, which is soft core," he says, gently directing the girl's head toward the inside of his thigh. "This is your second angle, which is hard-core," he continues, putting the girl's head directly between his legs. He gets up, gives the seat to Harry—who promptly opens his pants—and continues instructing the cameraman. "For soft core I want maybe thirty seconds of her head moving up and down. For the hard core all I want is the last ten seconds of the blow-job, and then the come shot right into her face." Short and sweet.

These specific directions are necessary, because Mansfield, more out of boredom than tact, will absent himself while the hard core is being shot. He also clears the room of everyone in the crew except the cameraman, explaining, "That's the way I shoot these." After an exchange of small jokes the participants get into position, the cameraman closes in, and what is generally known as "the action" begins. "Okay, just give me some notice," he calmly tells Harry as ejaculation nears, and then, a bare two or three minutes after it began, it's all over. "A mere act of oral copulation, haw, haw," Harry says, snapping his suspenders as the crew piles in the room again. The girl looks a bit flushed and is wiping her hands off with a tissue. "Let's open the window and air this place out," Harry says, and one of the technicians immediately complies.

Now that it is finished, this act of sex for cinema seems more than anything else mundane, so ordinary and so far removed from the dreamy fantasies of sexual wish-fulfillment that will drive untold numbers of men into dark theaters to see that act repeated on film. It is hard for most people to think of sex as everyday and old hat, just as it is hard to understand how inhabitants of concentration camps in World War II could treat another of creation's alleged mysteries, death, as routine, but the evidence is that they did. And here, too, contrary to what you might expect, an act that has aroused endless intense emotions throughout human history is nothing special, nothing special at all.

Harry's brown-haired partner is a perky twenty-three-year-old named Kathy. She has done other types of work, everything from secretarial stuff to a job in a meat-packing plant, but turned to hard core because it's better money than anything else and enables her to work for a while and then take it easy. Also, the other jobs were "very boring; my attention span was drained in a couple of weeks. I like the people in this business. I like being around this business."

She also likes being interviewed, volunteering without being asked that her favorite movie is *El Topo* and her favorite books *The Story of O* and Jung's *Memories, Dreams, Reflections.* She has been an artist's model and done still work and showed up this morning after being promised $50 just to appear as a backup, or, as it turned out, $200 to perform if the girl originally cast didn't show up. Not bad, but not as good as a very involved S-M and bondage movie she made that gained her $600 for four hours' work. On the other hand, though, she still has a few bruises from that one.

She comes from Duluth, Minnesota, and "started balling when I was fourteen. When you have nine months of winter, it's a nice way to keep warm." Being too young to have access to a car, Kathy started out in the great outdoors. "If you build a good windbreak and pack the snow real good, you can do it in forty-below weather and not get frostbite. Honest."

For the past year Kathy has been working in a massage parlor. "I'm particularly interested in sexual myths," she explains. "I took astrological charts of the weirdest people who came into the parlor, and now I'm working on an astrological text dealing with sexual aberrations."

For her, working in hard core is "mostly just a big fantasy trip," something that fits very well into her current relationship with her boyfriend. "Every once in a while we work out a heavy slave-master scene. We've been running it for a month now, and it's all incorporated into that."

Bob Mansfield returns about half an hour after he left, bringing with him two honchos from one of the bigger exploitation distribution houses. Vaguely greasy, with loud sportscoats, they are trying to look like they're too hip to care about the naked women running around, but since there's no other reason for them to be there, it doesn't come off.

Harry Reems, with his pants down and his shirt taped up so his rear end is visible, is busy pretending to be humping Kathy, flat on her back stark naked on top of his desk, her ankles up on his shoulders. What he's really doing is tickling her stomach causing her to erupt into a giggling fit. "Is this shining?" he asks the cameraman, pointing to his rear. "You've been a doctor so much," one of the distribution guys says weakly, "you ought to have an honorary degree." There is not much laughter.

The last scene of the day is going to involve giving a GI-type physical to four girls. "We're gonna line them up and, you know, use the old line, 'Bend over, cough.' We're gonna weigh each breast on a postal scale, things like that," explains Mansfield, pleased with the ideas. "It's all for gags, it's all played for sight gags."

The examining doctor is played by Harry Reems, complete with a nurse's hat, riding crop, and flashlight. The girls include Kathy, the two nurses from the afternoon before, and a new girl, all in various states of undress—panties but no bra, bra but no panties, a garter belt and stockings, a filmy negligee.

It's all supposed to be very light and ad-lib, with Harry weighing the breasts, pushing them to make sure they bounce back, cute things like that. None of the women are supposed to say anything, but that fourth girl—she can't seem to resist.

She is a strange one, first noticed by the go-for who let her in. "I never saw her before in my life, and she says to me, 'I need some make-up assistance, will you help me powder my pubic region?'" He declined, but she got the job done anyway, in gold no less, and now stands in the middle of the room with a teased-hair wig over her dazed, baby-doll face, striking poses in front of the mirror, tiptoeing back and forth. Kathy immediately wants this one's chart for her sex-and-astrology book, but the woman is so strange Kathy is afraid to go up and ask for it.

And she keeps saying lines, irritating Mansfield who can't understand why she can't understand she's supposed to keep her mouth shut. However, that crisis is soon superceded by a real one: The sound recording system suddenly refuses to work, and Mansfield has to make a series of angrier and angrier phone calls to the man he rented it from before it is decided that one of the crew will take a taxi down to the place and bring back some new stuff.

That trip will take more than an hour, and at least one observer decides it's not worth the wait. For even after short exposure, the making of a cheap blue movie becomes all those awful things—demoralizing, dehumanizing, de-what-have-you—that the decency crusaders are always yammering about. It gets to the point where you really don't want to look, you don't want to see another naked body for a long, long time.

Harry Reems seems to understand. "The excitement wears off, it turns into a job," he says at the door. "I'm getting to hate these things. I really am."

A month after *Doctor on Call* finished shooting, the Supreme Court came down hard on films of its ilk. And a month after that Bob Mansfield had made some decisions about what to do with it.

"Is it gonna be soft core? You better believe it," he said over the phone, revealing plans to shoot more burlesque-type sketches, splice them in, and change the name to *Dr. Feelgood*. "I don't think we'll be in a lot of trouble with this. It's not really a sex film *per se*; it's a comedy film," he says. "They'll have a lot of trouble calling it obscene."

As for the future, Mansfield is leaving sex to concentrate on horror films. He has a nice GP film coming up—"we're not going for the sex angle at all"—by the name of *The Niece of Dr. Jekyll,* and after that some other properties look promising. It all sounded so rosy that congratulations seemed in order, but that proved a bit too much to take.

"What do you mean, 'Everything's all right'?" Mansfield roared back over the phone. "We're out of business. Those guys put us out of business."

As Marlene Dietrich said to Orson Welles toward the close of *Touch of Evil,* "Honey, your future is all used up."

INDEX

243